CHURCH AND PEOPLE
IN AN INDUSTRIAL CITY

by

E. R. WICKHAM, B.D.

Canon Residentiary of Sheffield
Industrial Missioner

LUTTERWORTH PRESS

LONDON

Made and printed in Great Britain by
William Clowes and Sons, Limited, London and Beccles

CHURCH AND PEOPLE
IN AN INDUSTRIAL CITY

TO HELEN

PREFACE

THIS BOOK HAS grown out of a highly practical project of the Church in the Diocese of Sheffield, designed to relate the Church to the larger industrial institutions—notably the heavy steel and engineering industry—of the Sheffield area. The Industrial Mission, as it is named, was set up in 1944, when Dr. L. S. Hunter, the Bishop of Sheffield, invited the author to come to Sheffield to initiate this work. Since then it has developed in extent and depth with a growing staff of ministers and the active participation of an ever-growing number of laymen from all areas of industrial life. Essentially the Industrial Mission is a movement in which ministers and laymen are fellow-workers.

It has been impossible to work in this field over the years without asking many questions. Why are the churches so weak in the most heavily industrialized areas? How came the widespread estrangement of the working classes from the churches? Why the deep cultural divisions in society and the markedly different religious traditions and complexions of the different social groups that are still discernible? What might constitute serious mission of the contemporary Church in such areas, and since society as a whole is so determined and conditioned by the great industrial institutions of modern society, what constitutes an intelligent mission of the Church to the 'principalities and powers' of our age, beyond that abiding ministry to 'flesh and blood', to individuals, homes and local neighbourhoods? And if a ministry to 'principalities and powers' is valid, what national structure of mission is required if it is to be efficiently prosecuted? And many more ... loaded questions raising extremely controversial issues.

This study seeks to trace the process whereby the acute modern missionary problem (in the widest sense) has arisen, and to consider the kind of policy that might begin to measure up to its gravity. It takes the reader far back into Sheffield history to the beginning of its modern industrial shape, and leads him along a path of social detection that has certainly fascinated the writer.

The material of this study has been accumulated over many years, much of it of course distilled from histories, pamphlets, newspapers, and MSS relating to the Parish and City of Sheffield. No writer on Sheffield can fail to express his indebtedness to this rich store, and particularly to the most distinguished historians and antiquarians of the City—Joseph Hunter (1783-1861) the Unitarian minister, Dr. Alfred Gatty who greatly augmented Hunter's *Hallamshire* in length and value, and Robert Eadon Leader—who have provided the basic histories of the City.

The actual writing of this book, with the urging of many friends, was made possible by the award of the Sir Henry Stephenson Fellowship at the University of Sheffield, and I would like to record my gratitude to the Trustees for their generosity. To many people I express thanks for helpful comments and opinions; to the staff of the Local History Department of Sheffield City Library for their unfailing and courteous assistance; to Mr. J. H. Wood who enabled me to acquire some necessary books on Sheffield history, and most of all to great numbers of men in the steel industry of this area with whom I have learned so much about the problems and the possibilities of the mission of the Church in an industrialized society.

Sheffield   E. R. W.

CONTENTS

INTRODUCTION

THE WEAKNESS AND collapse of the churches in the urbanized and industrialized areas of the country should be transparently clear to any who are not wilfully blind, as also the intractable and chronic nature of the missionary problem facing the Church in our modern society.

Yet many factors obscure the situation and so divert our serious attention and will from the problem. There is our acquiescent assumption of the English Church as an age-old and venerable institution, perdurable as the English weather, which will go down the ages to the end of history—a great concept indeed to which Christians will subscribe—but which can veil the inertia of ancient institutions, and the fact that 'churches', as distinct from the Church of Jesus Christ, can have historical beginnings and endings. There is our weak sociological sense, and ignorance of the history of the case, that blind us to the extent and gravity of the problem. Wishful thinking and illusion can combine with energetic planning to suggest that things are not so bad—unconsciously our expectations have been scaled down, reorganization of parishes and the demolition of buildings rid us of hauntings from the past as we erect smaller buildings for far vaster populations in our cities. Our eager hearts leap at every evangelistic opportunity and are easily assured that the trough of the wave is passed and revival before us. There are even accommodating theologies that can reconcile us to the situation, though they jar badly with the national obligations of churches, particularly of the Established Church, and with the embarrassing demands of the population on the occasional offices of the Church. And always there is our busyness, and indeed our proper business in maintaining the Church and her customary work, and more than enough to do without worrying about impossible things we may have left undone.

The reasons popularly given, both inside and outside the churches, for the weakness and collapse are woefully superficial and betray ignorance of the process of history through which the churches have passed since urbanization and industrialization in the modern sense began some seven or eight generations ago. Indeed, unless we become better informed, in twenty years' time we may blame the nakedness of the scene upon television! We simply do not know what has happened to bring us to this pass. The writing of Church history—and there is a lot of it—should have provided us with expert information on the effect of industrialization on the life of the churches, revealing in the course of it the nature of the ever-growing mission problem. Unfortunately, 'Church history', with few great exceptions, is invariably about the Church abstracted from society, about ecclesiastical institutions, personalities or movements, in which the world in which they are set seems quite incidental. It is itself a disturbing symptom of the preoccupation of the Church with her own life and work, suggesting at best that society is but the raw material of her work, and revealing at worst a casual indifference to the wider life of the world in which the Kingdom of God is to be established and which she exists to serve. Either view was fatal in a period when the profoundest revolutions of history have taken place, and in which a wholly new world has been in making. Nonetheless the reasons for the estrangement of the population in general, and of the working class in particular, are peculiarly elusive. Discovered causes in turn become effects and go deep back into history, and social habit, changing slowly but inexorably in response to complex causes that are themselves the effects of other causes, becomes at any point the most operative immediate cause for participation or non-participation in the life of the churches. It is hardly surprising that we blame the 'two wars', or 'shift-work', 'education' or 'modern entertainment'.

Only a long historical pilgrimage can enable one to say, "Now I see how it happened." Even then we are not left with simple reasons and all our questions satisfied. We may be more baffled, and certainly more modest. But we have explanation, understanding and a recognition that only historical, sociological and psychological data can explain the situation into which we have come. Scales fall from our eyes, and the case is open for analysis and interpretation, lessons can be learned, prophecy may become a possibility and the demands of a missionary situation made clearer. The historical analysis of the problem is no post-mortem! The Church of God has a way of surviving her younger and more vigorous assailants, and even the cultures that they establish. But the disease is apparent; and only by understanding the history of the patient, how she got into this condition, and by a renewed understanding of her true function, can she be brought to health, to enliven and fructify her recalcitrant contemporary world instead of merely surviving it. The history of the case from the beginnings of industrialization is not good, but sound analysis suggests some surgical operations that are desperately urgent, the mental outlook if the patient is to be whole and function aright, and the tough environment she must adapt herself to if she is to regain her youth and escape the peaceful obscurity of old age. Certainly the history of the case assures us that, without deeper analysis and more radical overhaul, neither zeal, nor increased man power, nor money, nor even religious revival necessarily signify health, for the churches have luxuriated in all these at the very time that the disease was spreading.

This is an attempt to trace the effect of urbanization, industrialization, and an evolving new society, upon the institutions of the churches. It is an ecumenical study, and for our case-study we have taken the City of Sheffield. Necessarily it is local and detailed, and Sheffield is not Manchester, Birmingham or London, as Sheffielders would be the first to insist! But Sheffield is a good sample. Sheffield is a very great industrial city. Its geographical setting has given it distinct boundaries, its traditional trades and basic industry have given it clear social stratification, and the reactions of its townsmen to the successive phases and crises of the national life have been vehement and comparatively unblurred. To-day, the religious life of the City is weak, probably weaker than many other industrial centres, but historically its variegated religious life has borne rich and clear testimony to the characteristic piety or impiety of the different social groups that make up the nation. Within the contemporary Church of the City there is to be found a realism and a quality of work that might not obtain in a less grim missionary situation. Notwithstanding its distinctive character, often brutally distinctive, the broad generalizations and conclusions that emerge are substantially those of any large industrial city of the country, and the qualifications and details are incidental to the main conclusions. We should be unwise therefore to discount the evidence of Sheffield, and to take refuge in the attitude of George III—"Ah, Sheffield! Sheffield! Damned bad place, Sheffield!" We study therefore more than Sheffield—we study the rise and fall of the churches in an industrial order of society, and the emergence of the modern missionary situation. It may be useful to list some of those basic conclusions that emerge in the course of this study, some implications of which are examined in the last section. Briefly they are as follows:

1. From the emergence of the industrial towns in the eighteenth century, the working class, the labouring poor, the common people, as a class, substantially, as adults, have been outside the churches. The industrial working class culture pattern has evolved lacking a tradition of the practice of religion.

2. The increasing collapse of the churches from the beginning of the present century has been through the losses of the middling classes of society, the industrial and professional middle classes, the lower middle classes, the inhabitants of suburbia, tradesmen, black-coated workers, superior working people, etc.

3. There is an obvious sociological conditioning of both participation and non-participation in the life of the churches, of both 'faith' and 'unbelief', that calls for theological appraisal. A consequence is that the missionary endeavour (in the widest sense to include both making men Christian, and 'Christianizing' society) requires an impact on society in its structural and functional aspect.

4. The inadequate impact of the Church as a whole on the gradually emerging new society, and the ultimate erosion of the churches, are intimately connected with a theological deficiency that narrowed the concern of the Church to 'religion' and precluded the exercise of a prophetic role.

5. The inherited shape and structure of the local church are not adequate to the proper discharge of a missionary task in a highly urbanized and industrialized society.

There may be some who will resent any attempt at objective historico-sociological analysis of the Christian Church, on the grounds that sociology cannot grasp the substance of the Body of Christ, that the Church is defined spiritually, qualitatively, apprehended only by faith, and that it is sin to count the people. The social scientists of course would not concede this privileged position to the Church, and Christians should beware of claiming it either in the market-place or in the schools. They know her revealed to the eye of faith as the Body of Christ, the place where God is revealed, and man's sin forgiven, but they must also know that the Church is an historical institution, a social structure itself, colouring and coloured by the epoch and the social group in which she lives. They should know that this ambiguity belongs to the very nature of the Church in history, called as she is to 'baptize' the common life of men, and to become incarnate within successive cultures, and point them to God and their own true destiny. They should know too that this ambiguity is not minimized by any high doctrine of the Church, or by any restriction of the Church's frailty to the sum-total of the confessed sins of her members. Symbolically and mystically this contradiction finds expression in the early chapters of the Book of Revelation, where the frailty of the seven churches is all too apparent, and yet the seven stars in the right hand of the regnant Christ are the angels of the seven churches. That is to say that the Church is properly subject to historical and sociological analysis, even though the essence of her reality must elude an empirical sociology. Nor should this be conceded grudgingly. Historical and sociological analysis can be a modern mode of self-examination and the prelude to penitence, understanding and amendment of life. It also furnishes the Church with new tools, new measuring instruments, a map and compass for charting a strategy of mission. To reject the new instruments or to restrict their use to the 'social sciences' would be blasphemy whereby God is yet further banished to the shrinking area of the inexplicable and the arbitrary.

With these few introductory remarks the reader can embark on his historical pilgrimage, and be introduced to the City of Sheffield, with the wish that he will enjoy its colourful past.

Chapter 1

SHEFFIELD IN THE EARLY NINETEENTH CENTURY

SHEFFIELD is like a man's right hand. If you place your right hand, palm uppermost, and your arm in a north-easterly direction, with fingers widely spread, you have a rough map of the ancient parish, the fingers being streams running into the Don.

> "Five rivers, like the fingers of a hand,
> Flung from black mountains, mingle and are one."

In the palm the early township of Sheffield (as distinct from the wider parish) nestled on the end of a long spur running down from the Pennine and Derbyshire moors. Down the thumb from the north runs the River Don, turning north-east along the arm, into the broad flat valley that runs down to what was the village of Attercliffe, 1½ miles from the Market Place, and then on to the hamlet of Carbrook 2½ miles from Sheffield, where on its easterly side the parish joined that of Rotherham. A mile south of Attercliffe was the village of Darnall. Attercliffe-cum-Darnall constituted a township and chapelry within the parish, all of which was on the right side of the Don. It all falls in what is now called the 'East End of Sheffield'.

North of the Don in the loop made by the river was the township of Brightside Byerlow, including from the late eighteenth century at the very bottom of the loop, as suburbs of the Sheffield township, the populous areas of Wicker and Bridge-houses, and further afield in the byerlow the hamlets of Neepsend, Pitsmoor, Grimesthorpe and Brightside. Much of this township too, particularly Grimesthorpe and Brightside, falls in Sheffield's 'East End'.

We are left with the south and westerly townships, where the fingers of the hand extend to represent the valleys and streams dropping down from the lovely moors of Derbyshire which still form a large part of the City's area. From the moors several smallish rivers tumble down rocky drops into the city, to flow into the Don. There is the Rivelin from the due west, joining the Loxley from the north-west whose waters flow into the Don $1\frac{1}{2}$ miles north of the city centre. And parallel to the Rivelin, a mile south, runs the Porter Brook, joining the Sheaf (which gives Sheffield its name) running from the south-west, just before that river runs into the Don at the southern edge of the old Sheffield township. These streams, now much culverted and not easily viewed except on the outskirts of the city, are historically of great importance. From early times they turned the grinding wheels of the Sheffield cutlers and provided power for the tilt-hammers and thereby made possible the distinctive industry of the area. They also marked the divisions between the townships on the westerly side of the parish.

The area between the Sheaf and the Porter with the area north of the Porter and adjacent to the Sheffield town was the Township of Ecclesall Byerlow, containing the scattered hamlets of Whiteley Wood, Abbey Dale, Banner Cross, Bents Green, Button Hill, Sharrow and, nearest to the town, Crooks Moor, Broomhill and High Field. Beyond Sheffield it was the earliest populated township providing suburbs for the town itself, and in the first half of the nineteenth century the most handsome villas of the parish were situated in these suburbs to the immediate west of the town.

Two townships remain to make up the parish. The township of Upper Hallam fell between the Rivelin to the north and the Porter to the south, adjoining Derbyshire on the west and its easterly boundary two miles from the town centre. In area it was the largest of the townships with the smallest population, extensive wild country, with but small scattered hamlets at the beginning of the nineteenth century: Cross Pool, Fulwood, Nether Green, Ranmoor, Sandy Gate . . . which are now the names of Sheffield's most select suburbs.

The last township is that of Nether Hallam, north-west of Sheffield adjoining Ecclesall and Upper Hallam boundaries, comprising the hamlets of Upperthorpe, Walkley, Malin Bridge, Owlerton to the north of the township and the village of Crookes to the west. The Don separates it from the Brightside Byerlow. And Nether Hallam curiously had a detached member in the village of Heeley, two miles south of Sheffield.

All the remaining area, south and south-east of Sheffield, fell within the Sheffield township itself.

All these six townships now merge and make the City of Sheffield but in tracing the growth of the City, by the expansion of the villages and hamlets and the extension of the town itself, it is important to see the various community points from which the modern city grew. To the reader who does not know Sheffield, the townships and village names will mean nothing; but as flesh is added to the bones we shall see the growth of a great modern city that, notwithstanding its unique characteristics, could be any great industrial city in the North of England. The topography as we have delineated it is that of the late eighteenth-century maps and the early nineteenth-century directories.

Population figures put flesh on the topographical details, and the population increase is the easiest gauge of the growth of the town and parish. It is recorded that in 1615 the town itself contained 2,207 souls:

> . . . 725 which are not able to live without the charity of their neighbours. These are all begging poore.
>
> 100 householders which relieve others. These (though the best sorte) are but poore artificers: among them there is not one which can keep a teame on his own land, and not above tenn who have grounds of their owne that will keepe a cow.
>
> 160 householders, not able to relieve others. These are such (though they beg not) as are not able to abide the storme of one fortnight's sickness, but would be thereby driven to beggary.
>
> 1222 children and servants of the said householders: the greatest part of which are such as live of small wages, and are constrained to worke sore, to provide them necessaries.[1]

This survey made for Gilbert, 7th Earl of Shrewsbury, the Lord of the Manor, depicts a remarkable poverty compared with other towns of its size, and a wretchedness not shared by the other hamlets of the parish. An early nineteenth-century politically-Liberal comment on this social picture describes the town as "a mass of pauperism and dependence", not unrelated to the continued domination of the lord of the manor at Sheffield Castle, ". . . the presence of a noble family, combined with the remains of feudal subjection, paralysed the exertions of the artisans of Sheffield". This population, with perhaps a

---

[1] *Hallamshire,* Joseph Hunter, 1819. (Edition of Rev. Alfred Gatty, 1869, p. 148.)

further 1,000 in the remainder of the parish, had grown very little from the mediaeval period.

A census of the parish was taken in 1736 by order of the Church Burgesses,[1] and shows a considerable advance. In the town there were 9,695 people, and 14,105 in the parish. From 1801 there is the Parliamentary Census each ten years. The growth from then on, to the middle of the nineteenth century, is as follows:

Township	1736	1801	1811	1821	1831	1841	1851
Sheffield	9,695 (2,152 fams.)	31,314	35,840	42,157	59,011	69,587	83,447
Brightside-Byerlow	983 (211 fams.)	4,030	4,899	6,615	8,968	10,089	12,042
Ecclesall-Byerlow	2,352	5,362	6,569	9,113	14,279	19,984	24,552
Nether Hallam	(503 fams.)	1,974	2,384	3,200	4,658	7,275	8,897
Upper Hallam		797	866	1,018	1,035	1,401	1,499
Attercliffe-cum-Darnall	1,075 (245 fams.)	2,281	2,673	3,172	3,741	4,156	4,873
Total	14,105	45,758	53,231	65,275	91,692	112,492	135,310

In distributing the population over the six townships, during any time in the early nineteenth century there are several facts to be borne in mind. In the Attercliffe-cum-Darnall township, most of the population lived in the 'populous villages' of Attercliffe and Darnall, Carbrook being a much smaller hamlet. And it is important to note that after the later years of the eighteenth century nearly seven-eighths of the buildings and populations of the townships of Ecclesall-Byerlow and Brightside-Byerlow joined the town and provided its suburbs.[2] Thus in 1831, when the population of the entire parish was 91,692, 75,000 lived in the town and its immediate suburbs.

To put further living tissue on the topographical and statistical bones requires some description of the town at a certain point in time, and we select the 'twenties of the nineteenth century as a convenient period; a time when Sheffield had become a large industrial town, when much of the earlier eighteenth-century mode of life was still present, and yet when the shape of its industrial future is to be perceived. In

1 A lay body, incorporated in 1554 as the 'Twelve Capital Burgesses and Commonalty of the Town and Parish of Sheffield' to provide assistant ministers for the parish, to repair bridges and highways and to assist the poor. The Church Burgesses still provide for Church and charitable purposes.

2 It was this no doubt that accounts for Eden's *State of the Poor*, published in 1797, giving the population of Sheffield as 35,000.

1821 the population of the entire parish was 65,275, of whom about 55,000 lived in the township and its immediate suburbs. The total parish population comprised 13,795 families, of whom 11,196 were employed in trade, manufactures and handicrafts, 916 in agriculture, and 1,683 either in professional pursuits or unemployed. There were 15,045 houses in the parish of which no fewer than 1,664 were unoccupied, pointing to the depression of the time and an excess of speculative building.

The town was growing at a furious rate: by 1831 the population of the parish was 91,692—19,998 families, of whom 14,734 were employed in trade and manufacture, the reduced figure of 443 in agriculture, and 4,821 in professional pursuits or unemployed.

The following computation from various sources will readily show why Sheffield has been famed for cutlery and steel, and its menfolk denominated the 'sons of Vulcan':

Numbers employed in the Sheffield Cutlery and Edge Tool trades in 1824[1]		*Number of enterprises of one or more persons, in 1828*[3]
On table knives	2,240	143
On spring knives	2,190	177
On razors	478	80
On scissors	806	81
On files	1,284	80
On saws	400	60
On edge-tools	541	40 (in 1821)
On forks	480	15 (in 1825)

Numbers employed c.1830[2]		
In Britannia metal trade	600	12
In silver and plating trade	900	29

Numbers employed c.1830 in other typical trades of Sheffield		
As fender makers		19
As stove-grate makers		9
As iron and brass founders		43
As tilters, rollers and forgers, mostly on the rivers	*about* 2,000	24 (in 1825)
As steel converters and refiners		54
As anvil and hammer makers		5
As brace and bit makers		11
As auger and awl blade makers		12
As joiners' tool makers		20

---

[1] Sheffield Local Register, May 1824.   [2] White's Directory of 1833.

[3] Blackwell's Directory of 1828. Note: Some of the firms are engaged in the manufacture of more than one type of product. Nonetheless the striking feature is the large number of small enterprises in the Sheffield trades.

Numbers employed c.1830 in other typical trades of Sheffield	Number of enterprises of one or more persons, in 1828
As lancet and phleme makers .	12
As scythe, hay and straw knife makers	15
As shoe and butcher knife makers	21
As die-sinkers . . .	8
As nail makers . . .	11
As shear makers . . .	11
As skate makers . . .	10
As spoon makers . . .	8
As spade and shovel makers .	5

This list, including boys at work, and also some women in the metal and plating trades, makes a grand total of nearly 12,000 workpeople in the town engaged in the typical manufactures of Sheffield; a very imposing number when the total employed in the town (in the late 'twenties) was estimated at 15,000.

Clearly it was deeply marked by the concentration of such similar and integrated trades, and by the character of the men produced by them, as also was the atmosphere into which nearly 2,000 forges and fires belched volumes of smoke. But there were also all the other general manufactures, trades and professions of a large town. The 1825 Directory gives 36 boot, shoe and patten makers, 102 grocers, tea and flour dealers, 16 watch and clock makers, 5 brewers, 6 millers, 11 tallow chandlers. . . . There were medical facilities in the town, the Infirmary that had been erected in 1793 into which 704 patients had been admitted in the year 1822–3 and 1,833 treated as out-patients; the town directory shows the grim ratio of 25 surgeons to 5 physicians; and 27 druggists, the minutely detailed and allegedly successful workings of whose remedies were advertised in every issue of the local prints and to-day make gruesome reading for those with queasy stomachs. There was provision for culture and civilization; 8 music preceptors and instrument vendors, 8 tobacco and snuff manufacturers, 33 perfumers and hairdressers, 14 pawnbrokers, 7 inns and posting-houses, and no fewer than 231 taverns and public-houses.

There was food for the mind: the Free Grammar School that had been established in 1604, the Boys' Charity School, the

Girls' Charity School, two Lancasterian Schools for 620 boys and 350 girls, and six day schools in union with the National Society. In addition to these there were 35 private Academies, including those for 'ladies'. For adults there were several private circulating libraries, a Subscription Library in the Music Hall, a News Room, a Library for Mechanics and Apprentices, as well as 22 establishments of bookbinders and booksellers in the town. Sheffield boasted three newspapers at this time, the Tory *Mercury*, published on Saturdays, the more Liberal *Iris*, published on Tuesdays by James Montgomery, and the *Independent*, which had been started in 1819 by eager Liberals who were dissatisfied with the lukewarmness and almost-neutrality of the *Iris*.

Business men were fewer than in more commercial towns, but in 1825 there were 3 banks, 9 Fire and Life Insurance Offices, 11 accountants, 37 attornies, and 125 merchants and factors who were a very important group of men, bringing trade, selling Sheffield wares, distributing work, and many of whom were themselves proprietors of typical manufactories. There were clergy and ministers, of whom much more is to be told, and many others . . . butchers, bakers and three candlestick-makers.

But the character of the town was determined by its typical trades that had arisen centuries before in 'Hallamshire'— that area, larger than the parish, but of which Sheffield was the centre, and within which the "many smithes and cuttelars in Halamshire" pursued their crafts. The debate continues as to the date when the typical local trades began in this part of the world, but the origin is lost in the mists of time. The Local Register of 1830, proud of Sheffield as all its historians, has its first entry before A.D. 200 when "The artisans of Sheffield manufacture arrows for the Brigantes and Coritani (tribes of native Britons) who oppose the Roman invaders". If this can be believed it will not be hard to accept the tradition that Sheffield arrow heads won the battles of Crecy and Agincourt. And though every child in Sheffield must know that Chaucer in the Reeve's Tale mentioned the 'Shefeld thwytel' that the miller bare in his hose, Sheffield historians insist that it should be said in every book relating to the city "with a monotony that if wearisome is unavoidable"! But in 1565, in Elizabeth's reign, the records of the court-leet of the manor recite that a

jury of cutlers was impanelled to assign marks to different
manufacturers, to enrol indentures of apprentices and to levy
fines for infringement of regulations agreed on by the cutlers
and sanctioned by the Lord of the Manor. The first cutlers'
Ordnance belongs to this year "by the consent of the cutlers,
maker of knyffes and other occupacion wythin the Lordshyppe
of Halomeshire for mayntenance of the commonwelthe of
cutlers crafts and cuttelers occupacion according to the
aunncyants customes . . .".[1]

We have already seen that in the early seventeenth century
the leading townsmen, though poor, were craftsmen, and the
supreme importance of the local trades is clear by the Act of
Incorporation passed by Parliament in 1624, setting up the
Cutlers' Company "for the good order and government of the
makers of knives, sickles, shears, scissors and other cutlery wares
in Hallamshire and parts near adjoining". It required that
"all persons using to make knives, blades, scissors, shears,
sickles, cutlery wares and all other wares and manufactures
made or wrought of yron and steel, dwelling or inhabiting
within the lordship and liberty of Hallamshire, or within six
miles compass of the same, be from henceforth . . . in deed and
in name, one body politic, perpetual and incorporate, of one
Master, two Wardens, six Searchers, and four-and-twenty
assistants and Commonalty of the said Company of Cutlers in
Hallamshire". The number of 360 persons immediately enrolled
themselves members of the Company. The Act witnesses that
the greatest portion of the inhabitants are engaged in the
various cutlery crafts, making knives of the best edge, and
serve the most part of the Kingdom and many foreign countries.
It was nonetheless in part aimed at improving the quality of
the trade in general by securing control of unprincipled artificers who sold iron wares as steel, or employed a succession of
apprentices for less than a proper term and so flooded the craft
with under-skilled journeymen.

Natural advantages, we are told, made Hallamshire the
centre of the manufacture of cutlery and tools, as is still clear
to anyone who explores the modern city and its immediate
environment. There is local iron-ore, though at the middle of
the eighteenth century a third of the iron used for converting
into steel was Swedish; from the earliest times there was abun-

1 *History of the Cutlers' Company*, R. E. Leader, 1905.

dance of timber for charcoal, and rich seams of coal run under the town and extend to form the great South Yorkshire coal-field. Before the steam engine the streams running down from the moors provided power and turned the mills and grinding-wheels and worked the hammers. The wheels themselves were shaped from local outcrop gritstone, while clay and ganister for lining the puddlers' furnaces and for making crucibles is mined in the Don Valley, and limestone is quarried from the cliffs of Derbyshire and Yorkshire. A list of the Earl of Shrews-bury's rents drawn up in 1604 includes no fewer than 28 'cutlers' wheels' on the rivers of the parish, and a survey of 1637 tells us that "These rivers are very profitable unto ye Lord in regard of the Mills and Cutler wheeles imployed for the grinding of knives by four or five hundred Master Workmen that gives several marks".[1] No wonder that the same surveyor maintains that "All those things considered . . . this Mannor is not inferior to any Mannor in England as I suppose".

The first steam-driven wheel was installed in 1786, although water-power long continued to be used. The 1825 Directory of Sheffield lists 24 companies of rollers, tilters and forgers of iron and steel, which would have been among the heavier works of the period, and employing the greatest capital. They appear on all the rivers as 'works' and 'mills', in which the heated steel ingots were hammered, forged, rolled, flattened into sheets, and drawn into lengths of different shaped section. Many of the largest steel works of to-day have developed from the sites of those early tilt hammers. Also on the rivers and streams were the grinders' wheels going back long before the tilt hammers. Those out of the town where the streams ran most forcefully are described as being in highly picturesque settings, where the water falls down rocky channels or where dams had been built, overhung with richly variegated vegetation. Low buildings on a level with the dams were built and let off to different master grinders, each of whom would have a 'trough' and a wheel, or a grinder would take several wheels and employ journeymen and apprentices. Wherever the early grinding of knives, forks and razors is described there is reference to the deadly 'grinders' Asthma', made so much worse by the intro-duction of steam-power which increased the number of wheels in a given space, made work more continuous, and increased

[1] *An exact and perfect Survey and View of the Manor of Sheffield*, John Harrison, 1637

the volume of stone and metal dust. All grinders were to some extent affected, but dry-grinding and fork-grinding were particularly fatal. We are told that "a fork-grinder is an old cock at thirty" and it is certainly borne out by statistics. Between the years 1825 and 1840, when a national figure of 160 deaths per thousand occurred in the age group 20–29, the figure for Sheffield fork-grinders was 475, and when the figure in the country generally was 136 per thousand in the age group 30–39, the figure was 410. The grinders and their apprentices are generally depicted as a "rough half-civilized class", working hard when there was work, drinking hard all the time, devising rude practical jokes on one another, despising the doubtful protective measures of their time, and dying young.[1] And other hardships afflicted them:

> "When war is proclaimed our masters quickly cry,
> 'Orders countermanded', our goods we all lay by,
> Your prices we must sattle, and you'll be stinted too—
> There's few suffer such hardships as we poor grinders do."[2]

The importance of the streams and rivers to Sheffield's industry is thus very clear, but in addition there were all the scattered workshops in the town and in the surrounding villages and hamlets of the parish. Here too were the cutlers and the smiths plying their trades in a natural unostentatious way, within their own houses or in little workshops adjacent to the living house. R. E. Leader has preserved a good description of the old Sheffield smithy:

> ... You must picture to yourself a stone building of similar workmanship to common field walls, seven or eight yards long by four wide, and seven feet high to the rise of the roof. It is open to the slates or thatch. The door is in the middle of one side, with the fireplace facing it; and at either end is a hearth, with a bellows in the corner, and the 'stithy stocks' in their proper situations. The walls are plastered over with clay or 'wheel swarf', to keep the wind out of the crevices; sometimes the luxury of a rough coat of lime may even be indulged in. The floor is of mud, the windows about half a yard wide, and a yard long, have white paper, well saturated in boiled oil, instead of glass, or in summer are open to the air. In one corner is a place partitioned

---

1 *Vital Statistics of Sheffield*, G. C. Holland, 1843.
2 *The Grinders' Hardships*, Sheffield Songs, 1862.

off 'for t' mester' as a warehouse or store room, and on each side
are the work-boards with vices for hafters, putters together &c.
Over the fireplace is a paddywack almanack and the walls are
covered with last dying speeches and confessions, 'Death and the
Lady', wilful murders, Christmas carols, lists of all the running
horses, and so forth. Hens use the smithy for their roosting place,
and sometimes other livestock have a harbour there—as rabbits,
guinea pigs or ducks, while the walls are not destitute of singing
birds' cages. There are odorous out-offices close adjoining, and it
is essential that the whole should be within easy call from the
back door of 't' mester's' house.[1]

This picture must reflect the little cutlers' works back into the
sixteenth century; they ranged from the smallest establishments
of a single craftsman, free of the trade, working in his own yard
and making right out a particular kind of knife, or a journeyman working at home on some particular processes of knife-
making, to the works of the 'little mester' assisted by a brother
or a cousin, employing a few journeymen and apprentices.

Large works were the exception and the small average
number of men in an enterprise will be seen by an examination
of the 1824 list of the numbers employed in relation to the
numbers of enterprises. There is continuous reference to this
fact from many angles, and until the middle of the nineteenth
century it gave a unique characteristic to Sheffield among the
industrial towns. It was in part responsible for the early poverty
of the town, for any journeyman with a few pounds had enough
capital to set up on his own with all the attendant frailty that
went with it. The 'little mesters' were the easy prey of the
'trade vultures' who had contracted out small amounts of
work and single processes of manufacture, and could easily
haggle about prices, beat the craftsmen down and generally
exploit them. On the other hand such small units of manufacture had their repercussions on the workmen's side. Discipline was lax where there were no great factories to impose
the military-like industrial organization we associate with the
textile factories of this time; men took time off when they
wanted it and worked when they wanted to; they drew wages
in advance of work done for drinking or the races, which the
'mesters' freely allowed as a means of retaining them; trades
unions were hard to organize on a large scale, and could easily

1 *Reminiscences of Old Sheffield*, R. E. Leader, 1875.

disintegrate. With such conditions obtaining it is easy enough to see that in the eyes of a workman the greatest crime was not to "stick up for t' price", and that each claimed the right to settle matters "t' fountain 'ead". Such a background goes far to explain the traditional independence of Sheffield workmen.

There were exceptions; neatly built factories just off the town centre, of which Joseph Rodgers & Sons in Norfolk Street would be one of the largest, employing in 1825 between four and five hundred hands, cutlers to His Majesty, making the widest variety of the highest quality of cutlery, and silver and plated ware. A more typical larger works would be that of James Marsh & Co. who in 1818 employed 32 men, with a capital of nearly £10,000, and in 1822 had a total of £15,000 in customers' debts of which no less than £11,500 were from America.[1] But these are larger and more important works; more typical would be the little workshops adjacent to the living houses, followed perhaps by larger premises formed out of converted dwelling houses, forgers' hearths on the ground floor, with wheels and buffers in the first floor 'chamber' and the 'garret' above.[2] Clearly it is a very different picture from that of the early textile factories of Lancashire and the West Riding.

It was usual for apprentices to live with 't' mesters' until the end of the eighteenth century, when it became customary for them to live at home. If the social structure of pantomime times is evidenced under the old arrangement, the apprentices none-theless had hard times. They certainly became dexterous and skilful in the mystery of the craft; they may have been given a fortnight off a year for schooling and even taught the Bible. But an early indenture allows the cutler "to chastise him reasonably", his pay was nigh nothing, the dame required his services as well as the master, and he was probably "indiffer-ently fed and worse clothed". Yet Wilberforce described it as an increasing evil that apprentices no longer lived in the masters' household in Sheffield "now wives are grown too fine ladies to like it, they lodge out and are much less orderly".[3] From the early nineteenth-century picture it is possible to trace many modern characteristics of Sheffield industry—the team

[1] *Three Centuries of Sheffield Steel*, S. Pollard, 1954: pp. 9–10.   [2] *ibid.*
[3] *Reminiscences of Old Sheffield*, R. E. Leader, p. 180.

work in melting, forging and rolling, the "ingenious sub-division of labour" as a visitor to Mr. Rodgers' works described it, with the separate shops for forging and striking blades, the welding of tangs, grinding and polishing, and hafting in ivory and horn. And still to-day the process continues—rods of appropriate section bought from the larger steelmakers, to be forged into blanks, ground and polished outside and perhaps put together somewhere else.

No description of Sheffield can omit reference to its atmosphere, but even here the historians are loyal. Says Hunter, "the air is unquestionably salubrious. Epidemical diseases are rare: nor has it been found that effects injurious to the health of the inhabitants have proceeded from those sooty vapours". And Dr. Gatty adds, "Indeed, it has been said on medical authority, that the descending carbon acts disinfectingly". But the loyalty of modern citizens is strained here, as it would have been by the streets and sanitation of the town in the years gone by. Only an aged man, old enough to have seen great changes and make the comparisons, could write on such commonplaces as the streets and alleys of the town. Thus, at the middle of the nineteenth century, Samuel Roberts in his eighties could describe their condition in his early life. Channels ran down the middle of the narrow rough-paved streets, manure heaps lying in them for weeks together. Once a quarter, water was let out of the Barker Pool, an ancient small reservoir at Top-o'-t'-town, after notice from the bellman, in order to clean the more favoured streets. As the water gushed down the folk mopped and raked the streets, washed down houses and windows, and even their pigs, to the yelling of children, barking of dogs and swirl of the waters.[1] Few material advances in the nineteenth century can rival in importance the steady advance in the provision of reservoirs, piped water, sanitary invention, drainage and sewage-disposal and the byelaws relating to them, through the action of inventors, commercial companies and city fathers, even though the progress was continuously impeded by personal clashes, group interests and litigation.

The inhabitants were not without their amusements and entertainments. The eighteenth century had its crude diversions. There were the sports of bull-baiting, 'throwing at cocks' and dog-fighting. At the Sheffield Statutes, the cutlers' lads

[1] *Autobiography*, Samuel Roberts, 1849.

made sport of country bumpkins who came to be hired, of wandering Jews who had wandered more than seventeen hundred years, of Toms of Bedlam and Cousin Betties, poor insane creatures, beggars or impostors. There was racing and coursing, Christmas wassailing, horse-races at Crookes-moor until 1782 when the common was enclosed—which led to serious rioting. There were the high days and holidays, May-Eve known as 'Mischief Night', and May-Day, the fairs and the markets, and the day of the Cutlers' Feast. And there were always the taverns and the drinking and the many occasions for 'wetting' with ale, 'knock-em-down' and 'stingo' whose praises the popular rhymesters sang. Many of the riotous activities disappeared with the coming of the more sombre nineteenth century, but certainly not the drinking and "the stirrings in Sheffield on Saturday night". For the graceful section of 'Society' there was dancing at the Assembly Rooms in Norfolk Street, and playing-cards, tea and negus; at least so it was in the eighteenth century, although in the nineteenth the building was described as gloomy and neglected. Also there was the Theatre, loved of the gods of the gallery, who with their own King delighted

"To ger reit into t' gallera, whear we can rant an' rooar,
    Throw flat-backs, stooans, an' sticks,
    Red herrins, booans, an' bricks.
If they dooant play Nanca's fanca, or onna tune we fix,
We'll do the best at e'er we can to braik sum o' ther necks."

A wide range of shows was presented, in 1825 ranging from the representation of the Battle of Waterloo to *Hamlet*. In 1823 the Music Hall had been opened in Surrey Street for concerts of the Choral Society, for billiards and for the Literary and Philosophical Society that was begun at this time. They are all signs of the times, in which lectures and oratorios take precedence over dancing and the theatre for the serious-minded of society. So too the Cricket Grounds opened at Darnall in 1822 and in the Park in 1826, where each year Sheffield was wont to play Leicester, Nottingham and all England.

The large public meetings in Paradise Square, that became such a characteristic of Sheffield from the time of the French Revolution to their climax at the time of the Reform Act, must also be included among the large-scale public distractions.

They were much more, serious expressions of public opinion and of deep social stirrings at the birth of the modern era, but masses must have been drawn by the assembling crowds to see what was on. They will repeatedly appear as thermometer readings of the social temperature. Such democratic rumblings at the end of the eighteenth and beginning of the nineteenth century, not unrelated to economic depression and the spread of exciting news, is indicative of a growing interest in broader affairs by the people at large, and this in turn raises the question of the town's own administration at this time.

Not until the year 1843 was the town incorporated and able to boast its own mayor, aldermen and town councillors, and indeed until 1818 it had no advantage over the smallest town in the country in its administrative provisions. In that year an Improvement Act had been passed which set up a large body of the leading citizens as Commissioners of Police, comprising the Town Trustees, The Master and Wardens of the Cutlers' Company, with about 100 other gentlemen, who were empowered to levy a rate in the built-up area three-quarters of a mile around the Parish Church "for cleaning, lighting, watching and otherwise improving the town of Sheffield", and to appoint officers for those purposes. There was no police magistrate provided, and offenders continued to be brought before the West Riding magistrates for Sheffield, five out of seven of whom were clergymen in 1825, who occupied the bench at the petty sessions every Tuesday and Friday at the Town Hall. No writers speak highly of the administration before the incorporation of the town, and indeed before the improvement of 1818, though the town and parish had grown to such dimension, it was still administered by machinery that survived from the Stuart period and even the Middle Ages—the Overseers of the Poor with their restricted duties; the Town Burgery or Town Trustees (whose chairman, the 'town collector', was technically the leading citizen even if invariably overshadowed by the Master Cutler), and the magistrates of the West Riding, who rarely lived within the boundaries of the parish.

There is of course no end to the describing of a town, nor to the many unanswerable questions that crowd the mind about its past inhabitants. We can discover so much and yet still know so little. Nothing less than seeing through their eyes and thinking through their minds could really satisfy, and even then we might be as unthinking or as baffled by life and history as people are to-day who casually survey their contemporary world. Those who thought, reflected and wrote help us greatly, but just because they did these things they were not typical of the inarticulate masses. There are many gaps in this brief view of Sheffield in the early nineteenth century. One great gap is that of the churches, the chapels and the meeting houses, which we want to trace in greater detail, in relation to the age in which they appeared. But without the social context, as 'church history' unrelated to the town and community, they would be as stuffed exhibits in a museum.

Sheffield has had a notorious reputation, built up over many stormy periods of the national life. On more than one occasion lightning judgment has branded it 'disaffected'. Certainly it has played a robust part in that history of political and religious dissent that has terrified conservative contemporaries, and so often become the boast of future years. No city can claim a more 'radical' history in every sense in which that word has been used in successive periods. And this tradition has so marked the social life of the city, right up into the twentieth century, that its roots must be understood if the social attitudes of religious groups are to be understood throughout the period of industrialization in the eighteenth and nineteenth centuries. This entails some sketch of Sheffield at the time of the Civil Wars, and will also serve as a point in history from which to trace not only different social-political-religious traditions, but also the actual provision of religious institutions for the people. Apart from the old Parish Church they take their origin from the late Stuart, Commonwealth and Restoration period.

Chapter 2

CHURCH AND PEOPLE, FROM THE ENGLISH
CIVIL WAR TO THE FRENCH REVOLUTION

Religious provision at the time of the Civil War

THE OLD Parish Church in the centre of the township of
Sheffield was originally erected in the reign of Henry I.
Here for centuries the people of the parish had been
christened, married and buried. In the seventeenth century
this was the ancient church of the parish, as it still is, despite
many alterations, restorations and additions, as it passed from
dedication to St. Peter and St. Paul in the Middle Ages, to the
Holy Trinity at the Reformation, to St. Peter in the nineteenth
century, and to Cathedral status in the twentieth. To generations of Sheffielders it has been 't' owd church'.

The first 'church extension' was due to the reforming and
religious zeal of a succession of Puritan vicars of Sheffield, with
the practical assistance of leading citizens who shared their
views. The old chapel at Ecclesall, 2½ miles south-west of the
Parish Church, which had been originally provided by the
Abbey of Beauchief and fallen into decay, was rebuilt by
the inhabitants in 1622, as a chapel of ease. And an entirely new
chapel of ease was built at Attercliffe, two miles to the north-east
of the Parish Church, in 1630, again through the offerings and
practical help of the villagers under the leadership of local
gentlemen, Stephen Bright of Carbrooke Hall and William
Spencer of Attercliffe Hall. The petition to the Archbishop of
York for the dedication of the chapel speaks for itself:

> . . . within the parish of Sheffield are the villages of Atterclyff,
> Darnal, and Carbrook, wherein dwell many parishioners whose
> houses are most of them distant from the parish church two miles
> &c. by reason of the smal whide [width] cannot have room to
> stand in the parish church &c.—Therefore they the said inhabi-
> tants for the more public service of Almighty God, receiving of

3

Sacraments, marriages, churching of women, and burials, have at
their own costs and charges built a chappell in the said village of
Atterclyff, for them to resort thither for divine service &c. which
they humbly pray may be dedicated. . . .[1]

And the chapel was duly dedicated, *"Capella Jesu Christi
Salvatoris infra villam de Attercliffe"*, as a chapel of ease to the
Parish Church, it being required that all those on whose behalf
the petition was made should attend the Parish Church at
least once a year, on the Feast of Easter. It may be noted in
passing that if the petitioners did not exaggerate their case, if
indeed there was less than standing-room only in the pewed-up
Parish Church, it would seem that in the Stuart period people
in Sheffield certainly 'went to church', as the phrase goes. And
it is a reasonable assumption, bearing in mind the legislation of
Elizabeth enjoining, under pain of fine, diligent attendance at
the Parish Church on Sundays. And with a population of
2,207 souls in 1615 in the Sheffield township alone, standing-
room could well describe the condition on well-attended
occasions. We may note too that, after the building of the
Attercliffe Chapel and the repair of the Ecclesall Chapel, the
parish could be described as adequately and even well provided
with church buildings even though those in outlying hamlets
would have a considerable distance to travel judged by any
modern standard.

The Puritan élite

The puritanism of Sheffield was by no means restricted to
ecclesiastical matters. At the Civil Wars Sheffield is "represented by the royalists as being actively disaffected, while the
parliamentarians described the same feelings and the same
conduct by other terms" as Hunter delightfully expresses it.
It is impressive to discover how solidly Parliamentarian and
Puritan are both the clergy and leading citizens. From 1597
until the Restoration in 1662, all four successive vicars and their
assistant ministers were strong Puritans, the only exception
being for a matter of months in the years 1643 and 1644, when
a warm supporter of the royal cause reigned as vicar at a time
when the royalist forces were in charge of the town. One of the
vicars, Thomas Toller, was summoned to the Ecclesiastical

1 *Hallamshire*, Joseph Hunter, 1819. (Gatty's Edition, p. 407.)

Court in 1607 to answer charges that he was a Precisian and Brownist, that he was "no observer of the Book of Common Prayer, nor any way conformable to order". He promised to observe the Book and to certify on a certain day about signing the cross and wearing a surplice.[1] The influence of a sequence of men of such character cannot possibly be overestimated. The three most opulent families of the parish were the Jessops of Broom Hall who were patrons of the living of Sheffield, the Brights of Carbrook, and the Spencers of Attercliffe, and all of them were "decided Parliamentarian" in politics and Puritan in piety, of like mind to the clergy whom they appointed and with whom they were related and intermarried. Dr. John Bright for example, who was vicar from 1635 to 1643 following Thomas Toller, supported the Presbyterian party in the Church. He was uncle to John Bright (afterwards Sir John Bright) of Carbrook Hall, who raised troops for Parliament service in the district, becoming a colonel in the Parliamentary army, a commissioner for the West Riding to sequester "the estates of notorious delinquents", Governor of Sheffield Castle after it was surrendered to the Parliamentary army, and the holder of many important offices during the Commonwealth. Mr. Jessop, the patron of the Parish Church of Sheffield, married his sister.

Knowing so much of the political and religious sentiments of the leading gentry, it is tantalizing that so little detail exists of the attitude of the cutlers and the craftsmen. It is a safe assumption that they were more interested in their trade and their own internal relationships and organizations than in national politics. But it is also known that they had more sympathy with and were much more influenced by such local families than by the remote and feudal house of Howard, the Lord of the Manor and of Sheffield Castle that adhered to the King. And even if some caution is required in generalizing too widely from the Parliamentary claim that when General Crawford in 1644 besieged the Castle he was "welcomed with great acclamation and the many prayers of that well-affected people"[2] it is a royalist statement that maintains that the "people in the town, were most of them rebelliously affected".[3]

1 *Beginnings of Congregationalism in Sheffield*, H. H. Oakley, 1913: p. 19.
2 *History of the Cutlers' Company*, R. E. Leader, 1905: Vol. 1, p. 41.
3 Hunter, *op. cit.*, quoting the Life of William Duke of Newcastle, p. 136.

The Restoration of Charles II, with the inevitable reaction against the Puritans, not to speak of the Act of Uniformity that required every minister to give unfeigned assent to the 1662 Prayer Book that had been strengthened in those very features to which the Puritans took special exception, spelt crisis for the Church in Sheffield. It is important to realize that the Puritans were not merely good Protestants against the enormities of Rome, but sought that thorough-going reformation of which Geneva was the supreme example. They were opposed to the royal supremacy, to high-church episcopy, and a high-church prayer book, and were attached to Presbyterian or Independent forms of church order. Their moral conviction and strength of numbers are beyond question when it is seen that over 2,000 ministers throughout the country were either ejected or resigned their cures under the Act of Uniformity, including the Vicar and all three assistant ministers of Sheffield, and over 150 in the County of York.

At the time of the Restoration, James Fisher, a brother-in-law to Stephen Bright of Carbrook, was Vicar of Sheffield. He had been appointed in 1646, was described as "congregational in his judgment", and had certainly carried on the Puritan tradition of his predecessors. The Parliamentary Survey of 1650 described him as "an able, constant preacher"; he was appointed an assistant commissioner for ejecting ignorant and scandalous ministers in Yorkshire, and even in those Commonwealth days when he was Vicar of Sheffield he ministered to an independent "church of Christ", a spiritual association that was to be the nucleus of Nonconformity in the area.[1]

Bearing in mind the mood of Sheffield over the larger part of the previous hundred years, it is not surprising to find that all the Sheffield clergy were ejected. It appears that Fisher was removed before the Act of Uniformity to make way for that same vicar, the partisan of the royal cause who had reigned in Sheffield for a brief period in the years 1643 and 1644, when royalist forces had been in the town, and who had himself been ejected when the royalist garrison in Sheffield surrendered. It is of interest to our study to note that in 1660, when Fisher ceased to be vicar of the parish, he was allowed to rent rooms in the workhouse[2] from a sympathetic Burgery of Puritan con-

---

1 Hunter, op. cit., p. 290.
2 Records of the Burgery of Sheffield, J. D. Leader, 1897: p. 172.

viction, in which place he assembled the dissenting congregation until his committal to York Castle. It is in the West Bar
Workhouse that organized Sheffield Nonconformity can claim
to have had its first place of meeting. From 1662 they were
harsh times for the Dissenters. The three assistant ministers were
ejected, but, despite the Conventicle Act and the Five-mile
Act, Sheffield Nonconformity was kept alive among the
staunchest citizens and led, not only by the ejected ministers
of the parish (in between periods of imprisonment), but by
other able dissenting ministers who were able to take up their
abode in the non-corporate town. Groups were kept alive in the
parish, in Sheffield, at Attercliffe and at Shiercliffe, which were
able to blossom after the Declaration of Indulgence.

The Growth of Dissent

In 1672 Charles II granted liberty to Dissenters to exercise
their worship, from which date the growth of conventicles
became a practical possibility notwithstanding the restrictions
later to be re-imposed. The Sheffield Dissenters reconditioned a
building, the New Hall, in 1678 at the bottom of Snig Hill, in
the middle of the town, through the liberality of leading citizens,
and in 1681 Mr. Timothy Jollie was invited to minister to them
there. The nucleus of the congregation would have been the
independent church gathered by Mr. Fisher, the ejected vicar
of the parish, whose daughter Jollie married. Towards the end
of the reign permission was again withdrawn from the Dissenters
and Jollie was obliged to escape arrest by leaving Sheffield, but
returning in 1683 he was arrested and committed to York
Castle. From the time of his release until the Act of Toleration
his life was one of concealment alternating with flight.

Not unnaturally James II's Declaration for Liberty of Conscience in 1686 was welcomed by the Dissenters, though shrewd
if biased churchmen realized that the royal objective was to
weaken the Church of England by freeing all Dissenters, in the
ultimate hope of strengthening the small party of the Papists.
In Sheffield the Dissenters were elated and presented an address
to the King thanking God "for directing your royal majesty
unto the truest method of government which leaves entire to
God his absolute sovereignty over the souls of men". It is
interesting to note that after the event, when James II's objectives became clear, the Dissenters came under some criticism

for their act. It was nonetheless understandable enough, and the degree of toleration secured, followed by the rapid events of the Glorious Revolution and the accession of the House of Orange, ushered in a new era for the Protestant Dissenters, with striking consequences for the religious and social life of Sheffield. As early as 1686 a Dissenting Academy was opened at Attercliffe to train men for Christian ministry and, most important, a fine new meeting house was erected and opened in 1700, originally known as the 'New Chapel' or 'The Presbyterian Meeting House' and later, as to-day, the Upper Chapel. Its first minister was Mr. Jollie. It was the first significant Dissenting chapel in the town, and indeed, when built, the only place of worship other than the Parish Church. The building was conveyed to substantial citizens, "Thomas Hollis jun, citizen and draper of London; John Browne of Sheffield, gentleman; William Stead of the same place, mercer; Samuel Shore of the same place, Hardwareman; William Burch, Jonathan Smith, Benjamin Kirkby, Luke Winter, Joseph Fletcher, all of the same place, cutlers; Joseph and Samuel Sanderson of the same place, tanners; and John Crooke, the younger, tallow-chandler . . . in trust for the use of Protestant Dissenters. . . ."

We notice the solid core of cutlers and men of cutler families. There is however more general evidence at this period for the dissenting outlook of the leading cutlers of the area. Many of their names appear in lists of members of the dissenting body from as early as 1681, and we know that many more of them were forbears of strong eighteenth-century Dissenters. There is further evidence, intriguing to the Sheffield historian, in the long dispute between the cutlers and the Crown on the subject of the Hearth Tax. This tax had been imposed on domestic hearths in 1662, but when later it was extended to include the smithy hearths, the cutlers of Sheffield strongly contested its legality with the collectors. In the course of their protests they sought the assistance of Sir John Reresby of Thrybergh, a West Riding magistrate of royalist family and a courtier. Sir John did in fact press their case in the highest quarters, although the tax was not repealed until the Revolution, but in return he secured their promise of support for his candidate, a firm adherent of the Stuarts, at the forthcoming election of the Knight of the Shire. His memoirs show that, as he saw it, the

cutlers broke their word, voting instead for the Lords Fairfax
and Clifford, anti-Stuart Whig Lords descended from Parliamentary supporters, and his comment on the cutlers of Sheffield
reveals more than his disgust:

> ... Those that stood for Knights of the Shire were my Lord Fairfax,
> my Lord Clifford, and Sir John Kaye. The Sectaries and Fanatics
> stood for the two Lords, amongst which my friends at Sheffield
> who had been so much obliged to me on account of their chimney
> money and other things, did assist, and in opposition to Sir John
> Kaye, whom I had recommended as my friend; so much at this
> time did faction prevail over friendship. After this I concerned
> myself very little for the Sheffieldians. This was the second time
> the town had proved treacherous to this family; the first was in
> the beginning of the late civil wars, when my father being the
> next Justice of the Peace, and very kind and useful to them (before
> the breaking out of the war) was the first afterwards whose house
> they plundered; and we received more injury from that quarter
> than from all the rest of the Parliament's army.[1]

The incident and Sir John Reresby's comments illustrate the
political and religious sympathies of the cutlers, both as typical
inhabitants of the town and as prominent citizens within it. We
also know that many of the Master Cutlers and officers of the
Company of this period were Dissenters. One leading cutler
at least refused the office of Master because he refused to comply
with the requirements of the Test Act[2] though it would appear
that other members of the Company were occasional communicants at the Established Church in order to qualify for public
office.[3] We should not draw the conclusion that all the cutlers

---

1 *Memoirs of Sir John Reresby*, pp. 176–7.
2 *Sheffield in the Eighteenth Century*, R. E. Leader, 1901: p. 224.
3 The accounts of the Cutlers' Company have interesting reference to the Test
Act of 1673, in pursuance of which the officers of the Company had to present
themselves before the Quarterly Sessions.

1673.	Paid to Mr. Hill for 26 Certificates about taking ye Sacrament 13/6; for ye Act 12d., & for ye Companies charges to Leeds to take ye oaths & subscribe £6. 10. 7.	.	.	.	.	£7. 5. 1.
1674.	Charges of Companie to Doncaster & Rotherham about taking ye oathes & for their certificates	.	.	.	.	£4 17. 0.
1684.	To the Clarke for his journey to London, his certificates for ye Companies receiueing ye Sacrament in order to their takeing ye oaths, with Mr. Garland's fee about ye same, &c	.	.	.	.	£5. 18. 9.
	Charges expended att Barnsley & Doncaster sessions about taking ye oaths of allegiance & supremacie	.	.	.	.	£5 15. 11.

were Dissenters. The term 'cutler' is a wide one covering a whole craft from responsible burgesses to scallywags. Moreover we can assume that the townsmen were more publicly united politically than religiously, for though common economic interests united the town, before the Toleration Act and before the building of the Upper Chapel, to those who were not extremely zealous there was little inducement to religious dissent. From a late eighteenth-century list of pew holders we also know that there were highly respected members of the Cutlers' Company with freehold pews in the Parish Church. Clearly the picture is not monochrome, but, given the prominent social leadership of many Dissenters and the political complexion of the town as a whole, the reputation acquired by the Sheffielders is explicable.

The building of the Upper Chapel lifted the Dissenters' worship out of obscurity, and provided them with a fine public rallying point. It rapidly became the largest Dissenting congregation in Yorkshire, and we have proof of their strength in 1714. In that year Jollie died, and there occurred the first of those many schisms within Dissenting congregations which proliferated Independent churches all over the city. Certainly schisms within existing congregations rather than missionary zeal produced almost all the early meeting houses, witnessing both to the spirit of independence as well as to the affluence of members. The congregation of Upper Chapel were divided concerning the appointment of a successor to Jollie. The smaller number wanted his assistant minister, Mr. de la Rose, a High Calvinist, and the larger number, with the trustees, wanted a Mr. Wadsworth, said by his opponents to be inclined to the Arian heresy. The former group, 200 "mostly of the middle classes", seceded with Mr. de la Rose and built for themselves the Nether Chapel further down Norfolk Street. A contemporary list shows that 1,163 persons were left at the Upper Chapel, a prosperous and respectable congregation coming from all over the district, 75 of whom were freeholders in the county. This tells us much; and it suggests that the Upper Chapel had already begun its journey into Unitarianism—it is to-day the leading Unitarian
(note cont.)

Mr. Garland was Counsel who had advised the Company that the officers need not take the oaths yearly "none of them bearing any office civill or militarie, nor receiving any pay salarie &c from his Maje or place or trust from under his Maje."

(*History of the Cutlers' Company*, R. E. Leader, 1905: vol. 1, p. 245.)

chapel of the city, as Nether Chapel, the parent of orthodox
Calvinism, is to-day the leading Congregational Church.

The Religious Picture c. 1736

This brief historical and social sketch has been necessary to
explain the origin of the parties. It also sets before us the provision for worship at a point of time—the year 1736—for which
we have population figures, and before the picture was further
complicated by the birth of Methodism. The important places
of worship in the township have already appeared in the story.
There was the *Parish Church*. There were the *Upper* and the
Nether Chapels. And there were two other lesser, and less
public places—the Chapel of the *Shrewsbury Hospital*[1] where
services of the Church of England were conducted, and a small
Quaker meeting house which had been erected in 1705. Since at
this time, in 1736, the population of the entire parish was
14,105 (3,111 families) of which *9,695 (2,152 families) made up
the Sheffield township*, provision had clearly much worsened since
1615, when the Parish Church, by far the largest building, was
set amidst a population of 2,207. Quite apart from the question
of the kinds of people who regularly worshipped in the various
sects, we see here the beginning of a trend that was to continue
up to the present—the continuous outstripping of the provisions
by the population increase.

The need for further provision had in fact been realized long
before this date, and an odd story is associated with it. To meet
the shortage of accommodation, in 1720 a prominent gold-
smith, Robert Downes, and other principal inhabitants secured
ground on the southern edge of the town and money to build
a new church as a chapel of ease to the Parish Church, but
within the township. The 'New Church' or St. Paul's as it was
variously called was completed in 1721, a fine building in
Renaissance style, when serious disagreement arose between
Mr. Downes, the prime mover and contributor, the Vicar of
Sheffield, and the patron of the Parish Church of Sheffield,
each of them claiming the right of presentation. Such was the
deadlock that the church, fully built and furnished, remained

[1] An almshouse provided by the beneficent Gilbert, 7th Earl of Shrewsbury,
Lord of the Manor of Sheffield, who died in 1616. This fine Hospital still flourishes
under the patronage of the Duke of Norfolk.

empty and completely unused for 19 years! Indeed the census
of 1736 was ordered by the Church Burgesses to justify their
petition that it should become a parochial church. Robert
Downes ultimately took action that shows the mood of the
times. He secured a licence for the use of the building by Protestant Dissenters until such time that it could be used in the
service of the Establishment. There was prompt reaction. A
local solution was found and confirmed by Act of Parliament,
and the church was duly opened for public worship in May 1740
as a chapel of ease to the Parish Church.

From its opening the 'New Church', St. Paul's, had rented
pews and seats[1]—by that time an established practice in the

---

[1] The Parish Church of Sheffield was also pewed at this time but not in regular
shape as at St. Paul's. In the Parish Church box pews were irregularly placed and
of every shape and size; and had been held in freehold possession since the time of
their erection. The original date when the pewing of the nave began is not ascertainable. Certainly it was a gradual process, probably beginning in the late
sixteenth or early seventeenth century. Nor do we know whether open benches
existed in the nave before the pewing.

In the country generally, the private allocation of seats, and the erection of more
stately stalls and pews for more distinguished parishioners, can be traced to Pre-
Reformation times, but the Reformation gave great impetus to the practice. It
has been ascribed to a variety of causes—to the following of that precedent whereby the old chantries, abolished in 1519, often became enclosures where the manorial
family could sit in state; to the growing prestige of a middle class in society; as a
consequence of lay participation in the vernacular services of a Reformed Church
and the Puritan liking for long sermons, and even to exclude draughts in cold
churches. But there is a connexion between them, and it would seem reasonable to
suppose that all these factors have operated in varying degrees. The selling and
private appropriation of seating in the parish churches was in fact contrary to
common law, whereby all parishioners equally have rights within their parish
churches; but this did not prevent the widespread development of the practice.
It is of immense sociological value to know the exact practices that obtained.

R. E. Leader, who unearthed much of Sheffield's old history, informs us that in
the seventeenth century nearly every property owner in the main streets had a
freehold in the Parish Church belonging to or specified among the appurtenances
of his house. The earliest example he can cite is in 1625, when a title deed for
premises at the Church gates includes "chancellors order for ye seat in ye church".
It was sold in 1710 with the property by a Dissenter, and in 1796 when the property again changed hands "any pews, seats or sittings in the Trinity Church
belonging to the said premises" were expressly reserved from the sale. (Article
by R. E. Leader on Church Pews and Freeholds, *Sheffield Telegraph*, Aug. 20, 1907.)

In the eighteenth century the Parish Church was said to have been "one of the
most gloomy, irregularly pewed places of worship in the kingdom. It seemed as if
after the work of pewing had begun, every person who chose had formed a pew
for himself in his own way, to his own size, height, and shape. There were several
galleries, but all formed, in the same way as the pews; some of them on pillars,
and some hung in chains" (Samuel Roberts, *Autobiography*, p. 13). There were at
this time 134 pews on the ground floor, and 163 in the Loft or Gallery, and a

"Plan of Pews in the Old Worship House in Sheffield" towards the end of the eighteenth century gives the names of the pewholders, and shows that most of the pews were appropriated. (Fairbank Collection M.B.448, Sheffield City Library.)

In 1800 the archdeacon at his visitation signified his intention to improve the decayed condition of the church, and a document of 1802 authorizing restoration says "the seats, stalls, and pews in the body, and the lofts and other parts, are moulderous, rotten and decayed, and are moreover irregular and incommodious, and greatly unsuited to the rank, style and condition of life of the present owners and occupiers thereof". In fact the entire nave was rebuilt during the course of several years, and new orderly pewage was installed, the owners paying their share of the pewing costs "as their property will thereby be improved". The new nave with pewed ground floor and gallery was opened in 1805, and commissioners were appointed to re-allot the sittings totalling about 1,500, first to those who had been seatholders in the former nave, then to "parishioners . . . paying Church assessments, as are or shall be for the time being destitute of Seats Stalls Pews or Sittings upon such terms and conditions as the Twelve Capital Burgesses and Commonalty shall deem meet and reasonable" and next "to set apart the rest and residue (if any) of the said new Seats Stalls Pews and Sittings and also the vacant spaces and the Forms and Benches placed therein to and for the use and accommodation of the Poor. . . ." (Repewing Allotment—plans and details of the Trust, 1806. Borthwick Institute of Historical Research, York.) In 1807 the free seats were duly determined. There were about 100 of them apart from the benches for the boys and girls of the Charity School. There were a few in the gallery behind pillars, and the rest were downstairs, behind the three-decker pulpit, and mostly behind pillars. In two of them, the stoves were placed. (See Plan showing the New Pewage as executed, at the Borthwick Institute of Historical Research, York, and the Minute Book of the Church Burgesses, July 2, 1807. See Appendix III.)

Once the pews were allotted and acquired, they could be sold, sublet, auctioned or bequeathed. Possession was part of a man's material assets. Leader gives evidence of Pew No. 69 being sold in 1817 for £105, and again in 1819 for £115, and yet again in 1847 for £100—It was one of the finest placed in the church, seating six persons. (*Sheffield Telegraph*, Aug. 8, 1907.)

Apart from the freehold possession of pews, it was possible to rent them. The first price list for the new church of St. Paul's quoted 2s. 6d. yearly for each sitting in the best pews, 2s. in the next quality, and 1s. 6d. in the last. For a pew of the last type the cost would have been a week's wage of a labourer, and a substantial part of that of a journeyman cutler.

Typical notices of auctions are as follows:

TO BE SOLD BY AUCTION, by Mr. Bardwell, on Tuesday, June 12th . . . at Mr. Peech's, Angel Inn. A seat (No. 6) in St. Paul's Chapel, containing 5 sittings, belonging to Mr. Gregory, a Bankrupt.

Likewise the 3rd seat under the North Singing Loft in the Old Church, containing 5 sittings.

(*The Sheffield Register*, June 8, 1792)

AUCTION BY MR. BARDWELL, at his Auction Room, Sheffield . . .

Lot 13.   A pew in the north gallery of the Parish Church of Sheffield No. 20.

Lot 14.   Two Sittings lettered F,G. in the Pew No. 23 in the same gallery.

Lot 15.   Four Sittings lettered A.B.C.D. in the Pew on the north side of the middle aisle in the same Church No. 49.

N.B. The above premises are of the nature of Freehold. . . .

Lot 18.   A Pew in the north gallery of St. James Chapel, Sheffield, No. 36.

Lot 19.   A pew in the same gallery No. 59.

towns. It was a custom dating from the pewing-up of the old parish churches from the sixteenth century, and it became a characteristic feature of new churches and chapels of ease erected by the Establishment from the seventeenth century, as also of the large, permanent chapels and meeting houses of the Dissenters in the growing towns from the time that they were erected. The practice was to persist even into the twentieth century, and although the provision of free seats was continuously increasing from the early nineteenth century, we shall see that the custom had profound consequences for the relation of the churches to the common people. It is not clear whether all the seats at St. Paul's were appropriated, but most if not all were privately allotted, and a considerable sum of money was to be raised through rents. The perpetual curate was to be maintained, the existing Vicar of Sheffield was to receive £30 per annum, £48 per annum was to go to the Downes family for ever, and a Trust was empowered to let the seats "upon such terms that they be not less than four shillings each upon an average". It was not a 'proprietary chapel' as such, but, like others to be built later, can have been little different in practice. Such arrangements hardly suggest that the poor were expected to 'belong' in an age when they were many.

There is further data to add to the picture as we build it up at this period. In 1743 returns were made to the Archbishop of York in answer to his visitation questions.[1] The two meeting houses of the Dissenters, the Upper and the Nether Chapels are mentioned and "it is supposed that the number of both the congregations may amount to 700 and sometimes more". The Quaker meeting house is also mentioned. At the Parish Church the Sacrament of the Lord's Supper was administered

(note cont.)

Lot 20.   A Pew in the South gallery of the same chapel No. 16.
Lot 21.   A Pew in the West gallery of the same chapel No. 29.
Lot 22.   A Pew on the ground floor of the same chapel No. 34.
Lot 23.   A Pew on the same floor No. 39.
Lot 24.   Two shares in the Leeds and Liverpool Canal.
Lot 25.   Two shares in the Chesterfield Navigation.

N.B. The above premises are of the nature of Personalty. For a view of the Land and houses apply to the respective tenants, and of the Pews and Sittings, to the Clerks of the Church and chapel.

> (Handbill advertising sale on 28th April 1806 in Sheffield City Library. Special Collection No. 5194.)

[1] *History of St. Paul's Church, Sheffield*, Rev. W. Odom, 1919.

on the first Sunday of each month and on the Great Festivals—
"On Palm Sunday, Good Friday, and on Easter Day last about
500 in all did communicate at the old church". At St. Paul's
"about 40 usually (communicate each month), but on Festivals
perhaps one hundred". The Sheffield Local Register notes that
in 1736 there were 172 members of the Society of Friends
(36 families) and 246 Roman Catholics (57 families). It would
seem that there were about 250 families of Independents and
Presbyterians. All these figures refer to the township of Sheffield,
at a time when the population was (at 1736) 9,695 in 2,152
families.

In the absence of further social detail to fill in the gaps, we
are perhaps tempted to conclude too much from these figures
in seeking to discover the extent to which the community as a
whole was Christian in a practising sense. Do the numbers of
worshippers refer to adults? What was the number that worshipped in the churches of the Establishment who were not
regular communicants? No doubt the numbers of worshippers
referred to represent very minimum figures of adherents. And
if this supposition is correct it would seem that a very considerable part of the township's inhabitants did take their part
in worship. But what kind of people were they? Our knowledge
of the proprietary nature of the churches and chapels of the
time—the Parish Church and St. Paul's of the Establishment,
and the Upper and Nether Chapels of the Dissenters, coupled
with our general knowledge of the social group that was the
mainstay of the Old Dissent in the eighteenth century, does not
encourage us to think that the poorer common folk 'belonged'.
It may well form a picture (typical of so much of the future) in
which the more established and respectable members of society
found their places in church and meeting house, and indeed in
places that were their own, the less firmly rooted in society
and the flotsam and jetsam much less so, if at all.

It is a view strengthened by our knowledge of the crudeness
of much eighteenth-century Sheffield life, a crudeness by no
means confined to Sheffield, but markedly in that town with its
tradition of ancient roughness. Hunter, writing of this period,
says that "the want of a due mixture of persons well-educated
and of a superior situation in life, rendered Sheffield at this
period less distinguished by the elegancies and refinements of
social life than by the feelings of independence and rugged

honesty, by hospitality, and a rude and boisterous conviviality".[1] This courteous euphemism hardly conceals the coarseness, by no means solely artisan, of much eighteenth-century
Sheffield life. Taking all these factors into account, there is
little to suggest that the practice of piety was universally
observed. John Wesley's general criticism of the country, of
"that English sin, ungodliness, that reproach of our nation,
wherein we excel all the inhabitants of the earth", would have
found ample evidence in eighteenth-century Sheffield.[2]

*Rapid expansion of Independency towards the end of the eighteenth
century*

By 1736 the population increase was under way but not out
of hand; from then on the increase became heavy, partly due to
natural increase, partly to the new arrivals from outlying districts through the increasing operation of Enclosure Acts, and
the promise of work and wealth. From 14,105 in 1736, the
parish increased to 45,758 by 1801. Further provision for
worship was made, or perhaps we should say, further provision
for worshippers was made, and deserves to be studied in some
detail, since it is in the second half of the eighteenth century
that the social groups of the nineteenth and twentieth centuries
begin to emerge clearly, and their religious expressions as well
as their social prestige are seen in their religious edifices, and
the way of life within them.

A new religious factor comes on to the scene just after 1736.
'Methodistical' preaching first began in the parish in 1738 in a
very small way, a trickle that was to become a mighty river.
Numerically it was without importance for many years, nor
were its building provisions of significance until near the end
of the century, except in the early years as an object of ruffian
violence. But an influence began to be exerted both locally and
nationally. In due course the local growth must be examined,
and its influence calculated.

But the large increase of chapels in the last quarter of the
eighteenth century did not come from the Methodists but from
the Independents, and yet not until late, and after the Methodists had taken root. Nether Chapel, the orthodox Calvinist
Independent Chapel, had been erected in 1714; yet not until

1 *Hallamshire*, Joseph Hunter, p. 153.   2 *Journals*, Nov. 25, 1787.

1774 was a further chapel provided in the town, and even then not designed to meet a growing population but the needs of a group who seceded from Nether. But it was the beginning of a spate of Independent building. Was the Methodist influence at work in this expansion of Independent facilities? Dissenting historians tell us that "to the preaching of the Methodists, both calvinistic and arminian, the dissenters owe a considerable increase both in the number of congregations and hearers".[1]

In 1771 there were only two or three hundred members of the Methodist society, but among their number were both conformists and nonconformists, and they had a zeal that was to be infectious. Later in the century, too, clergy and dissenting ministers were theologically influenced in great numbers by the new, warm, evangelical religion. Less so in the eighteenth but greatly in the nineteenth century was the Established Church in Sheffield brought into the evangelical tradition. Some infectious influence may have been at work amongst the Independents, not least on the mode of preaching, but quite sudden vigorous activity there certainly was, even though schism within congregations appeared to be the common immediate cause of expansion. They mostly stemmed from the mother Independent congregation at Nether Chapel. Disagreement over the appointment of a new minister led to a secession from Nether, amongst whom was Mr. Edward Bennet, a well-to-do sugar refiner who built a chapel for them in *Coal-pit Lane*, in 1774. The same group built for themselves a new and handsome chapel in *Howard Street*, in 1790. In 1780 *Lee-croft Chapel* was put up by seceders from 'Mr. Bennet's faction'. Another group of Independents erected *Garden Street Chapel*, in 1780 (which was later to house a Wesleyan group). Following disagreement with the minister a further secession from Nether Chapel took place leading to the building of *Queen Street Chapel*, in 1784, by a group of wealthy men.

Thus five Independent chapels were built in the town itself between 1774 and 1790, which with Upper and Nether Chapels and the Quaker meeting house gave eight buildings to the Old Dissenters, as against three of the Establishment— the Parish Church, St. Paul's, and one other, St. James's, which had been built in 1788. It is an interesting comparison.

The conditions of building the new church of St. James point

1 *History of Dissenters*, Bogue and Bennett, 1808.

only too clearly to the kind of people it was to provide for. To hold 660 people, it cost £3,000 which was raised in shares of £50 each which entitled the subscriber to a pew as a free-hold inheritance, and a family vault under the Church. Though a chapel of ease to the Parish Church, it stood adjacent to it, and was in fact a proprietary chapel for select people. Almost a century was to pass before the galleries were made free and open. The Church of England erected no further churches until 1821, by which time the population of the parish had reached 65,275! Clearly the masses of the people were not in the national church, nor expected to be.

But neither should it be assumed that the Old Dissenters were flooded with the common people. Substantial and im-posing though the Independent expansion is from 1774, as has already been pointed out, it should not in any way be regarded as planned provision for an increasing population. Independency never thought in those kind of terms anyway. No doubt the secessions left the parent congregations greatly weakened in numbers, only gradually to be repleted from grow-ing children, from families enlarged through marriage and birth, and by new members who took a pew in the chapel and entered with their kith and kin into the social group of the chapel. Before 1850 we have no detailed evidence of the ratio of appropriated to free seats for all the Dissenting chapels[1] but they were supported by pew rents, and it can safely be assumed that the free seats, where they existed at all, were few in number; which suggests on the one hand the sense of possession of their chapel by the group of families making up the member-ship of the church, and on the other the feeling of exclusion that would mark the attitude of outsiders even were they to consider the possibility of attendance. A typical arrangement is to be seen from the records of the Queen Street Chapel, where in the year after its opening in 1784, "to defray the incidental ex-penses thereof, such as candles, fire &c., Casual Repairs . . . there shall be three collections in the year on the most remote days from Quarterly Payments of the Seat Rents, say 5th

---

[1] Departing from Sheffield to the adjacent parish of Rotherham, John Guest's *Historic Notices of Rotherham*, 1879, gives a plan of the pews in the first Independent chapel—the Masbrough Chapel, erected in 1764. All the pews are rented and allocated by name, and the rentals are given on the plan. It was no doubt a typical arrangement.

Sabbath after. . . . No money to be received but in the above manner."[1] The most typical members would be merchants, 'little mesters' of modest substance, manufacturers, tradesmen and superior craftsmen . . . the "bones, muscles, and sinews of civil society" as Dissenters of the period have been called.[2]

*　　*　　*

The birth and growth of Methodism

We must retrace our steps and go back behind the spate of Independent chapel building into the middle years of the century, to trace the trickle that was to become Wesleyan Methodism, and the spring of 'experimental religion' that was to water all churches in the Evangelical revival. Sheffield has a rich source of information on the origins of Methodism in the area through one of the earliest studies of local Methodism ever compiled. In 1823 James Everett published his *Historical Sketches of Wesleyan Methodism in Sheffield and its vicinity*. Everett was (note cont.)

Plan of seats in the first Masbrough Chapel.

			£5 5s. 0d. per yr.
43 £2 per yr.	**23** 10s. per yr.	**22** 10s. per yr.	**1** £1 10s. 0d. per yr.
	24 10s. per yr.	**21** 10s. per yr.	**2** £1 7s. 0d. per yr.
42 18s. per yr.	**25** 10s. per yr.	**20** 10s. per yr.	**3** £1 4s. 0d. per yr.
41 16s. per yr.	**26** £1 10s. 0d. per yr.	**19** £1 10s. 0d. per yr.	**4** £1 4s. 0d. per yr.
40 16s. per yr.	**27** £1 7s. 0d. per yr.	**18** £1 7s. 0d. per yr.	**5** £1 per yr.
39 16s. per yr.	**28** £1 4s. 0d. per yr.	**17** £1 4s. 0d. per yr.	**6** £1 per yr.
38 16s. per yr.	**29** £1 per yr.	**16** £1 per yr.	**7** 16s. per yr.
37 12s. per yr.	**30** 18s. per yr.	**15** 18s. per yr.	**8** 16s. per yr.
36 12s. per yr.	**31** 16s. per yr.	**14** 16s. per yr.	**9** 16s. per yr.
35 12s. per yr.	**32** 12s. per yr.	**13** 12s. per yr.	**10** 12s. per yr.
34 12s. per yr.	**33** 12s. per yr.	**12** 12s. per yr.	**11** 12s. per yr.

[1] *History of Queen Street Chapel*, 1933.　　[2] Bogue and Bennett, *op. cit.*, 1812.

4

himself a Wesleyan minister who had lived some years in the
town during which he had quarried his information, much of it
being first-hand material supplied by three local patriarchs,
first-generation Methodists who lived respectively to the great
ages of 107, 94 and 95! Their engraved features, warts and all,
adorn his book together with engravings of the earliest Methodist preaching houses. James Everett will feature again in this
story, since he became one of the most famous Methodists, if
one of the most infamous and renegade Wesleyans, being one of
the three ministers ejected from the Wesleyan Connexion in the
middle of the nineteenth century at the time of the Reform
agitation in that denomination. He became the most famous of
the Wesleyan Reformers.

How did Methodist preaching first invade Sheffield to begin
its massive history? Why did it make such continuous progress,
and amongst what kind of people? There are in Everett's
rambling story enough facts, hints and asides to discover
answers to these questions. John Wesley made the first of his
many visits to Sheffield on June 14, 1742, and he came with
special intent "having a great desire to see David Taylor, whom
God had made an instrument of good to many souls, but not
finding him there, I was constrained to go forward immediately; however the importunity of the people constrained me
to stay, and preach both in the evening and in the morning".[1]
They met the following day for the first time. It was this David
Taylor who began evangelical and open-air preaching in the
parish and district of Sheffield in 1738. He is described as "an
itinerant preacher out of Leicestershire", in which county he
had been a butler, but in that year he came to reside with the
family of Mr. Wardlow, a Dissenter living at Fulwood, a rural
hamlet on the Derbyshire side of the parish. Apparently from his
arrival he was wont to practise those warm, lively pastoral
habits that at this time were uncommon among both Churchmen and Dissenters, praying with people in their homes,
exhorting them in the open, and singing with them in their
cottages. At Heeley, a village in the parish one mile south of the
township, "a few serious people associated with him, who were
afterwards denominated Methodists, and who may be considered as constituting the first Society belonging to the body in

1 *Journals*, June 14, 1742.

these parts".[1] Taken to Thorp to preach, a village six miles north of Sheffield, he "probably consecrated the very first barn, that is, in connexion with Methodism, as a temple for the public worship of God".[2]

John Wesley's own comment on his meeting with David Taylor is most illuminating and hints at his own newly-adopted missionary strategy: "I found he had occasionally exhorted multitudes of people in various parts; but after that, he had taken no thought about them, so that the greater part were fallen asleep again".[3] In fact, Everett tells us that many of those first converted by Taylor's preaching were sustained by their frequent attendance on the preaching of the Rev. Mr. Dodge, the curate of the Ecclesall Chapel, who was attached to the Methodists and "frequently wept over his auditors while enforcing the great truths of the Gospel", all of which procured him many enemies among the less devout members of the Establishment. But Everett also affirms that numbers were lost, not only because Taylor failed to organize a society on Wesley's pattern, but also through his gradual lapse into that 'German stillness' that Wesley, the Churchman, the Englishman, and the activist, continuously wrestled with in his own early itinerancy.

But a seed had been sown in Sheffield, a few had been mightily awakened, and, in spite of theological tensions bound up with the clashing personalities of preachers, Methodism had come to birth in Sheffield. James Bennet, probably a master grinder, had provided a little meeting house in Cheney Square, under the shadow of St. Paul's, in 1741, which witnesses to David Taylor's success in preaching and exhortation whatever John Wesley may have said about him! The little house in Cheney Square was completely destroyed by rioters in May 1743, and a second preaching house was erected the following year in the adjoining Pinstone Lane, the largest subscription coming from James Bennet. It was built as an ordinary dwelling house "with a view to beguile the turbulent" while it was in building, the stone flagged ground floor becoming the preaching room. But crisis dogged the members, and this house was lost to them, possibly through Edward Bennet, the son of their benefactor, becoming a Calvinist. An optician, Mr.

---

[1] Everett, *op. cit.*, p. 6.   [2] *ibid.*, p. 5.   [3] *Journals*, June 15, 1742.

John Wilson, built another house for them, a dwelling-house-preaching-house, probably in Burgess Street, which was tenanted by a filesmith, Henry Alsop, who has the honour of being the first class leader in Sheffield. But this too was the scene of rioting in February 1746, and in the course of a week of disturbance the house was completely demolished by the mob. John Wilson sought a warrant against the rioters, but the justices declined to take action until redress was secured through the magistrates at York, who fined the ringleaders and sentenced the Sheffield magistrates to rebuild the house.[1]

It is hardly surprising to read the comment of a man who was alive during these times, that the "Methodists in Sheffield were few and feeble". Foes without are now replaced by dissensions within. Apparently the rebuilt house was used both by the Methodists, properly so-called, led by John Wilson, and the Calvinistic Methodists led by Edward Bennet "at the head of Mr. Whitfield's interest"—"Calvinism would probably be preached in the morning, and Arminianism in the evening; and thus the minds of the people were often distracted with jarring sentiments, and this was not all; when any were awakened under the Methodist preachers, the persons belonging to Mr. Whitfield's party employed every method to gain them over to their creed".[2] The Wesleyans were ultimately driven out, procuring a warehouse in Mulberry Street in 1757 which they converted into a small preaching room, twelve yards by ten yards. It seems that there were five classes at this time, meeting in the homes of members.

Clearly, Methodism grew from humble and troubled beginnings; but it grew steadily, though very slowly, and in the face of public obloquy, suspicion and mob violence, and in spite of dissension within its body at a fluid time of its history, before organization was perfected and before its relation to existing theological traditions was worked out. Within a few years the Mulberry Street room was too small for the congregation, and in 1763 it was enlarged to twelve yards by eighteen yards, and a gallery put in; and it had the austere marks of the

---

[1] Charles Wesley writing in his *Journal* of the Sheffield rioters says they "exceeded in outrage all I have seen before. Those of Moorfields, Cardiff and Walsall, were *lambs* to these. As there is no King in Israel, I mean no magistrate in Sheffield, every man doeth as seemed good in his own eyes."

[2] Everett, *op. cit.*, p. 111–2.

early Methodist preaching houses—seats without backs, and
the sexes segregated on either side of the building. A further
serious split weakened them in 1764, when a preacher of the
Sheffield Circuit, Mr. T. Bryant, led a secession from the
Connexion. John Wesley had himself written that year that
"T. Bryant's staying another year in the Sheffield Circuit
would neither be good for him, nor for the people. I know his
strength and I know his weakness . . .", a view not unconnected
apparently with the fact that several years before he had been
ordained by a Greek bishop on a visit to England, which seems
to have given the preacher an improper arrogance! But
Bryant was unsuccessful in his attempt at getting hold of the
Mulberry Street Chapel, and within a year or two the seceding
body built *Scotland Street Chapel* where Bryant ministered to an
Independent congregation until his death, when the building
became the first home of the Methodist New Connexion in
1790.

In 1766 the first figures of membership were published at the
Annual Conference, and the Sheffield Circuit numbered 583
members. Not this number in Sheffield, however; the circuit
covered a great area embracing Doncaster, Worksop, Retford,
Mansfield, Chesterfield, Bakewell, Barnsley and Rotherham.
By 1771 when this large circuit had 652 members Sheffield had
between two and three hundred members in the Society. It
was in fact a small number of committed membership after
more than thirty years' labour. It is important to note that the
exact number of Society members was registered, and they
were organized in classes. In 1757 there were five classes in
Sheffield; in 1771 there were thirteen comprising the two or
three hundred members, and Everett has preserved for us the
names of the class leaders with the houses where they assembled
their members each week.

Besides members, there were of course the interested
'hearers' from the very beginning—it was implicit in the very
idea of itinerant preaching—but before the 'sixties the general
wider interest does not seem to have been great. In August
1761, John Wesley had preached outside the little Mulberry
Street preaching room "to thrice as many people as it would
have contained", but it could not have been a great crowd. But
from the 'sixties, with persecutions subsiding and a solid nucleus
formed, great numbers not avowedly Methodist were caught up

in the revival, while as the years went by the presence of Wesley himself in the town became the occasion of even greater public gatherings. Not only was Methodism taking root as a self-contained movement with its own identity, but it was also fertilizing the religious life of the whole community.

Certainly the Vicar of Sheffield did not minimize its importance. In his returns to the Archbishop of York's visitation of 1764 he opined that "the numbers of Dissenters is very large but cannot be well determined. Many persons go to their meetings who declare that they have no other reason for not going to church, but the want of room. The sect of Methodists is at present the most numerous here, the Independents next, then Presbyterians, and Quakers the fewest . . . the Methodists have very frequent meetings generally once in every day, and often twice ; their congregation is a great concourse of people consisting of some from every sect and many who profess to be members of the established Church of England".[1]

It is interesting to note that although the Independents were to erect five chapels in rapid succession after 1774, whereas the first large Wesleyan Chapel was not erected until 1780, and that remained the only large one until the turn of the century, the Vicar of Sheffield should have placed the Methodists first in numerical strength in his returns of 1764. At least it is evidence of the strong impression the Methodists were making on the public mind, and suggests the wide diffusion of their influence. This widespread interest and influence is evidenced when John Wesley came to Sheffield in 1779, on Thursday, July 15, a venerable and national figure, and preached in Paradise Square, as he says in his *Journals*, "to the largest congregation I ever saw on a week day". It was clear too when he came the following year to preach at the opening of the new Wesleyan Chapel in Norfolk Street; on the Sunday following he preached at the Parish Church at eight in the morning and "there was afterward such a number of communicants as was never seen at the old church before. I preached again at five; but very

---

[1] Returns of James Wilkinson, Vicar of Sheffield, to the Archbishop of York, 1764, at the Borthwick Institute of Historical Research, York.

It is more than probable that this enthusiastic week-day activity on the part of the Methodists was connected with the decision made in December 1764, that Evening Prayer should be publicly said at the Parish Church every evening at 7.00 p.m. after the ringing of the bell. (*Records of the Church Burgesses*, Dec. 5, 1764.) Sunday evening service was introduced in 1778.

many were constrained to go away".[1] It was a sign both of his own personal influence and that of Methodism—it also affords evidence that members of the Established Church were finding their spiritual home among the Methodists, for in the returns of 1764 the number of Easter communicants at the Parish Church was given as 850, while in 1780 they were down to 340, a number that was reduced to little over 200 by the end of the century; and yet John Wesley tells us that the numbers soared "as was never seen at the old church before" on that July Sunday of 1780 when he was present for the celebration.

The social composition of Methodism

What kind of people were the early Methodists? It is fairly clear that from the beginning when David Taylor began his preaching a very mixed group were stirred. There were people of substance—James Bennet a gentleman Dissenter and prosperous master craftsman, a number of women, several of quality, John Bennet a gentleman of leisure of Chinley (who became one of Wesley's closest associates, and married Grace Murray). After the earliest days there is Mr. Johnson of Barley Hall, Thorp, "a pious family some of whom were the first fruits of Methodist zeal", with whom John Wesley frequently stayed when he was in the vicinity. There was John Wilson the optician who provided a chapel, and his nephew Thomas Holy, Esq., "a substantial merchant". There was James Vickers, the inventor of Britannia Metal in Sheffield. . . . And yet poor people were there too. As Everett says, "not only were persons of respectability brought to an experimental acquaintance with the truth of God in this revival, but the poorest of the poor".[2]

David Taylor sang with the cottagers at Heeley and preached in the open at Sheffield Moor, and clearly too the more substantial patrons like Mr. Johnson of Barley Hall provided the opportunity for the preachers to meet their labourers and humbler fellow-inhabitants, inviting them to the hamlets, accommodating them, and placing a barn or some such building at their disposal. In outlying areas beyond the parish we read of the preachers bringing their influence upon lead-miners in Derbyshire, "a most savage race". Of Ecclesfield, a

---

[1] *Journals*, Sunday, July 2, 1780   [2] Everett, *op. cit.*, p. 149.

village just outside the parish carrying on Sheffield trades,
Everett says "Few places stood more in need, not only of
evangelizing, but of civilizing . . . the village was deemed the
Sodom of all the neighbouring places", and here too the
Methodists began the reforming process. A letter from the Vicar
of Rotherham to the Archbishop of York complains that "there
are weekly meetings established in several parts of this parish,
which occasion much disturbance, on account of some of the
impious doctrines inculcated by the itinerant teachers of this
sect, who for the most part are mechanics".[1] Of the Sheffield
society, Everett tells us concerning the Mulberry Street preaching house that "Such was the general poverty of the Society . . .
that it was found impractical to pay a person for taking care of
the chapel; and hence the principal members kept the key,
locked and unlocked the doors alternately. The few persons
who possessed the property had large demands made upon their
benevolence from various other quarters".[2] Again, the general
lack of wealth in the society is evidenced by small sums of
money granted to Sheffield by the Annual Conference, £5 in
1766, £8 in 1769. . . . It is inconceivable that an Upper or a
Nether Chapel could have needed such grants from outside the
area.

Clearly, Methodism in the eighteenth century was not led by
the "principal inhabitants" as the more modish Dissenting
chapels could claim to be. In fact Methodism at this period
defies sociological label, being a purely religious-revival movement, and not the stereotyped religious expression of a social
group. The movement had its more substantial patrons, but
they were converted by the new religious experience; some were
Dissenters, some were of the Establishment and continued to be,
some were worldlings who had no previous seriousness to their
faith. And by taking their faith outside the normal institutions
and proclaiming it among the people, it meant that men and
women, rude, poor and even brutish, and outside the religious
institutions of their time, could hear the Gospel, respond and
find their place and new status in the class meeting. The contempt in which the early Methodists were held, both by those
who were well-to-do and by the masses of the common folk, is
sufficient evidence of the social insignificance of their body.

1 Everett, *op. cit.*, p. 65.   2 *ibid.*, p. 65.

Justices, gentry, merchants and master manufacturers do not attack their own social group, and the 'mob' at this period did not throw mud, dirt and dead cats either at their own masters or at a solid group of their own kind. The evidence is thus many-sided, and can even look contradictory, but the pieces can be fitted together.

We have already traced the growth of Methodism, slow for twenty-five years, and then faster. In 1771 there were between two and three hundred members in Sheffield, and fruitful years lay ahead. In 1780 the first proper chapel was erected in Nor-folk Street, a large one, and on June 29 John Wesley himself preached at the opening of the new house, "thoroughly filled with rich and poor", as he says in his *Journals*. Undoubtedly the new chapel in the centre of the town must have given dynamic to the movement. In 1784 Sheffield town had 630 members; in 1788 there were 746, and when the aged Wesley made his last visit to the town and preached in the Norfolk Street Chapel on Wednesday July 9 of that year, he could write that "the house was much crowded, though one of the largest in England . . . in the morning (following) at five we had an evening congregation and the people seemed to devour the word. Here and at Hull are the two largest morning congregations which I have seen in the Kingdom".[1]

By 1795 there were 1,820 members, and by 1796, the year before the first secession led by Alexander Kilham, the high figure of 3,099 was attained. For some years people had been pressing in. Methodism had indeed travelled far from the days of the converted dwelling house, the warehouse and the attacks of the mob. The persecutions were a thing of the past; Meth-odism had persisted and men of substance had espoused it, and the new Norfolk Street Chapel crowded with a cross-section of the town was measure of the new status accorded her. This "large and commodious" building, capable of seating about 1,300, took on characteristics of the Dissenting chapels which are important to note. Although poorer members helped in its building after their day's work it cost £3,090 to erect, and the first six years' seat rents, in total £668, went towards the sum.[2] But there were free sittings for the poor—several hundred of

---

[1] *Journals.*   [2] *History of Norfolk Street Chapel*, T. A. Seed, 1907.

them—far more than any other single church, chapel or meeting house in the town provided, and an 1828 comment on the
Norfolk Street Chapel shows the good reputation that the
Methodists had in this matter. Norfolk Street Chapel, it was
said, "is a large and commodious place of worship, capable of
seating about 1,300 people, and contains a large proportion of
free sittings, a mode of accommodating the poor, of which
Methodism may be justly proud, having herein set an example
which has been worthily followed by other religious denominations who are anxious that to the poor the Gospel should be
preached".[1] And certainly Methodism had a following among
the poor to use the free sittings. But nonetheless the sense of
possession and of 'belonging' on the one hand, and that of
inferiority or exclusion on the other, stemmed from the practice of rented seats; they were to acquire ill-repute as the nineteenth century wore on, and there must have been a very
different 'feel' in Norfolk Street, though a much grander one,
than in the converted warehouse of Mulberry Street, especially
after the early Methodist practice of segregating men and
women on different sides of the building, as happened in Norfolk Street to begin with, gave way "to the preference of individuals, and the comfortable adaptation of family pews".[2]

The social advance and growing prestige of Methodism is to
be seen in these little details, and even more so with the building
of the Carver Street Chapel in 1804, "elegantly fitted up, with
extensive galleries of the crescent form", on the western edge of
the town, which drew off many of the more well-to-do from
Norfolk Street. It had pew sittings for 1,150 and free seats for
350; again, a very high proportion for those days. At the time
of building it was said to be the finest chapel in the whole
country, and it still stands in the middle of the city, a superb
building of its kind, with features both austere and rich.

The estranged poor

Although exact measurement of the extent to which the
people of Sheffield took a regular part in public worship is not
possible, it is fairly deduced that the bulk of the poorer folk, the
most hard pressed and least securely rooted in the community,

---

1 Blackwell's *Directory and Guide to Sheffield*, 1828.
2 *A Description of Sheffield*, c. 1830.

did not have their seat or pew in church or chapel, and that they would not have had a sense of 'belonging' even had they used the free places, which in any case were wholly insufficient for their numbers. True, the evidence at the period under review, the later decades of the eighteenth century and indeed the earlier years of the nineteenth, is circumstantial; it is not until the eighteen-thirties that we have forthright social documentation. But the conclusion is fairly deduced, and brings the excluded social group into court for examination.

Although the classes in English society have been as rigidly fixed as anywhere in the world, their edges have invariably been blurred. This was more true in Sheffield than in other industrial areas, where the proximity and merging of social groups was assisted by a variety of local factors. There was no resident aristocracy; there was no large purely merchandizing group, and—most important—the nature of the Sheffield trades, calling for little plant and capital, made many more little working masters, who themselves had been apprentices and journeymen and socially hardly removed from their own workmen. This makes it harder to isolate the poor as a social group, and harder also to define the limits of the artisan class. Nonetheless the poor we have always with us, though their characteristics, attitudes and self-consciousness change from age to age. There were the 'begging poor' of the seventeenth century, the 'mob' in the eighteenth, the 'labouring poor' of the nineteenth, and the 'common man' of the twentieth. They, their descendants, the social group that they comprised at any time, have in fact constituted the mission problem of the Church throughout the period of industrialization, whether the fact was recognized or not.

Their unrecorded attitudes to life, to 'religion', and to the churches of their time are what we would most like to know and understand. Their most commonly recorded reaction to society is in the cry of the poor and afflicted, but the eighteenth century in Sheffield is not one of abject desolation. On the contrary, it was in general a thriving century with no sign that the social problem was out of hand until the latter years. There was continuous demand for labour, wages were good, and both Arthur Young and Eden in their visits to the town were impressed with the high general earnings, the industry and the good standard of living of tradesmen, artisans and labourers.

The reasons were several, an expanding trade with the rest of the country, the opening of Continental markets, and the notable inventions of silver-plating, 'Sheffield plate', the polishing of hardened steel, and Huntsman's invention in 1770 of cast steel—all of which gave impetus to the local trades. The social picture is less one of poverty and distress than of industry, sturdy independence and joviality on the part of the workmen, if also of coarseness and drunkenness. Inevitably there was distress. We read of a great riot in the town in 1774, occasioned by a rise in the cost of coal, in which the mob burned the wooden railway and coal stage, paraded the town and were dispersed by muskets. There must have been many outbursts, instinctive group reactions when pressures were beyond endurance, but they are not the major note of the century.

The scene changes however in the last decade; the simple reaction of the labouring poor gives way to a much more complex picture in which strands quite separate in origin are tangled together, tighter here, looser there, and all coloured by the shattering events of the French Revolution. It spelt the birth-pangs of the modern age, and brought the political problem and acute social tensions to the fore. Social unrest was rife in the country by 1791, and in July of that year we read of the crowd destroying the gaol, liberating the prisoners, and proceeding to attack Broomhall, the residence of the resident justice James Wilkinson, who was none other than the Vicar of Sheffield. They burnt his furniture, library and hayricks, for which one of the mob was subsequently hanged at York. By July 1795, between four and five thousand were applying for help to the corn relief committee. Throughout the year 1800 there were disturbances, riots, and attacks on flour mills and shops through the high price of provisions. In March 1801 "upwards of 10,000 persons receive the benefit of the very liberal subscription entered into for the relief of distressed objects in the parish; so unprecedented is the wretchedness arising from the excessive high price of all the necessaries of life".[1] Clearly the distressed poor, as a large social group capable of an ugly mood, have emerged by the end of the eighteenth century, and a social problem rears its head that no public subscriptions, corn and compassion societies, or abounding personal philanthropy could dissolve.

[1] Sheffield *Iris*.

The political affinity of Radical Dissenters and the artisan class

Although with every conceivable reaction, the French Revolution shook the country in a quite unprecedented way, and Sheffield became a byword for sedition, privy conspiracy and rebellion. A local newspaper of 1793 asserts that "Sheffield is stigmatized as being a seat of ignorance and disloyalty",[1] but the generalization conceals the distinctive attitudes and reactions of the different social groups to the news from Paris. Initial attitudes in some quarters changed out of all recognition as the Revolution itself passed through the successive phases of the Bastille, the Terror, the wars, and the years of Napoleon. Sheffield radicals of the middle classes who in 1790 were sympathizing with the 'people' of France struggling for freedom, in 1794 were joining the Loyal Independent Volunteers to resist the Jacobins, with more than an eye on the prospect of trouble at home. And while in Birmingham in 1791, mobs in a 'Church and King' mood were wrecking the houses of middle-class Dissenting reformers for alleged Republicanism and sympathy with the revolutionaries abroad, in Sheffield in 1792 thousands of people were celebrating the success of the French revolutionary armies in the Netherlands at the ox roasting![2]

It is a perplexing period to unravel, once the generalities of national history give way to the successive events in the local prints. It is tempting to say that the middle-class Dissenters reacted in such a way, the Wesleyans and the Church of England in this way, and the workmen so. . . . Such clear-cut lines rarely exist between either religious or social groups in Britain. But distinct and diverse reactions from distinct quarters are visible and they have strong social and religious colouring. Certainly the 'radical' reputation of Sheffield was upheld! And the radicalism was not solely middle-class, at least in the mind of Authority as a report on Sheffield to the Secretary of War makes clear:

> . . . At Sheffield . . . I found that the seditious doctrines of Paine and the factious people who are endeavouring to disturb the peace of the country had extended to a degree very much beyond my conception; and indeed they seem with great judgement to have chosen this as the centre of all their seditious machinations, for

---

[1] Sheffield Local Register, Apr. 26, 1793.   [2] *Ibid*, Nov. 23, 1792.

the manufactures of this town are of a nature to require so little capital to carry them on that a man with a very small sum of money can employ two, three or four men; and this being generally the case there are not in this, as in other great towns, any number of persons of sufficient weight who could by their influence, or the number of their dependents, act with any effect in case of a disturbance. As the wages given to the journeymen are very high, it is pretty generally the practice for them to work for three days, in which they earn sufficient to enable them to drink and riot for the rest of the week, consequently there can be no place more fit for seditious purposes.

The mode they have adopted for spreading their licentious principles has been by forming Associations on terms suited to the circumstances of the lowest mechanics, of whom about 2500 are enrolled in the principal Society, and that it may not be confined, they allow any man to be present who will pay 6d for admission. . . .[1]

This does not refer, as one might at first think, to trades union activity which was undoubtedly increasing from 1790, but to associations of a wider cross-section, pressing for political reform, of which the Society for Constitutional Information was formed in December 1791. The "ideas of 1789", trade combination and outbreaks of mob violence all combined to terrify the authorities, and the symbol of them all was seen in Tom Paine. But Tom Paine did not distribute his own books in Sheffield, although it is an interesting fact that he had connexions with Rotherham at the Masbro' works of Thomas Walker, where he was occupied for a long time on building a model of the Southwark Bridge which was cast at that works! The fact is that there were intelligent and influential men in the town who found the ideas of Paine exceedingly congenial, whatever may have been their later reactions to the excesses of the French revolution and the tyranny, and they were Dissenters. And it is significant that there were no 'Church and State' mobs in Sheffield to molest them, as in many other large industrial towns. Samuel Roberts, a famous Sheffield silversmith, a social reformer, and conservative in political views, writes in his autobiography that "to many, even professed ministers of the Gospel, it (Tom Paine's *Rights of Man*) appeared

---

[1] Colonel De Lancey (Deputy Adjutant to the Secretary of War) June 13, 1792. H.O. 42/20—quoted in *The Early English Trade Unions*, A. Aspinall, 1949: p.4.

to become dearer than their Bible, and their visits to their
flocks were made with the Rights of Man in their pockets, to
induce them to read it".[1] Again, we are told that Jehoiada
Brewer, the Calvinist minister of Queen Street Chapel, enter-
tained "somewhat ultra Liberal opinions . . . at a time when
such avowal rendered a man liable to be reproached with being
associated with infidels in the assertion of the necessity of parliamentary reform, and in the advocacy of the claims of civil and
religious liberty".[2]

There is intriguing evidence of the attitude of 'Sheffield' and
of the role of radical Dissenters, in the great public meetings
that were held in the course of 1794, at a time when the most
repressive legislation was being hurried through Parliament,
and when the courts were filled with Government prosecutions
of anything that savoured of 'reform', or 'sedition', terms that
were synonymous in the official mind of the time. Sheffield has
always enjoyed large public meetings and demonstrations, and
certainly 1794 had its fill! A wide variety of causes coalesced
under the banner of Reform—peace and liberty, opposition to
the war with France and to the presence on English soil of
Prussian mercenaries, demand for Parliamentary Reform and
the abolition of slavery, and protest against the imprisonment
and transportation of reform-martyrs. On all these issues
Sheffield was kept informed, and her passions roused, by the
Society for Constitutional Information, and the Friends of
Peace and Reform, and other *ad hoc* groupings that the political
reformers set up for various propaganda purposes. It is, of
course, common history that middle-class 'philosophic Dissenters' inspired by such national figures as Price and Priestley
were zealous for Parliamentary reform, in the joint interest of
civil and religious liberty, but the consequence of this in a town
where the conservative Church influence was slight, Dissenters
many and without any sense of inferiority, and the people unmoved by 'Church and State' appeals may not be so well
known. Sheffield was such a town.

In August 1793 war was declared on revolutionary France,
and a Public Fast with an appropriate religious service was
proclaimed by Authority for Friday, February 28, 1794. No

1 *Autobiography*, Samuel Roberts, 1849: p. 44.
2 *Reminiscences of Old Sheffield*, R. E. Leader, 1875: p. 174.

doubt the order of service was duly used in Sheffield as elsewhere, but a huge counter-demonstration against the 'blasphemy' of the Fast was organized in West Street by the Friends
of Peace and Reform, attended by between five and six
thousand people. Its proceedings were remarkable, being at
the same time politically ultra-radical and wholly religious. It
began with prayer, concluded with a hymn written for the
occasion by James Montgomery and sung to the tune of *Old
Hundredth*, and a Serious Lecture was delivered by " a gentleman
from Halifax" which in fact was a sermon in which the Bible
had been ransacked to find every possible text to attack "the
venal tribe of Kings, Courtiers, Priests and their accomplices",
particularly any that might favour a National Church; the
whole address in the passionate interest of civil, political and
religious liberty, and the cause of Christ, Peace and France.

> ... Gallia must in spite of all her foes prevail. She will establish
> her Republic, and depend upon it, the Gospel will soon flourish
> there; nay ... but it does now flourish; the ministers of God are
> there propagating his word with success, so that to say the
> people are all atheists and without religion, argues weakness,
> ignorance, and wickedness. ...

The address had been written by a labouring mechanic; the
chairman of the meeting, the late secretary of the Sheffield
Constitutional Society, was duly arrested, and both the London
Corresponding Society and the Society for Constitutional
Information sent resolutions congratulating the Sheffield
Friends of Peace and Reform. Certainly the ideas of Tom
Paine had penetrated Sheffield, but the wholly religious sanctions of a popular Sheffield meeting on the controversial issues
of political reform are not due to Tom Paine but to the influence of radical religious dissenting opinion. And it witnesses
to the common interest at the time of certain middle-class and
artisan groups. No doubt it is idle, but it is also fascinating, to
speculate what the future might have held had this particular
axis been maintained.

A much larger meeting was held a few months later on
Castle Hill, on April 7, organized by the Friends of Justice,
Liberty and Humanity "to consider the propriety of addressing
the King, in behalf of the persecuted Patriots, Citizens Muir,
Palmer, Skirving, Margarott and Gerrold; also of again peti-

tioning the House of Commons for a Reform of the Representation of the People, and to determine upon the propriety of petitioning the King for the total and unqualified Abolition of Negro Slavery". Notwithstanding the inclemency of the weather, from ten to twelve thousand people assembled at three o'clock that Monday afternoon to hear Henry Yorke, of national fame, speak on behalf of the 'reform-martyrs' who had been transported to Botany Bay, whose trials (says G. M. Trevelyan) had been "among the worse pages in our judicial and political annals".[1] Naturally enough, Yorke was arrested, and tried at York for sedition and incitement and for using such dangerous phrases as 'levelling', 'revolution', 'a word about arms'. . . . He was found guilty and sent to prison. Yorke in fact strongly denied the accusation of incitement to armed revolution, claiming that he stood for no more than reform in the representation of the people and for shorter Parliaments, and that Earl Fitzwilliam, President of the Whig Club who was present at the trial, did as much. He conducted his own defence, calling among other witnesses two Independent ministers who gave the most direct and uncompromising evidence to his innocence, one of whom was the Rev. Moses Taylor, minister of Howard Street Chapel. So much so, that the Prosecution began his reply with a vehement over-all attack on members of "that holy profession", when "minister after minister . . . swore with confident memory and perfect recollection, negativing every word spoken by honest and plain men. . . ."[2]

Not too much significance should be attached to the vast size of these public meetings; Sheffield has always liked a holiday and a lively meeting, and one of them was a public fast day and a 'holiday', and the other was on a Monday, when men who were in employment and could afford it frequently took a 'Saint Monday'. But it showed large interest, and also a radical-religious-middle-class element in the leadership of public opinion. It shows something of the climate of opinion in Sheffield to say the least, and at the famous treason trial of Thomas Hardy, the founder of the London Corresponding Society, at the Old Bailey later in the year, several members of the Sheffield Society for Constitutional Information, themselves under arrest, had to give evidence, and the reports of the

[1] *British History in the Nineteenth Century*, G. M. Trevelyan, 1922: p. 70.
[2] *Trial of Henry Yorke*, Henry Yorke, 1795: p. 173.

5

Sheffield meetings found in Hardy's house were particularly scrutinized as evidence against him.[1] Remarkably for the times, Hardy and his fellow-prisoners were acquitted, but quite typically the Sheffield Friends of Reform dined together to celebrate his release and that of the five members of the Sheffield Constitutional Society.[2]

We must not assume a general political maturity amongst the masses: far from it. When middle-class reformers had later entered fully into the spirit of the war against Napoleon, one of them writes in his diary of the dangerous political ignorance of much working-class opinion, and quoted the typical views expressed in a public house: ". . . everything is wrong in this country, from the King to the Constable, and Bonaparte is an honest fellow. I insisted upon the despotic nature of the French government, and the great freedom we enjoyed. They would not believe me. Speaking of the Duke of Wellington, they said he was driven from Madrid. I told them he was in advance of it and pursuing the retreating enemy. They said the rich always pretended to know better than the poor . . ."[3]— a chance conversation in a pub recorded by a mildly radical middle-class Dissenter, but giving some insight into popular opinion in some quarters. Nor again must it be assumed that Dissenting opinion was solid, and certainly, as has already been evinced, it was not unchangeable. We have noticed the attitude of some Independent ministers, but it must also be noted that in 1805 on December 5 when a day of Thanksgiving was observed for the victory of Trafalgar, the Minister of Nether Chapel preached on "England's greatness, and the effect of the Divine Power", and against "such contemptible scribblers as Paine, who while living is sunk almost into oblivion",[4] and no doubt all the churches and chapels evinced similar sentiments on that great day. But the years before are not thereby erased.

The Toryism of Church and Wesleyan Methodism

It would be a gross understatement to say that the Church of England and the official Wesleyan outlook would have had no

---

[1] *Memoirs* of James Montgomery, vol. 1, 1854: pp. 184–5.

[2] Sheffield Local Register, Dec. 26, 1794.

[3] *The Diary of Thomas Asline Ward*, 1812; "Peeps Into The Past", Bell and Leader, 1909, p. 191.

[4] *Sermon on the Day of Thanksgiving at Nether Chapel*, by J. Dawson, Dec. 5, 1805. Sheffield Library Local Pamphlets, vol. 44.

truck with the democratic reform agitation with all its Jacobin
undertones. This at least is a generalization that can be safely
made. John Wesley himself had been both a High Churchman
and a Tory, and his journals give ample evidence of his loyalty
to the Constitution and King George, and to his complete lack
of sympathy with the American colonists in their criticisms of
the British crown. And the Wesleyan Methodist Conference
persistently continued Wesley's Toryism and 'No Politics'
rule and imposed it throughout the Connexion at terrible cost
in membership, well beyond the middle of the nineteenth
century.

The evidence for this at the time of the French wars is
patently clear in the secession of 1797, led by Alexander Kilham against the paternalism and autocracy of the Wesleyan
Conference, in the interests of more democratic government in
the Connexion. It was essentially a religious movement he led,
but Kilham was greatly influenced by the new ferment of ideas
stemming from the *Rights of Man* and the French Revolution,
and the seceders he led were nicknamed 'Tom Paine Methodists'.[1] In fact he drew off the democratically minded and so
rendered the Wesleyan parent body more monochrome in its
social views. Interestingly Sheffield Methodism was probably
the most disaffected, due no doubt to the long and strong
influence of the Dissenters. In 1796, the Wesleyan Connexion
numbered 3,099 members in the town; in 1797, the year of the
secession, it was reduced to 1,857, with a further drop to 1,080
by 1804. The New Connexion began with only 5,000 members
spread over the towns of the North of England, so that Sheffield
clearly had more than its share! In Sheffield the New Connexion members took over the old Scotland Street Chapel in
the very year of the secession and Kilham himself came to be
their minister until his early death in 1798, and his own words
witness to the welcome he was accorded and the appeal of his
views. "I never preach on Sunday mornings at eight or on a
weeknight, without having about 1,500 hearers, and on Sunday
evenings we do not know what to do".[2] The secession in 1797
of 'Methodism's oldest daughter' is indirect but good evidence
of the official and general attitude. The complexion of the

[1] *Methodism and Politics*, E. R. Taylor, 1934: p. 85.
[2] *Centenary of Methodist New Connexion in Sheffield*, 1897. Sheffield Library Local
Pamphlets, vol. 74.

New Connexion would be less easy to ascertain, but it would have political affinities with the Radical Dissenters, it would contain a greater admixture of the lower orders, and certainly it would show a more vital 'experimental' expression of religion than the Old Dissenters.

It must not be assumed, because the formative radicalism of the period was most articulate in Dissenting circles, that all Dissenters held such views. Their long experience of political disability as well as theological attitude predisposed them to political reform, in an age that was stirred by such possibilities. But also they had prospered in their callings, and particularly in the non-chartered towns like Sheffield where they had taken strongest root, and were among the leading manufacturers. If on some scores they were drawn to support democratic causes, as indeed we have seen they were, on other scores they could have an instinctive and shrewd fear of democracy, not to speak of revolution, that challenged them as a socially privileged group. Both elements and the tensions between them persisted, and continued in the heart of the Liberal Party of the nineteenth century, which was so strongly sustained by Radical Nonconformity.

Contemporary historians of the Dissenters made clear the simple operation of 'sin' in the lives and attitudes of Dissenters, as they prospered in trade and business, and as their disabilities were removed. Early zeal, they say, could not be maintained; some "sighed for a more modish faith to appear with grace in the fashionable world", trade and commerce often led them "into the course of this world and fashionable folly", and some in chapel "yawned out the hour, and those who slept began to consider that sleeping at the meeting house was dearer than at church".[1] This is national comment, and less true of Sheffield, where their strength precluded any sense of social inferiority and where the Church of England lacked a higher social class that wealthy Dissenters might have sought to enter. In Sheffield they could 'be themselves', to take a more 'Whig' or a more 'radical' attitude according to disposition and their own reactions to contemporary events.

But these qualifications notwithstanding, the strong dissenting radical element in Sheffield at the birth of the modern era

---

[1] *History of Dissenters*, Bogue and Bennett, 1812.

stands clear, likewise its capacity at times to give leadership to the most radical views within the artisan group. Clear too by the end of the eighteenth century is the distinct and different religious colouration of the different socio-political groups, traceable back to the seventeenth century and pointing forward to the pattern of the nineteenth. The several destinies of the religious bodies were to be closely shaped by the histories of the social groups they inhered. We see also the artisan group with its own identity, politically unformed but no longer aptly described as the 'begging poor', and capable of an ugly mood towards more privileged groups when prodded by adversity. Their general estrangement from all the religious bodies will become apparent as we trace their expansion into the nineteenth century.

Chapter 3

CHURCH AND PEOPLE IN THE 'BLEAK AGE',
1800–1850

AFTER THE remarkable spate of Independent Chapel building in the 'seventies and 'eighties of the eighteenth century, and the rising of the first Wesleyan Chapel in Norfolk Street, there was surprisingly little extension by any of the denominations for a period of nearly forty years. A few extra chapels witnessed both the growth and the schisms within the Methodist body, but these apart, there was little activity until the eighteen-twenties, when the National Church made some massive provision, if not in the numbers of buildings, certainly in their structural aspect! The year 1821 therefore is a good one in which to recapitulate, and take stock of the provision made by the churches in relation to the population. Most of the buildings have already appeared in the tracing of the denominational origins; they are not so many at this time that they cannot be individualized, and their social complexion is important to grasp in any historical and sociological study of church and society. The population had risen steadily; by 1821 the total of the parish was 65,275, of which about 55,000 lived in Sheffield township and its immediate suburbs.

Provision of the Churches in 1821

Providing the ministrations of the Church of England there were the three churches, the Parish Church, St. Paul's and St. James', and also the Shrewsbury Hospital Chapel. The churches together provided accommodation for about 4,000, and with the two chapels of ease outside the township, at Ecclesall and Attercliffe, were served by eight clergymen. We have already examined the appropriated nature of the sittings in the churches of the township, and in measured words we have evidence that at this time, about 1821, "there were not 300 sittings for the poor in all the churches (Established) of Sheffield, though the population must have exceeded 60,000". It was the striking comment of a clergyman of the town given before a Royal Commission.[1]

The public reaction to this situation finds colourful expression in the controversy at this time on the levying and collection of church rates—a matter on which passions ran high in Sheffield. We see too the unchallenged strength of Dissenters amongst the ratepayers. A Vestry Meeting was called in 1818 to examine the accounts of the church-wardens, and to report on the necessity of a church rate upon the parish. A committee was appointed, which came to the unfavourable conclusion that "(we) cannot forbear remarking that the claim of those who are called the owners of the pews in the Parish Church to have an exclusive property in such pews, is at variance with the general law; and that if they intend to persist in their claim, it is well worth their attention to consider whether it be proper to suffer the church-wardens to call upon the rest of the parishioners to assist them in providing the expenses . . . in a church, which according to their claim, is for their own exclusive benefit; and your Committee would beg respectfully to remind the seat-owners that the rest of the parishioners maintain their own religious establishments, without having or seeking any assistance whatever for them".[2]

The matter was put even more bluntly at a Vestry Meeting in the chancel of the Parish Church in September 1819, when a proposition for a church rate of 2d. in the pound was lost in favour of an amendment "that the expenses of providing necessaries of the performance of divine service ought to be defrayed by the pew owners, who have excluded the rest of the parishioners from the use of the church, and claim an absolute right to their pews".[3] This was the majority view of a public meeting of the ratepayers, and the attitude of Dissenters is certainly expressed within it. But it is also a revealing insight into the public mind. Many later attempts were made to levy

[1] Report on the Trades of Sheffield and Moral and Physical Conditions of young persons employed in them, made under authority of the Royal Commission of Inquiry into the employment of children in trades and manufactures not under the Factory Act. J. C. Symons, 1843.

[2] Report of Committee to examine accounts of the church-wardens, Aug. 8, 1818. Sheffield Library Local Pamphlets, vol. 60.

[3] Sheffield Local Register.

a rate, but without success. Sheffield was one of the very first towns in the country to have done with church rates and may even have been the first. By the time the issue was a national battle cry of militant Liberal Nonconformity, Sheffield at least was not disturbed by it as a local issue; this particular battle had long been won!

Then there were the chapels of the Old Dissenters, an imposing list, and even in 1821, after no building for thirty years, still making greater provision than any other religious group. There was the Upper Chapel, variously denominated Presbyterian, Arian, and Unitarian, "well-pewed, three large galleries" with several ministers, all scholarly men, in its service, containing the doyen of Sheffield Nonconformity. There was the meeting house of the Quakers in Fig-Tree Lane, "capable of containing 1,200 people, but rarely so filled"; they were described as "a numerous body in 1819", and a prosperous if austere one. The Independent Calvinists had five chapels in the town, Nether Chapel, Howard Street, Lee Croft, Garden Street and Queen Street, each with a minister. Some picture of the organization of the chapels can be gained from the history of the Nether Chapel, the oldest of the Calvinistic chapels. In spite of the fact that the membership of the society appears to have been extremely small for many years and passing through bad times according to a modern history of the chapel, a contemporary guide to the town alleges that "it is in contemplation to remove this building, which is much too small for the congregation, and to erect an elegant and commodious chapel on the same site". The fine new chapel was built in 1827, subscribers of ten guineas and more being entitled to a piece of land for burial. The advertisement of opening says that the chapel is built for 1,000 persons, with a gallery for 350 school children . . . "a very eligible and convenient part of the body of the chapel (besides the upper gallery, open at the evening service) affording together accommodation for 400 persons, will be entirely free; which our poorer neighbours are respectfully and affectionately invited to occupy".[1] It would be interesting to know whether the poorer neighbours availed themselves of this generous offer. In fact the Old Dissenters, as the Church of England, can hardly have expected great demands upon their free seats. The Upper Chapel had 50 free

[1] *Lights and Sidelights of 200 Years of Nether Chapel*, 1916.

out of 900, Howard Street 100 free out of 637, Lee Croft 57 out of 475, and Garden Street had 420 seats none of which was free.[1]

In 1821 there were three groups of Methodists in the town. The parent Wesleyan body had the two fine chapels in Norfolk Street and Carver Street, which have already featured in the origin of the Society. There was one other Wesleyan building in suburbs adjoining the town, north of the Don at Bridge-houses, a small plain preaching house, whose history serves to show both the numerical and the social advance of the Methodists. In 1795 a very humble preaching room had been made of a barn where the Sheffield poet, James Montgomery, in 1802 associated "with some of the poorest of Christ's flock". In 1808 the society erected a small plain brick chapel, and developed a most vigorous social life, with Sunday schools, classes, district visitors, a library and secular evening schools, with a large and devoted group of teachers, superintendents and committees. They must have burst the walls of the old chapel, until 1834 when they built a second larger chapel, "a chaste and beautiful Grecian structure of freestone, an ornament to the place, and an honour to the persons by whose taste and liberality it was erected".[2] It accommodated 750 persons, and "in order to meet the circumstances of all classes the pews are let at the following extremely moderate rates:—The best sittings are 5s. per half-year; the rest from that amount to 2s. per half-year . . . there are from two to three hundred free seats for the accommodation of the poor".[3]

Whatever a later generation may have said of the practice of seat rents and whatever sense of separation between the "sheep and the goats" may have followed the practice, the long influence of Bridgehouses Wesleyan Chapel over the best part of a century, in a very populous and poor part of the town, justified those measures without which no chapel would have been there. But the growth in stability and prosperity, though not rivalling the Independents, is marked. It is a measure of the social, moral and religious elevation of those who had been among the poorest, as it is of the advance that the social group of a chapel could make in a generation. By 1821 this process

---

1 Figures from 1853 Ordnance Survey Map.
2 *Centenary Record of Bridgehouses Wesleyan Methodism*, 1911 : p. 31.
3 *ibid.*, p. 34.

within Wesleyan Methodism was well advanced in urban areas, where large chapels were a practical proposition and where a stratum of society was continuously growing that was neither proletarian and destitute, nor wealthy and rooted in the older churches. In 1827 there were 2,106 members of the Wesleyan Connexion in the town, but several times this number would have been hearers; they were regarded as a now "influential sect". Four ministers of the Connexion were resident in Sheffield. Then there was the Methodist New Connexion, the more democratic Kilhamite body, meeting at the Scotland Street Chapel, the first flush of its enthusiasm no doubt having passed with the turbulent years of the 'nineties. They had their own minister.

There was also an obscure congregation of Independent Methodists, who had seceded from the Wesleyans, and built for themselves Townhead Cross Chapel in Bow Street in 1821, "maintaining as an indispensable rule of faith, that their ministers should not receive any wages for their services. . . . It is a plain square building, calculated to hold a large congregation. . . . The preachers are working men from amongst themselves . . ."[1] We should like to know more of this body.

The Baptists, who had begun to meet in the Coalpit-Lane Chapel in 1806, had built for themselves a chapel in Townhead Street in 1814; they had their own minister. The Roman Catholic Chapel in Norfolk Street "capable of containing a numerous congregation" had been erected in 1816, following the use of a large room attached to a house of the Duke of Norfolk. And in 1821, the one other congregation in the town was in the Coalpit-Lane Chapel, "occupied by that deluded sect called Johannaites, who notwithstanding the detection of Johanna's imposture by that stern determinator death, yet maintain that she possesses the efficacy of salvation to all mankind".[2] Odd religion is by no means confined to the twentieth century!

Such was the total provision in the town and its immediate suburbs in 1821, when the population within this area was about 55,000. It is interesting to note that although so little additional provision had been made in the previous thirty

---

[1] *The Picture of Sheffield*, T. Ramsay, 1824: p. 154.   [2] *ibid.*, p. 155.

years, years of social unrest and war, judged by modern standards the total provision, possibly 14,000 places, was very
considerable indeed. Moreover we have taken stock of the
situation on the eve of considerable expansion. It appears too
from the evidence adduced that in the main the provision was
for the better sort of people, or at least the type that could rent
a pew each half-year at the cost of a day or two's wage. It is
possible to trace a multi-layered social gradation through the
denominations, and the congregations within them, from the
wealthiest to the poorest for whom some very slight provision
was made in the free seats. Below this thick religious sandwich
were the artisans and the labouring poor, whose typical members could not have, and probably did not want, a share in the
cake.

Provision in the outlying areas of the parish

For a body claiming to be the Church of the nation, both the
limited provision and the social restrictiveness of the Church of
England is outstanding in the period under review. Perhaps the
National Church assumed her inherited place in society too
easily, when clergy were leading public notabilities in whom
the conservative exercise of social power was vested, and while
the masses came to her for baptism, marriage and burial and
accorded her the undisputed title of 'the Church'. And indeed, short of ceasing to be the Establishment, it is hard to see
what could have been done, so legally bound was the Church,
so lacking in any freedom of manoeuvre and so at ease
and compliant in the situation. It was a lameness that
weakened the Church of England from the beginning in all the
industrial areas of the country, and from which she has never
recovered.

We have seen the provision made by the Church of England
in the town, at the Parish Church, St. Paul's and St. James',
and the facts speak for themselves. The position in the outlying
parts of the parish was no better. The whole area east of the
township fell within the chapelry of Attercliffe, where the
Attercliffe chapel of ease was to serve the Byerlows of Attercliffe-cum-Darnall and Brightside. Yet in 1821, in Carbrook,
Attercliffe and Darnall alone, there were 3,172 "consisting
chiefly of colliers, mechanics, and manufacturers of cutlery

and hardware", while the chapel "would not contain more than 450 to 460 persons, besides which the seats and pews being entirely private property, no provision at all was made for the poor".[1] The Nonconformists on the other hand were well ahead. The Wesleyans had a chapel at Attercliffe in 1803, where there had been a preaching station seven years before the erection; at Darnall there was Methodist preaching from 1796, and a chapel from 1823. The Independents had a cause at Attercliffe from 1760, it is said, and certainly a chapel there from 1805, and at Darnall there was a chapel by 1828 after some years in which the members had used a cottage and a hayloft. All of these were in the Attercliffe-cum-Darnall Byerlow, and across the river Don, in the Brightside Byerlow, there were Wesleyan chapels at Bridgehouses in 1808, at Grimesthorpe in 1809, and several other preaching places appear on the plans early in the century. This is an astonishing setting in which to find the solitary episcopal chapel in so large an area.

The situation was similar in the larger area west of the township, in the Byerlow of Ecclesall, and Upper and Nether Hallam. Far to the south-west was the one chapel of ease at Ecclesall, which had been built in 1788, replacing the restored chapel of 1622; it contained 700 sittings, 580 of which were let at an average of 2s. a sitting per annum, and 120 of which were free.[2] Only a multiplicity of widely dispersed centres could possibly have met the needs of so huge an area, so much of which was wild rough country, in which the many little hamlets were completely isolated from all that were not in their own little valley. The Nonconformists provided between them such a multiplicity of centres. There had been an old Dissenting meeting house at Fulwood since 1724; the Methodist New Connexion had chapels at Walkley in 1819 and at Heeley in 1826, and there were Wesleyan chapels at Owlerton in 1825, Heeley 1826, and at Ranmoor from 1783 and Whiteley Wood from 1789. And in addition to these solid centres there had been a score of preaching places over the area, in almost every small hamlet, many of them going back to the end of the eighteenth century and most of them appearing on the Wesleyan preaching plans, but several of them established by the New Connexion

---

[1] ibid., p. 251.   [2] Hunter, op. cit., p. 349.

and the Primitive Methodists. Clearly, in these rural outlying parts of the parish, the Church of England could not compete with the flexible, mercurial habits of the Methodists. It was to have significant consequences for Sheffield, as urbanization proceeded, and the little hamlets became the oldest suburban centres of a large city.

Expansion of the Church of England and the Methodists after the Napoleonic Wars

After the long war with France, it was realized that the provision made by the Church of England in the industrial towns was grossly inadequate to the population increases, and that great numbers had become Dissenters in part through sheer lack of space in the national churches. This was the background to the Act of 1818 by which Parliament voted £1,000,000 for building churches in the populous centres. It was generally called 'the Million Act', and the sum was subsequently increased by the Treasury, besides stimulating much voluntary effort. Sheffield was granted four of these 'Million' churches, but there were serious limitations to the scheme from the commencement. The clergy appointed had no parochial cure or stipend, and their support was to be derived from fees and pew rents. Nearly half of the seats were to be free, but the places allotted to the poor were in the less comfortable parts of the churches and many of very little use at all, although this was in keeping with the custom of the day in both churches and chapels where free accommodation was available. The four Sheffield churches were massive Gothic structures designed to last for ever, and even the bombs of the Second World War could do no more than blast them. Little hope had the Chartists of burning one of them down in 1839 with flaming tarred paper floated against it!

St. George's on the west side of the Sheffield township was the first. The memorial stone was laid in 1821 in the month of George IV's coronation, and under the stone was laid a glass jar containing a set of coronation medals, and a eulogy by James Montgomery to Napoleon Bonaparte, the tidings of whose death had just reached the town. The church was consecrated in 1825. It was to seat 2,000, and the handbill advertising the opening made reference to the seating arrangements.

"Many of the pews in St. George's Church, being now tenanted, persons will be in attendance to shew Strangers into Vacant Sittings. The public are informed that there are upwards of a thousand free seats for those who are unable to take paid sittings".[1] It rapidly became the best attended church in the town, and the free seats too were well occupied, according to James Montgomery, speaking at a public meeting some time later on the vexed subject of church rates.[2] St. Philip's on the north-west side of the town was consecrated in 1828, St. Mary's on the south side in 1830, and Christ Church in Attercliffe in 1826. In each of them the provision was for 2,000, with about 800 seats free and unappropriated.

It would be interesting to know the way in which the new buildings were occupied. Were there large numbers of people waiting for the day to rent a pew for the first time? Did they desert another church for the newer one, perhaps more conveniently placed, or more modish and attractive? Were other buildings denuded as a consequence? There is evidence that all these things happened to some extent, although the story would vary from church to church. But it cannot be doubted that there would be many people, especially in the new suburbs where the churches were erected, who would be brought to attend and belong by the very opening of a fine new cream stone building, an event of greater public note than would be the case in the twentieth century.

Neither were the Nonconformists inactive, or more accurately neither were the Methodists inactive. The Old Dissenters in fact remained the least active of all the denominations, the only contribution being made by the Independents who put up two or three smaller chapels in outlying parts of the parish, and one large one in the town, Mount Zion, in Westfield Terrace in 1834—their only addition to the town itself between 1790 and 1854. It is remarkable to see how the Independents, who produced such a crop of buildings between 1774 and 1790, quite suddenly cease to expand as a new denomination comes on to the scene. The outstanding Nonconformist activity after 1821 for many years, both in the township and in the more outlying centres of population of the parish, is Methodist, Wesleyan and New Connexion, both of which were endowed

---

1 *St. George's Church, Sheffield*, J. E. Furniss, 1925.
2 Sheffield *Iris*, Feb. 5, 1828.

with a flexibility that was admirably suited to the fast expanding town. Large Wesleyan chapels continued to arise in the town, at its growing edges. Thus a handsome Gothic building, the Ebenezer Chapel, was built in Moor-fields in 1823, in dignified keeping with the former two large chapels in Norfolk Street and Carver Street. It contained 1,579 places, of which 366 were to be free. The Park Chapel was completed in 1831 in the populous south-eastern Park area of the town. Originally the entire lower floor was to have been free, but such was the demand for seats that it was decided to make only the two top corners at the back of the gallery, and five pews in the bottom, free and unappropriated. The rents are recorded. In the gallery the seats were 4s. 9d. in the front row per half year, 4s. in the second row, 3s. 3d. in the third row, 2s. 6d. in the fourth, 2s. in the fifth, and 1s. 6d. in the corners, and 3s. for the seats in the bottom of the chapel.[1] Not large sums, it would appear on first sight; but for a small family it could mean half a working-man's wage for the week twice a year. No doubt superior artisans with steady work in good trades could manage it and did, and many such men would have been Methodists.

But the Methodists did not restrict their later building to large chapels. In the outlying villages and hamlets of the parish, both the Wesleyans and the New Connexion Methodists produced humble meeting houses and little chapels wherever preaching centres had produced a nucleus of the faithful. Preaching places occur on the early preachers' plans long before there were chapels. They began as open-air stations, or in houses or barns, in a gentleman's hall at Whiteley Wood, and at Fulwood in a public-house, where the publican's wife would suspend a white sheet on the brow of a hill whenever the preacher came—the house held two licences simultaneously, one as a public-house and one as a house of prayer.

There were in fact two ways in which the Methodist chapel could be born; by a brand-new building that the existing members of a congregation would subscribe for, or by the embryonic growth of a little indigenous group, from a preaching centre to a barn or school, and later a small chapel and then a larger one, all in the same locality, or even on the same site.

1 *History of Wesleyan Methodism in Sheffield Park*, J. J. Graham, 1914: pp. 62–66.

Methodism had in fact grown in this kind of way in the beginning, as the antecedents of Norfolk Street Chapel clearly show.
The rapid development of Methodist chapels is therefore understandable, at a time when the Church of England moved slowly,
massively, and ponderously, a dinosaur among smaller livelier
mammals. The Methodists had complete local freedom to
develop in their own flexible way; their buildings could be
makeshift and economical; they could start 'causes' or stop
them, or remove them elsewhere, and above all they were
rooted in local groups far too small to be considered for episcopal chapels of ease. They required only a preacher, who could
be a layman, and zeal—and they had both. Where the National
Church required an Act of Parliament, a grant of money, an
educated gentleman and a crop of lawyers, the Methodists required only a friendly barn and a zealous preacher! The fact
that the Methodist chapels could grow fashionable, and take on
all the characteristics of a stable pew-renting congregation, did
not prevent the more humble developments elsewhere. It was
one of the secrets of the spread both of the first Methodism, and
a.so of her later offshoots, many of which spread precisely because of their reversion to the earlier methods. Hence the
multiplication of Methodist chapels, large and small, the
headache of anyone who would track them all down!

The public recognition of this Nonconformist expansion,
particularly of Methodism, finds expression in an incidental
comment in the 1833 Directory of the town:

> ... As in many other places, the million act came too late to sup-
> port the former dignity and superiority of the 'mother church'
> in Sheffield, for we find there are now in the town no fewer than
> 22 places of worship, wholly unconnected with her . . . and in-
> clude amongst their numerous congregations a large portion of
> the most opulent and respectable families.

By 1841, when there were 112,492 people in the entire parish,
there were 13 churches of the Establishment with sittings for
about 15,000 hearers, of which at most 6,000 were free, while
there were 37 Nonconformist chapels, capable of seating
25,000 of which less than a third were free.[1] As at earlier periods,

---

[1] After 1841 (and some may well say before) the number of buildings becomes
too large for their separate historical treatment, even were it possible to do so
with them all, and once the distinctive character and origin of each religious group

when the total provision had been set against the population we can say that, judged by modern standards, it was very considerable indeed.

* * *

The Evangelical élite

And what of the reaction of the people to this array of churches and chapels? Certainly they must have been impressed by the continuous building of such fine edifices, and it is hard to-day to imagine that the huge, dark, begrimed buildings were once cream limestone, or redbrick, set among new industrial housing or suburban villas. Clearly large sections of the community were no mere onlookers. The very existence and continued proliferation of buildings witness to the Christian convictions of a large growing social group, to their zeal, vigour

(note cont.)

is traced, the individual details even where obtainable belong only to highly specialized local interest. Beyond a certain point, the wood is more important than the trees, especially when there are so many trees. In the appendix there is an historical chart showing the development in each denomination. There are no doubt omissions and errors in connexion with smaller Methodist chapels, but the list is probably as complete as can be made.

The following is the total list in 1841 within the boundaries of the old parish of Sheffield:

Church of England: The Parish Church; St. Paul's; St. James'; St. George's; S* Mary's; St. Philip's; St. John's; Christ Church, Attercliffe; Ecclesall Church; Christ Church, Fulwood; St. Thomas', Crookes; Holy Trinity, Darnall; the Shrewsbury Hospital Chapel.

Wesleyan Methodist: Norfolk Street; Carver Street; Ebenezer, Moor-fields; Bridgehouses; Park Chapel; Brunswick Chapel; Owlerton; Crookes; Heeley; Manor; Attercliffe; Darnall; Grimesthorpe; Ranmoor; Whiteley Wood.

Methodist New Connexion: Scotland Street Chapel; Walkley; Heeley; South Street, Moor; Malin Bridge; Attercliffe.

Protestant Methodist: Surrey Street; Stanley Street.

Primitive Methodist: Bethel, Cambridge Street.

Independent: Nether Chapel; Lee Croft; Garden Street; Queen Street; Howard Street; Mount Zion, Westfield Terrace; Attercliffe; Darnall; Fulwood.

Baptists: Townhead Street Chapel; Portmahon Chapel.

General Baptists: Worship in the Assembly Rooms.

Unitarian: Upper Chapel.

Quaker: Meeting House in Fig-Tree Lane.

Roman Catholic: Chapel in Norfolk Row.

Johannaites (the Johanna Southcott sect): Assembled in the Free Masons' Hall.

and generosity, and to the success of the Evangelical Revival, not only sustained within Methodism, but deeply influencing both Independents and the Church of England. Sheffield was no Jane Austen world, no Barsetshire; in Sheffield there were no fox-hunting clergymen, no ministers "standing on the same holy ground as the pheasant and the partridge", in spite of the proximity of the moors! Nor were there absentee pluralist vicars or starving curates. From early in the century Evangelicalism was firmly entrenched in Sheffield Christianity. The appointment of Thomas Sutton, a strong evangelical churchman, to the living of Sheffield in 1805, which he occupied until his death in 1851, was responsible for a long sequence of evangelical clergy in the parish, and in 1841 the advowson was purchased by a few individuals to ensure the appointment of a successor with similar views, with the result that the clergy were much in line with the essential theological outlook of the Nonconformists.

There were of course ecclesiastical rivalries, and differences of social slant and political susceptibility which could be passionately roused when controversial issues were publicly raised, but all the churches were solidly evangelical, throughout all the phases that Evangelicalism itself passed right up to the twentieth century. The few later High Church exceptions prove the rule. And this gave the Sheffield churches a common bond, within the extremes of an evangelical Unitarianism and the more revivalist wing of the Methodists. It was no mere guide-book language that in 1824 offered "humble tribute of praise to the benevolent and unremitting zeal of the clergy. Their lives appear devoted to the best interests of the people; their doctrines are alike free from the taints of the world and the illiberality of sectarian feeling . . . while we think there are few towns where the Dissenting preachers are so deservedly respected".[1] Nor was the vigour confined to religious activity. All those many causes that Evangelicalism initiated or espoused were strong public causes in Sheffield, widely supported by Christians of all denominations except where strong political undertones divided the Establishment and Nonconformity. Apart from these issues, they both vied with one another and supported one another in the same good works, in Sunday

1 Ramsay, *op. cit.*, pp. 147, 157.

ship in the town will not be found to contain accommodation for above one third of its inhabitants, and are they filled by regular attendants? Not by far. Look at the families surrounding your dwellings, and you perhaps see a solitary instance where a whole household of several persons are regular attendants. . . ."[1] It is true enough that the élite ordered the public affairs of the town, but it was set within the growing mass of the 'artisan class' and the 'labouring poor', who by their very numbers and problems more and more coloured the town, even though they remained for generations inarticulate, and except for industrial disturbances generally unrecorded.

Hitherto the general alienation of this class from the churches has been a matter of deduction from circumstantial evidence, but in the 'thirties and the 'forties there is forthright evidence to support the assertion; it is middle-class comment, literate comment, but its objective accuracy need not be questioned. And it reveals much more than the fact of general alienation; it also reveals the gulf between the churches and the common people, their respective moods and their increasing irreconcilability. Some of the local material deserves to be quoted in some fulness.

Considering the early evangelical zeal for foreign missions, for the abolition of slavery, and for the care of the poor, it is surprising how late in time there is either public awareness or stirring of conscience about the *missionary* problem at home. Perhaps it was assumed that Sunday schools and a degree of day school education for the children of the poor, with some increase of free accommodation in the new churches and chapels, was sufficient to meet the problem—in which case the religious bodies must have been singularly uncritical of what their efforts had failed to do. Perhaps this is a persistent weakness of zealous Christians. And perhaps the most serious lacuna was the failure to understand the nature of the social problem determining the lives and thinking of the people, and its significance for the Christian Church. It is easy to be wise after the event, but there were prophets with words for those that had ears to hear.

An early prophetic word came from Dr. Thomas Arnold,

---

[1] *Sermon by Mark Docker*, Jan. 12, 1817, on "The state of the times, and God's controversy with a guilty people". Sheffield Library Local Pamphlets, vol. 53.

and touched on both the missionary and the social aspect of the problem. He exposed the theological weaknesses of the Church, averring that Evangelicalism handed over the temporal affairs of men either to natural laws or the devil, and that High Churchmen retreated into the religious institutions with a sectarianism quite foreign to the idea of a National Church—"I cannot understand what is the good of a National Church if it be not to Christianize the nation, and introduce the principles of Christianity into men's social and civil relations, and expose the wickedness of that spirit which maintains the game laws, and in agriculture and trade seems to think that there is no such sin as covetousness, and that if a man is not dishonest, he has nothing to do but make all the profit of his capital that he can."[1] This plea for the social, moral and intellectual application of Christianity to the total life of the nation was his continuous concern, which he ever felt to be a blind spot in a narrow evangelicalism. It led him to a practical consideration of what was demanded of the Church in terms of planning and reorganization, which he developed in great detail in his *Principles of Church Reform* in 1833. Thomas Arnold out-thought the Church of his day by generations, and not yet have we matched his teaching.

Nor did the missionary problem in the large towns escape him. In 1832 he was invited to publish a series of Letters in the *Sheffield Courant*. They do not relate to the Sheffield situation as such, and indeed as a guest contributor he was unnecessarily flattering to the situation there; but the general situation, as he saw it, is only too plain. "There is a strong popular feeling against the political opinions of the clergy, particularly of the bishops and other dignitaries among them. . . . Hear the cry with which the bishops in particular are now assailed in every part of the kingdom, and most loudly in the great manufacturing districts. Whence comes the special bitterness with which they, above all the other anti-reforming peers, are everywhere attacked? Whence the hatred with which the whole order of the clergy is sometimes attacked? Is it not because the people have never been made to feel the full amount of the good which an established church may and ought to effect . . .? Is it not because in our large manufacturing towns the church has allowed thousands and tens of thousands of its members to grow

[1] *Life of Dr. Arnold*, A. P. Stanley, 1858: vol. 1, p. 227.

up in misery and in ignorance; and that a step-mother's neglect is naturally requited by something of a step-mother's unpopularity . . .?" And speaking of the causes of Dissent, he instances the "utter insufficiency of the Church, in populous towns, as a religious society, that men's feelings of Christian union, and all their social propensities as Christians, desire some better satisfaction than to be members of a parish of 10,000 or 20,000 souls . . . and in forming themselves into distinct religious society when so situated, the Dissenters acquired a bond of charity more than they had before, but I know not what bond it was their conduct violated. . . . Was it fit to wait for money enough to build an expensive church, rather than licence the first room, or the first court-yard that could be found, wherever the inhabitants of the parish became too numerous or too remote to attend the Parish Church?"[1]

This general picture takes on rich local corroboration in the long open letter to Sir Robert Peel on Church Extension in Populous Towns, written by John Livesey, the incumbent of St. Philip's, one of the four 'Million' Churches granted to Sheffield. He wrote in 1840, twelve years after its consecration. His parish contained

> . . . 24,000 labourers and mechanics (about one fourth of the entire population of Sheffield); there is one church; and until very recently only one clergyman. The church contains 800 free sittings, and accommodates 1,200 in the pews. . . . Now surely it will be thought, in such a teeming population, the accommodation, especially the free sittings, will be eagerly sought after. Alas, the reverse is true. The wealthier classes, in tolerable numbers, are found occupying the pews; but the free seats are too often thinly tenanted. To what shall we attribute this indifference to Divine ordinances? . . . The prevailing reason, I am assured, is the *force of inveterate habit* . . . they tread in the steps of their fathers, and are neither impressed with the obligation, nor feel the desire, of obtaining religious instruction. . . . *The moral condition of the people is precisely what might be anticipated.* . . . Can it be surprising that the profane doctrines and licentious practices of the Socialists, so congenial to the animal appetites of the ignorant, find numerous abettors? It is quite natural that in such a population, the demagogue and political firebrand will find abundant materials for sedition, treason and rebellion. . . . There

---

[1] From *Thirteen Letters addressed to the Editor of the Sheffield Courant on our social conditions*, Thomas Arnold, 1832.

is indisputable evidence, that the ramifications of the late Chartist conspiracy were deep and numerous in this district. Two at least of the class-meetings of those unhappy and infatuated men were statedly held within its precincts. . . .[1]

This tells us a great deal about John Livesey and the clerical viewpoint as well as about the people of his parish. But he was a man of character—he never wore a surplice in the pulpit after 1847, when the church-wardens presented him with an address, thanking him for giving up so popish a garment—and he spent a week imprisoned in York Castle for a false entry in the burial register after his sexton had been found guilty of providing a body for dissection at the Infirmary Medical Hall! He was a shrewd man. His letter went on to analyse the "spirit of Independence" pervading the operative class, making them reluctant to accept gratuitous accommodation, so that since the unendowed churches required high pew-rents to maintain the minister, the free seats are "generally vacant, or tenanted by a few aged and infirm persons, together with the children of the Sunday school". As a solution he proposed that there should be many more small buildings, that large parishes should be subdivided into smaller ones, and "mechanics' churches" built by the labouring classes themselves with small shares, and trifling annual rents entitling each contributor to a pew and a family grave site. . . . "The Church in our towns is too exclusively the church of the Higher Orders. Mechanics' churches would bring under the salutary influences of the doctrines and rites of the Establishment, that part of the population which has hitherto been so grievously neglected. When a church is reared on this plan, a congregation is at once secured, every member of which is personally interested, and feels himself and his family identified with its success. The dear-pew and free-sitting system, I am convinced, will not succeed among the operatives of a town population. They have a feeling of English Independence . . . which leads them to desire a place which they can call *their own*."

He is aware that some have deprecated all classification of pews and distinction of prices, and advocate an exclusively poor man's church, "but this is carrying things to a ridiculous

[1] *Mechanics' Churches—a Letter to Sir Robert Peel on Church Extension in the populous towns and Manufacturing Districts*, by John Livesey, M.A. Sheffield Library Local Pamphlets, vol. 103.

Symons, and concluded that something under one-third of the
boys and girls had any schooling at all, and that the average
length of schooling of those who did attend was only 9½ months;
it is not surprising that of 2,267 children visited in 15 schools,
only 1,228 could read fairly and only 829 write, so that "two-
thirds of the working-class children are growing up in a state of
comparative ignorance".

Symons speaks of the vicious influences exerted on the youngsters—drinking and promiscuous sexual intercourse begin at an
early age, women's language is often "twice as bad as men's",
and the younger generation spend Sunday tossing coins, dog-
fighting and drinking in the beer-shops and "London kind of
gin shops", where they sit with their sweethearts until late at
night. The superintendent of the police, giving evidence, was
sure that the morals of the youth were worse than in Manchester and Leeds, where the factory system prevented them
running wild in the same manner. Altogether Sheffield young
people to-day can feel they have made considerable advance!
And the youngsters were not merely being 'called', as they say
in Sheffield; all who gave evidence saw them as victims, and
Ebenezer Elliott waxed eloquent on their behalf, insisting that
"after labouring at a distant mill or shop from light to dark, six
days in seven, neither children nor adults will voluntarily seek
the imprisonment of school or church" and that the only cure
is a compulsory system of national education, and the repeal of
all monopolies. It is inconceivable that the Corn-Law Rhymer
should have lost an opportunity of preaching his gospel before
a Government Commissioner.

Dr. Holland does more than propound facts; he interprets
their meaning and ventures moral and religious judgments.
His researches into social conditions apparently brought him
more and more into sympathy with the working classes, and
certainly detached him from the buoyant middle-class Radicals,
amongst whom many of his conclusions must have been highly
uncongenial, for the Radical press lampooned him as an erst-
while Whig who now supported the Tories, and as an advocate
of trades unions, who had once been a Radical. But the
sufferings of the poorer people shocked him to the core,
whether he was considering the appalling mortality rate of
infants, the early death of grinders, the filthy streets or the
fitfulness of trade. Thus in the five years 1837 to 1842, of a total

of 11,944 deaths in the Sheffield registration area, no less than 6,710 had been of children nine years and under, and 8,068 had died under thirty years of age; while the different mean age at death within the different social classes strikes him as "exhibiting astounding difference in the value of life".[1] The trade cycle occupied him in a number of writings:

> ...A period of prosperity invariably begets one of adversity; and as inevitably does the latter lead to the former. Long continued good trade gives full employment and enhanced remuneration and stimulates production, until at length it exceeds the necessities of both home and foreign markets. During a season of excessive demand, the artisan riots in the affluence of his means and his conduct is frequently marked by dissipation, neglect of work, and a disregard of the certain necessities of the future. This state of things which seems inevitable, is prejudicial in the extreme to his mental, moral and physical improvement ... at one moment (there is) insufficient to purchase the common necessaries of life, at another, gratifying the gross indulgence of the appetite. . . .

On the subject of the habits of worship of the working class in Sheffield, he is emphatic: "The artisans generally are not frequent attendants on a place of worship. It is stated, on authority which is the result of inquiry, that not one family in twenty is in the practice of visiting either Church or Chapel, indeed it is a duty in the performance of which the working classes are exceedingly lax, and the evil is not to be cured by the creation of religious accommodation. . . ." In fact he is a severe critic of the spirit of rivalry that has animated the different sects, whereby places of worship, indifferently attended, have been multiplied beyond the real demand. His hopes are reposed in education rather than proselytism. And he has some

---

[1] Details of the average age at death of different classes in the suburban, rural, and town districts of Sheffield in the three years 1839, 1840, and 1841, are given in *The Claims of Labour*, Sir Arthur Helps, 1845:

	years
Gentry, professional persons and their families	47.21
Tradesmen and their families	27.18
Artisans, Labourers, and their families:	
(a) Employed in different kinds of trade and handicraft common to all places	21.57
(b) Employed in the various descriptions of manufacture pursued in Sheffield and its neighbourhood	19.34
Paupers in the workhouse	25.51
Farmers and their families	37.64
Agricultural Labourers and their families	30.89

shrewd comments to make upon the growing class of prosperous and comfortable manufacturers, expressing the fear
that "what they have lost in the grossness of their vices, they
have gained in the refinements of their hypocrisy and dis-
simulation . . . the concentrated feeling of the present age is the
adoration of wealth. This embodies every virtue, and is associated with every talent, and religion seems not, in any degree,
to modify the thirst for it, or to abate the ardour of the pursuit.
The love of the world grows with the contemplation of the
things above". It was a hard saying, and possibly unfair as a
generalization, but it also shows an acuteness of judgment not
common in the period. Albeit in more refined language it
certainly expresses the common judgment of the later working
class on the religion of their employers.

The evidence for this estrangement from the churches of
the adult working class, estimated by Symons and Holland to
be two-thirds of the community, seems conclusive, and it could
be supported by a mass of evidence on the national situation ;
so much, that it is strange how little of it appears in conventional church history. But this still leaves unsaid most of the
things we would like to know about the attitude of the ordinary
workmen towards the variety of religious facilities, that so few
of them used. Social habit, always the major determining factor
in a social group, would operate strongly, as the incumbent of
St. Philip's had clearly seen when he ascribed the indifference
to "the force of prevailing habit . . . they tread in the steps of
their fathers", but we can be certain that a whole range of
attitudes would exist, from a gross, brutish, infidel one to that
of the converted Methodist poor, with the bulk between these
extremes too engrossed with their own affairs to think much
about it, but whose moral sense, if tied to the scrappiest religious
knowledge, would be coloured by that Christianity of Church
and Dissent that meant 'religion' to the people, and was
disseminated in some way by almost every social agency at
work. We would like to know their heartfelt hopes and fears,
which is stuff of which religion is in fact compounded, in the
face of poverty and distress, frequent births and so frequent
burials of their little ones. In many ways the early nineteenth
century was a stoical age, and even had they left records, these
would probably witness to a mute fatalism that was also a
characteristic of other classes, who also were not free from

catastrophic visitations of cholera and suchlike, even if their chances of both resistance and recovery were better. And it was the mood of all the pulpits in the face of human vicissitude. Sustained open revolt against the lot of the poor, and the demand for a new order of things, belong to a later period of political self-consciousness.

*   *   *

Emerging social groups

During the first two decades of the century the periodic outbursts continued in the form of riots against the high prices of provisions, attacks on meal and flour shops, and parades with poles aloft bearing loaves of bread dipped in blood. And the reactions were the old-fashioned ones: the Riot Act read, the militia called out, and a public subscription for the aid of the unrelieved poor and those who were not in trade combinations. As far as political stirrings went, there was the continued uneasy partnership between the middle-class radicals, with some of the more mature elements of the journeymen mechanics and craftsmen. After the hectic days of the French Revolution period, the issue of reform had slumbered or smouldered while the nation was engaged on a long hard war, but even before Waterloo it was a live issue in Sheffield in relation to which the various political groupings became defined.

In June 1810 a large public meeting was held in Paradise Square, organized by the Friends of Parliamentary Reform, to petition for a reform in representation of the people and to return thanks to Sir Francis Burdett, their national leader, who was in the Tower, declared guilty by the House of Commons of a breach of privilege. It was the beginning of a movement that was to issue in the Great Reform Act. And the Tory element in Sheffield appears as a distinct group. Immediately after the public meeting, the Master Cutler, the Town Collector, the Church Burgesses and 300 merchants and manufacturers published a declaration dissenting from the objects of the meeting. It was probably as many as could be mustered in support of the Tory viewpoint.

By 1817 the country was seething with discontent. The good years of trade following the conclusion of war were giving way to inflation, unemployment and bankruptcies; Habeas Corpus was suspended by an alarmist Government and any

reform agitation was regarded as Jacobinical. In January a
large public meeting was chaired in the Square by a fiery
Sheffield Radical, Thomas Rawson, a brewer of Pond Street,
to petition for reform of Parliament, and the annual election of
members by all who pay taxes. In March of that year no fewer
than 21,500 people signed a petition for reform, which was duly
presented to the Commons by Sir Francis Burdett. And again,
it was immediately followed by a loyal and dutiful address,
ultra-loyal according to Sheffield Whigs, to the Prince Regent
"from the Wardens and (part of) Company of Cutlers, clergy,
gentry and others of the town and neighbourhood". The
simpler riots of the poor interspersing the reform meetings
both strengthened the reformers' hands, and at the same time
embarrassed them, as a dangerous movement, often of workmen, against whom they were compelled to take police and
military action. The fact is that the élite of Sheffield contained
men of varying political views. There were some who were of
the Established Church and solidly Tory, a few at the other
extreme like Thomas Rawson who were out and out Radicals
and willing to work with the most Republican-minded leaders of
the workmen. And between them were the 'reformers' as many
of them liked to be called, as distinct from 'radicals', who were
genuinely eager for reform within certain limits, but wary of
extreme demands, and opposed to anything that smacked of
violence. They were often in the ranks of the Old Dissenters.

Their dilemma is well seen in a person such as Thomas
Asline Ward, one of Sheffield's greatest characters, who was
Master Cutler that very year, and a prominent member of the
Upper Chapel. His diary[1] shows that he had taken a leading
part in the 1810 agitation and had even framed the requisition
that went to Parliament; later he was President of the Political
Union in Sheffield for securing the Reform Bill, and we find
him disgusted by the brutality of Peterloo. Yet on the other
hand we find him offering himself as a special constable in the
riots in Sheffield, and he was highly critical, if not to say
snobbish, in his attitude to the lower rank reformers, the
'Annual Parliament and Universal Suffrage' men, who were
asking for something quite different from the general run of
middle-class reformers. Ward did in fact call himself a 'moderate reformer' and not a Radical—"I wish for Reform, but

[1] *The Diary of Thomas Asline Ward,* pub. 1909.

would have it gradual, that the change might be felt and proved before another be made". But he would not sign the loyal address and place himself with the Tories in the Cutlers' Company. He well represents the uneasy alliance between the gentlemen and the working-class reformers. Only a few apparently, like Thomas Rawson, were tough enough to ignore the tension.

At the time of the 'Peterloo Massacre' in 1819, the different social groups and their typical reactions become quite clear. Sheffield public opinion was appalled by the news from Manchester, and a great public meeting demanded that justice should be done on those who had committed the atrocities. Again the immediate Tory reaction was a loyal declaration from many freeholders and other inhabitants to the Prince Regent. On the other hand, a few months later we see one John Blacker, the 'King of the Gallery', committed to York for collecting mobs and inciting the unemployed to riot, while on August 15, 1820, a silver gilt cup purchased from the penny subscriptions of journeymen and mechanics of Sheffield was presented to Earl Fitzwilliam on the occasion of his dismissal from the Lord Lieutenancy of the West Riding, having incurred royal displeasure for sympathizing with the victims of Peterloo.[1] These various reactions show at least four social and political groups in the period, and there were subtle distinctions within them.

The climax of the mounting reform agitation was of course the Reform Bill itself, issuing in a universal excitement that entirely eclipsed every other interest. The leading social group of the town was almost unanimously behind the Bill with a religious fervour, the working-class reformers grasped at it as both a hope for their plight and a victory over privilege, and zeal infected the entire population. Never had there been such a solid demonstration of Sheffield radicalism as in the years of 1831 and 1832. When news came on October 8, 1831, that the Bill had been defeated by the Lords, within a matter of hours a requisition came to the Master Cutler for a public meeting, and almost 20,000 people turned out the next day in protest with black flags, effigies, and to the sound of muted bells; the members of the Political Union even felt obliged to offer their services to the magistrates for the maintenance of public peace and property! In May the next year, 20,000 assembled to pray

1 Sheffield Local Register.

the Commons "to exercise their undoubted privilege of with-holding supplies until a redress of grievances was obtained", and to pray the King "to recall his late ministers and by an immediate creation of peers, to secure the success of a constitutional reform". Within an hour of the news reaching Sheffield that the Bill had received its third reading, the people celebrated with discharges of fire-arms, ringing of bells, and raising of flags. The official celebration on June 18 was attended by 30,000 people, with the 5,000 members of the Political Union each bearing a medal struck for the occasion. Sheffield had never known such a day, and never before can the town have appeared so unified and jubilant.

The Chartists

It is common historical knowledge that the Reform Act was a victory for the middle classes, giving them franchise and members in the new industrial boroughs; Sheffield was to have two members, with 3,504 eligible to vote. The election, a noisy affair in which five people were shot dead, took place in December, when four reformers of varying Liberal hues contested the two seats. But within three or four years there were political stirrings among the working-class reformers, who felt they had been cheated by the Reform Act, and refused any longer to shout at the hustings for Liberal candidates whom they could not elect. It was the beginning, a small beginning, in the political self-consciousness of the working class over against the interest of other groups. It had been stimulated by the reform agitation stemming from the previous century, that had led to the Reform Act, and the flames were certainly fed by the long period of bad trade after the Napoleonic wars. From 1820, after a few good years in which there were still shortages of war to be made up, there was a long period of fitful trade, alternating between unemployment and starvation wages on the one hand and brief periods of frenzied activity on the other.[1] Nor had the new representation in the House of Commons the economic consequences that some had hoped. In the late 'thirties and early 'forties the situation deteriorated into the worst slump within memory. In August 1842, it is recorded that of 25,000 adult men in the local trades, only 4,000–5,000 were in full work with average earnings of 18s. a week, 17,000 in

1 *Report on Unemployment in Sheffield*, A. D. K. Owen, 1932: pp. 5–10.

part-time work, averaging 9s., and 3,000–4,000 were totally unemployed.[1]

At the annual meeting of the Society for Bettering the Condition of the Poor, the chairman, James Montgomery, reported that "the visitors have never had knowledge of such a state of privation, suffering and helplessness, as appears to be the lot of our labourers and artisans at the present time. Since the year 1837 there has been a most disastrous turn in the trade and manufactures here. . . . The oldest inhabitants of Sheffield cannot remember a crisis of calamity so general. . . . The labouring classes have been going down into abject destitution, in spite of every effort they have made to support themselves, while the relief that the parish can offer (with difficulty contributed by impoverished ratepayers) falls much short of the necessities of those who are compelled, however reluctantly, to ask it".[2] The same events that stimulated the middle-class manufacturers to press on for the repeal of the corn laws and all monopolies, gave birth to the Chartist agitation among the workmen for their own political representation. It showed the first open break between the middle-class liberalism and the working-class radicalism, however far ahead the effective political expression of it was to be.

As one would expect, the waters of Sheffield were deeply stirred. The open cleavage appeared at a meeting at the Town Hall on December 14, 1837, which the Master Cutler had been asked to convene, to petition for the 'Ballot'—the next constitutional objective of the middle classes. A group representing the 'Sheffield Working Men's Association' proposed a significant amendment:

> . . . That the landowners and capitalists now monopolise representation in both Houses of Parliament, in manifest injustice to the working classes. It is therefore the opinion of this meeting that a petition be sent to the Legislature, praying for an extension of the suffrage to all classes of Her Majesty's subjects, in order that all may have equal justice; for Vote by Ballot, in order that the voter may exercise his right with independence; and for shortening the duration of Parliaments, that the represented may have a sufficient control over the representative.

The amendment was lost, and the Committee of the Association addressed an open letter to the working men of Sheffield venti-

1 Sheffield Local Register.   2 Sheffield Iris, Oct. 11, 1842.

lating their grievances, that the "champions of the Ballot without Extension of the Suffrage" had endeavoured to terminate their business before the working men could get to the meeting, although the Association had given notice that they intended to move the amendment. It was followed by a printed address that was widely distributed among the working people of the town in the January following, setting out fully the aims of the Working Men's Association. It had been formed "because the members despair of ever obtaining social and political equality except by their own exertions. . . . The Whigs and Tories must fight their own battles, for let either side win, we are sure to be the losers. . . . The people are rising, but it is in peace; they will gain the victory but it will be bloodless. . . ." The objects are fully set out—Universal Suffrage is first in importance; the Ballot is necessary to give freedom in the exercise of one's right; short Parliaments to prevent the dishonest representative from forming nefarious connexions; and the abolition of a property qualification for members. Substantially they are the points of the Charter, although not until May was the Charter itself published. They solicit the full support and membership of the "*sober* and industrious of the working classes" of Sheffield. It is an interesting document, and probably the first working-class political manifesto published in the town.

The summer of 1839 saw the beginning of public 'Chartist' demonstrations, not only in Sheffield, but all over the country. From July there were nightly meetings, Sunday preaching in the open air, and when, in August, meetings were banned by the magistrates, they declared a policy of "holding small class meetings, similar to the Methodist class meetings for the purpose of concentrating our strength, for the holy purpose of effecting our *Just*, *Legal* and *Constitutional* Object, the People's Charter".[1] The national decision of the Chartists to hold a Sacred Month in August was expressed in Sheffield by mass procession of the Chartists to morning service at the Parish Church, as happened in many other industrial towns of the North; and as a direct encounter of the Church with the working people it is worthy of report. The Chartist leaders intimated to the Vicar that they would attend and desired him to preach on the first six verses of the fifth chapter of St.

[1] *ibid.*, Dec. 17, 1837.

James's Epistle! A vast concourse marched from Paradise Square after singing one of Ebenezer Elliott's Corn Law hymns, and duly filled the Parish Church "to the exclusion of a majority of the respectable seatholders". One of the assistant ministers preached the sermon, but from Proverbs 24—"My son, fear thou the Lord and the king: and meddle not with them that are given to change", in which the workmen were warned of the wickedness and desperate hazard they were pursuing, and "exhorted to a serious and diligent pursuit of those better things which the Gospel of Christ held out to them".[1] One gentleman during the service had his pocket picked! Again on the following Sunday the workmen filled the church, which was densely packed before 10 o'clock, and on this occasion their choice of the text from the Epistle of James was granted, but with the following five verses! The tone of the address can be gathered from excerpts of the preacher's words: "In addressing them as his dear poor brethren, he would exhort them to patience unto the coming of the Lord. They must endure long suffering and endurance. Their troubles were sent by God and they must be ready to bear them. If they were poor they must be contented, for if they had the riches of others their responsibility would be greater. . . ."[2]

On the fourth Sunday there was fighting and shouting in the service, in spite of the Vicar preaching on John 21:22–3, "What is that to thee?" in the course of which "he inquired whether God had not furnished every man with abundance of employment, if he attended to his own affairs, leaving all other events to the mercy of God?"[3] One of the seatholders asked men to vacate his pew and was refused; the holder claimed he had paid £6 a year for it, and the broil ensued. In the course of the following week, the Vicar and church-wardens appeared before the magistrates on behalf of the seatholders, to ask why they had not been given protection on the preceding Sunday, and a clerical magistrate on the bench "apprehended that every seat was the freehold of the owner as much as his own house was. Persons ought therefore to be protected in the occupation of their pews". In the course of the proceedings the Vicar made the point that the seats were the subject of sale and purchase.[4] On the following Sunday morning, September

---

[1] Sheffield *Mercury*, Aug. 24, 1839.
[2] *ibid.*, Aug. 31, 1839.
[3] Sheffield *Iris*, Sept. 10, 1839.
[4] Sheffield *Mercury*, Sept. 14, 1839.

15, the last on which the Chartists sought to attend church, the police were at the church gates with cutlasses, and only "decently dressed individuals" were allowed to pass; a matter that the Chartists were not slow to notice, and which their spokesman made much of in any paper that would print the story.[1]

Demonstrations continued for some months, culminating in a conspiracy aimed, it was said, to burn the town; but it led to the arrest and imprisonment of the leaders, and little further active demonstration took place. The Chartists confined themselves apparently to attending the growing volume of Anti-Corn-Law meetings, and moving amendments—consistently defeated—demanding the implementation of the whole Charter. Like the national movement, Chartism in Sheffield petered out ingloriously, and no more is heard of the Working Men's Association, that had run up a membership of about 2,000, and boasted "some hundreds of respectable persons".

There were a number of reasons for its failure. It was early deserted by some of its strongest and most respectable supporters who had given it status in a radical public eye; thus Ebenezer Elliott asked for his name to be erased from the list of supporters as early as May 1839 on the ground that the Chartist Convention was advocating physical force, and far from seeking the repeal of the Corn Laws was defending monopoly, so "fighting the battle of the aristocracy under the people's colours", and certainly the headstrong policies of the 'O'Connorites' seemed more in evidence than the quieter policy of the Association. But neither did they carry all the leaders of the working class. In Sheffield, a trade union delegate-conference had been called in September 1839 to consider "the policy or impolicy of joining the Chartists, in the capacity of Trades' Union societies". The opponents of formal amalgamation argued that it would damage the proper object of the unions with wage issues, divide the members and could lead to suppression of the unions by law; but in spite of the counter-appeal by members of the conference who were also on the committee of the Working Men's Association, the proposal to join officially with the Chartists was heavily lost.[2] Nonetheless all the members claimed to be supporters of the Charter, but the large majority wished to keep the unions clear

[1] Sheffield *Mercury*, Sept. 21, 1839.   [2] Sheffield *Independent*, Sept. 7, 1839.

of political involvement. It led the disillusioned Bricklayers' delegate to write: "Trades Unions are for botching up the old system; Chartists are for a new one. Trades Unions are for making the best of a bad bargain; Chartists are for a fresh one; and everyone must admit that Trades Unions partake of the tampering spirit of monopoly".[1]

The time was simply not ripe, and much water had to flow under the Don bridges before Universal Suffrage could be a practical proposition. The only group who were strong enough to carry a nation-wide agitation without being pricked by the bayonets of the militia, or bruised with the bludgeons of the police, were the industrial middle classes, and they were resolutely set on the issue of Corn Law repeal and Free Trade. It is not surprising that many of the leaders of the working-class Chartist agitation threw in their lot with them, forming the Sheffield Mechanics' Anti-Corn-Law Association Committee, in December 1839, appealing to the working class to support the repeal movement, and the Chartists to give up their opposition after the example of no less a person than Ebenezer Elliott.[2] The outward and visible sign of the political realism of this point of view was seen in Sheffield in the replacement of Chartist riots by monster demonstrations and petitions for the repeal of the Corn Laws, the abolition of monopolies and all restrictions on the importation of food, and for Free Trade. No doubt it was good for the nation and it was to end in a further great victory for the industrial middle classes.

Social and religious alignments

It was to be expected that with the enfranchising of the borough, bringing practical politics on to the doorstep of the town, the distinctive political interests and groupings would become more defined. There were the Tories, expressing themselves in the 'conservative interest'; although an old-fashioned Whig, even an early Radical, could well become conservative in his political views, as did no less a person than the aged Christian poet, James Montgomery. Then there was the great Reform party, claiming the support of the Whig principles, and campaigning for the repeal of the Corn Laws, for the remission of the duty on iron and for Free Trade in general in the interests

[1] *ibid.*, Sept. 14, 1839.   [2] *ibid.*, Dec. 14, 1839.

of expanding exports and cheap imported food. At home they were opposed to all restriction on trade or industry. And there was the unenfranchised working class, its politically conscious element being divided between the Chartists and the more sober section, apparently including most trades union leaders, who were more concerned with employment and good wages in their trade than political theory, or who at least intended to keep them separate. This latter element, after the Chartist flare-up, was clearly predisposed to rely, for its political hopes, upon the passing of liberal measures. But the great mass at this period, even if they appeared at the public meetings in the Square, would feel quite outside the world in which decisions were made, as in fact, they were; they could work when there was work, or near starve if there was no work; they could strike for a few weeks, and small numbers might resort to 'rattening'. But, as a group, there was no question of their views being taken into account.

It is possible to see something of the religious alignments of these different groups. They are probably not surprising but they show the existence of distinct group attitudes and judgments, and the sociological roots of the modern mission problem are set in this period. We have already considered the evidence of the general estrangement of the artisan class from the churches, although the merging of its upper stratum with the more 'respectable classes' should be borne in mind—men such as those in the silver and plated manufactures, and in the high-class cutlery trades, saw makers, men drawing high wages, in strong unions, restricting entry into their trades, most of them able to read and write, and with a little deposit in the Savings Bank; men of sober and regular habits, who would find themselves in congenial company in a small chapel, and with little taste for rioting or dissipation. There have always been such men in the highly skilled, older trades of Sheffield, usually in the employ of very old-established companies. But they were not typical of the growing artisan class.

The really buoyant, cock-a-hoop group were the newly represented, politically aggressive manufacturing class, the victors of 1832 and eager for further freedom in trade, industry and religion. Its core was lineally descended from the Old Dissenters, and their religion was expressed in Nonconformity, whether Independent, Unitarian, Quaker or one of the newer sects, but hardly in Wesleyanism. It was to become the Non-conformist backbone of the great Liberal Party. The political strength of the Reform party was truly amazing, and the Tory minority stood no chance against it. All four candidates in the first election, and all three in the 1835 second election were Liberal reformers. At the 1837 general election a conservative candidate stood, but received only 655 votes out of 4,817 cast. Even a Chartist in 1847 got 326 votes, and it was not until 1880 that Sheffield returned a conservative member to Westminster. The small conservative interest was mainly represented by Lord Wharncliffe of Wortley Hall, outside the parish, the clergy and local gentry of the Pitt Club, and a few hundred merchants and manufacturers, together with the leading Wesleyan ministers. As individuals they were distinguished and influential; as a political group they were swamped in a sea of Liberalism. Certainly the Church and the Wesleyan Methodists were openly regarded as conservative, and fearful of the popular demands of the times.

There is some interesting corroboration of this in connexion with the 1835 election. It was before the days of the secret ballot, and the Poll Book shows the way the 3,587 electors voted for the three reform candidates: Mr. John Parker, Mr. James Silk Buckingham, and Samuel Bailey "the Bentham of Hallamshire". It is very revealing, especially one extant copy, in which a contemporary computor has marked with the letter 'c' the reliable conservative supporters (although they had no candidate of their own).[1] Almost all the clergy and Wesleyan Methodist ministers receive the mark and generally abstained from voting, while not a single Independent minister has it, each giving his two votes to the liberal candidates of his choice, or his plumper to one. So with the leading laymen; those whom we know to be distinguished Churchmen or Wesleyans all receive their conservative mark! The 1837 election provides less subtle evidence. In the election that year a conservative stood for the first time in the borough; it was open knowledge that he appeared under the special patronage of Churchmen and Wesleyans, and a political pamphlet of the time attacks the "high Tory Wesleyans and high Tory Churchmen" and the clergy and ministers by name for trying to foist a Tory on

[1] Copy in the author's possession.

the people of Sheffield.[1] Needless to say, he was defeated in so staunchly reforming a constituency.

With religious denominationalism and political convictions contained by the same dividing lines, it is natural that social cleavages should be doubly hardened, especially as the years went on and 'politics' assumed a more and more central position in the public mind. As religious dissent and political dissent had reinforced one another in the previous century, so political Liberalism and liberal Nonconformity fed one another in the nineteenth. And it was inevitable that religious issues should become political ones. So John Parker, who sat at Westminster for Sheffield for many years from the very first election, knew his electorate, and that he had nothing to fear from the opposition of Churchmen when he asked indignant questions in his election literature about the Church, and aired the grievances of Dissenters, demanding how the registration of births, marriages and deaths invaded the safety of the Church, why Dissenters could not officiate at marriage ceremonies, why the universities shut out half the nation, and why Dissenters should pay church-rates?[2] It was sound Liberal tactics for the rest of the century, as the Liberal candidates in Sheffield knew well. It indicated both the solid political unity of Liberalism and Nonconformity, as well as the political divisions between the churches. And it was the way to win an election in the borough. But neither on the other hand did John Parker need to consider the opinions of the 'working classes' who let out 'the most discordant yells' at his nomination—though invariably top of the poll, he was never a popular candidate with the workmen; neither popularity among the workmen nor sympathy towards them was a requisite for success. So much so, that Tories and Chartists seemed to have more political sympathy with one another! In Sheffield, the Liberals had nothing to fear. The economic barometer after the disastrous slump of 1842 was set 'fair' for a generation, and the victories of Liberal politics lay ahead. Philosophers and poets were with them . . .

---

[1] *An exposure of the extraordinary combination of certain Wesleyans and Churchmen to foist a Tory on Sheffield*, by a Plain Man, 1837. Sheffield Library Local Pamphlets, vol. 55.

[2] John Parker's election pamphlet to Sheffield, Dec. 1834. Sheffield Library Local Pamphlets, vol. 56.

> "Cloud trades with river, and exchange is power:
> But should the clouds, the streams, the winds disdain
> Harmonious intercourse, nor dew nor rain
> Would forest-crown the mountains; airless day
> Would blast on Kinderscout."[1]

Even God was with them in their zest for political freedom and economic laissez-faire, as Mr. William Ibbotson of the Globe Steel Works demonstrated, more prosaically, in his address to the workmen in the file trade when they had gone on strike for an advance in wages, and been locked out for eight weeks in 1836:

> . . . while the foreman gets his 30s. or 40s., the striker whose labour is more severe only receives his 20s. or 30s.; while he that has served an apprenticeship obtains his 20s. to 30s., the learner and the mere labourer gets his 10s. to 18s. In all these cases the God of nature has established a just and equitable law, which man has no right to disturb: when he ventures to do so, it is always certain that he, sooner or later, meets with a corresponding punishment. That law is the natural operation of things, and in proportion as man, by trickery, manoeuvre or an abuse of power, violates this law of nature and equity, in the same degree does he receive his reward. Thus when masters audaciously combine, that they may effectually oppress their servants, they insult the Majesty of heaven and bring down the curse of God upon themselves, while on the other hand, when servants unite to extort from employers that share of profit which of right belongs to the master, they equally violate the laws of equity. . . . The master manufacturers of England were foremost in their struggles to secure that glorious reform in Parliament which I doubt not will end in the moral and political regeneration of the world . . . singlehanded, you must submit to receive merely the share of profits which the God of nature assigns you . . .[2]

When all the nuances are taken into account, the co-inherence of denomination and social group is very clear, despite the blurred and fascinating growing edges of expanding classes. Clear too is the social, political and religious isolation of the working-class group. Naturally enough the fortunes of the several denominations were intimately bound up with the fortunes of the different social groups, and from the middle of the century the stage was set for the leading actors, even if the working-class group had still to wait some decades in the wings.

[1] Ebenezer Elliott, the Corn Law Rhymer—*The Ranter*.
[2] *Address to the Workmen in the File Trade*, Wm. Ibbotson, 1836. Sheffield Library Local Pamphlets, vol. 6.

Chapter 4

CHURCH AND PEOPLE IN THE YEARS OF
RELIGIOUS BOOM, 1850–1900

The estrangement of the working classes

B Y THE MIDDLE of the century there are many indications
of an awareness on the part of the 'powers that be' of the
vastness of the populations in the new industrial areas,
and of the general widespread alienation of the artisan classes
from the churches; a matter to which the Establishment and
the appropriate agencies in Government were to give official
consideration. A number of factors combined to open the eyes
of the authorities. There had been the deep depression of the
late 'thirties and early 'forties and the waves of working-class
agitation arising from it, which in spite of the collapse of
Chartism with its last nation-wide spasm in 1848 had alarmed
the authorities. There was the growing awareness of the grim
social scene through census figures, blue-books, the reports of
Poor Law Commissioners and the Home Office, and statistics
on drunkenness and crime, all of which were reported in great
detail in the growing volume of daily and weekly newspapers.
And there were spokesmen for the depressed—evangelical states-
men, often Tories; novelists like Charles Kingsley, Disraeli,
Mrs. Gaskell and Dickens, writing on new themes, depicting
new characters and harrowing pictures, all insisting with their
varying emphases, interests and literary qualities that, as
Dickens put it, "men are creatures possessing affections, feelings, fancies—a whole world of emotions that lie outside the
ken of the older school of political economists". There were the
diatribes of theorists, men like Richard Oastler screaming that
"the Factory-System compels individuals to war against the
Church" and Thomas Carlyle thundering on the "Condition-
of-England question". All these and many other factors were
prising open the eyes of authority and of the public at large.

The response of the religious authorities, whether looked at in terms of survey of the situation, analysis or church building, was in fact very considerable and on a scale that renders any later response amateurish. It was the last period for example in which the Established Church admitted a proper obligation to have provided accommodation for the entire population, as though it was still expected that the whole people should be Christian in a practising sense—a hopelessly unrealistic expectation no doubt—but indicative of a view of her proper relationship to the nation at large, and one that was to recede in the years ahead. Some of this thinking is embodied in reports on the national scene, which, although not directly descriptive of Sheffield, nonetheless illuminate the situation there.

It had been proposed that in the 1851 census returns people should be asked to declare their religious affiliation, as a means of assessing the religious condition of the country; but this was rejected on the grounds both of impropriety and of its doubtful reliability. Instead, Horace Mann, a barrister, was asked by the Registrar General to organize a great voluntary count of all the people worshipping on a certain Sunday throughout England and Wales.[1] The response from the churches was almost complete, and on March 30, 1851, apparently a fine day, the count was made by an army of assistants. As one would expect, the occasions given for dispute about the significance of the figures were legion, but nonetheless a general picture was secured. The population of the country in 1851 was 17,927,609; the total sittings provided by all the denominations amounted to 10,212,563, of which 53 per cent. were appropriated. It was calculated that, had all attended other than those prevented by physical disability or needful occupation, 58 per cent. or 10,398,013 would have taken their place at worship. In fact there were 7,261,032 attendances at some religious service that day, although this figure included 'twicers' and also Sunday school scholars who actually appeared in church. To-day, of course, we should regard this as an astronomically high proportion, as indeed it was for the time, witnessing to the solid church-going practice of an immense social group. The Sheffield figures, when the population of the municipal borough was 135,310, are as follows:

[1] *Sketches of the Religious Denominations . . . & the Census,* Horace Mann, 1854.

Denomination	Places of Worship	No. of Sittings			No. of Attendants			
		Free	Appropriated	TOTAL	Morning	Afternoon	Evening	TOTAL PER DAY
Church of Engl. .	23	6,815	11,797	19,562	6,291	2,934	5,656	14,881
Independent .	10	1,112	3,974	4,486	2,283	413	1,854	4,550
Partic. Baptists	2	220	1,250	1,470	831	—	624	1,455
General Baptists	2	250	500	750	362	—	527	889
Soc. of Friends	1	800	—	800	136	80	—	216
Unitarian .	1	50	850	900	650	—	350	1,000
Wesleyan Method. .	16	3,067	7,412	10,479	5,282	960	4,319	10,561
Meth. New Conn. .	5	402	1,550	1,952	1,000	—	1,183	2,183
Primitive Meth.	1	350	650	1,000	977	—	1,550	2,527
Wesleyan Assoc.	2	90	580	670	241	—	161	402
Isolated Congregs. .	2	350	—	350	50	—	60	110
Roman Catholic .	1	—	950	950	2,000	—	2,000	4,000
Catholic Apostolic .	1	320	—	320	140	100	250	490
Jews . . .	1	500	—	500	27	—	—	27
Wesleyan Reform. .	2	—	—	—	30	100	—	130
Totals .	70	14,326	29,513	44,189	20,300	4,587	18,534	43,421

Considerable though these figures seem to us to-day, Horace Mann's view of the national scene was a disturbing one. Commenting on the "alarming number of non-attendants" revealed in the census he defines the attitude of the several social groups:

> ... It is not difficult to indicate to what particular class of the community this portion in the main belongs. The middle-classes have augmented rather than diminished that devotional sentiment and strictness of attention to religious services, by which, for several centuries, they have so eminently been distinguished. With the upper classes too, the subject of religion has obtained of late a marked degree of notice, and a regular church-attendance is now ranked amongst the recognised proprieties of life. It is to satisfy the wants of these two classes that the number of religious structures has of late years so increased. But while the *labouring* myriads of our country have been multiplying with our multiplied material prosperity, it cannot be stated that a corresponding increase has occurred in the attendance of this class. More

especially in cities and large towns it is observable how absolutely insignificant a portion of the congregation is composed of artizans. They fill perhaps, in youth, our National British and Sunday schools, and there receive the elements of a religious education, but no sooner do they mingle with the active world of labour, than subjected to the constant action of opposing influences, they soon become as utter strangers to religious ordinances, as the people of a heathen country. From whatever cause, in them or in the manner of their treatment by religious bodies, it is sadly certain that this vast, intelligent and growingly important section of our countrymen is thoroughly estranged from our religious institutions. . . .

He goes into the causes for this estrangement. First he puts "social distinction" prevailing in the churches, which interestingly is still one of the first reasons given by workmen, even though the justification to-day is so much less. But Mann contends that the existence of rented pews and free seats, and the placing of them, deters people from attending, and confirms their view that religion is a purely middle-class luxury. Nor does he think that the "broad line of demarcation which on week-days separates the workman from his master can be effaced on Sunday by the removal of a physical barrier". In a world apart, the labouring people have no desire to mingle with the higher orders, but desire to be "exclusively confined to their own order". Again, the churches are criticized, says Mann, for their indifference to the social conditions of the poor, although he admits that clergy and ministers can now be found in the foremost leadership in schemes of improvement. Then there is the "misconception of the motives of the ministers", for the labouring classes distrust them, and draw the "hasty inference" that their work is purely pecuniary, or official duty. And he makes a profound point in saying that the deplorable conditions in which people live and from which they cannot escape are more positive and influential teachers than any others can be, and that a home situation that "forbids all solitude and all reflection" (by which the spiritual life of middle-class families is nourished) precludes any religious progress for the workmen and their families.

He is under no illusion that the mere provision of further church accommodation can be a satisfactory solution since "teeming populations often surround half-empty churches, which would probably remain half-empty even if the sittings were all free", and he is led to the conclusion that absence from religious worship "is attributable mainly to a genuine repugnance to religion itself". This in itself is an important observation, and he goes on to analyse his own statement. "Infidelity" he thinks is exaggerated, but nonetheless "an unconscious secularism" is widespread in the class that is "engrossed by the demands, the trials or the pleasures of the passing hour, and ignorant or careless of a future. They are never or but seldom seen in our religious congregations, and the melancholy fact is thus impressed upon our notice, that the classes which are most in need of the restraints and consolations of religion, are the classes which are most without them". Horace Mann certainly provides forthright evidence of the estrangement of the working classes, and his evidence, though not his perspective, is supported by that of Frederick Engels, writing of the 'forties, that "among the masses there prevails almost universally a total indifference to religion, or at the utmost, some trace of Deism too undeveloped to amount to more than mere words, or a vague dread of the words infidel, atheist, etc . . .".[1] And Engels forecast that being "unconsciously and merely practically irreligious . . . necessity will force the working-men to abandon the remnants of a belief which, as they will more and more clearly perceive, serves only to make them weak and resigned to their fate, obedient and faithful to the vampire property-owning class".[2]

Mann and Engels certainly provide indisputable evidence of the *fact* of estrangement and of indifference, and yet the very failure of Engels' prophecy should make us wary of putting too simple a construction upon such phrases as "unconscious secularism" and "practical atheism". In a sympathetic context they are fair enough, but too baldly asserted they distort the truth; not only the comparative successes of working-class expressions of Methodism, but even more so, the persistent and emphatic rejection of explicit atheism right up to the present, suggest that the vague assumptions and residual beliefs prevailing among the working classes were more complex than might be thought from their religious practices. And whereas Engels looked forward to the extinction of religious superstition,

1 *The Condition of the Working Classes in England in 1844*, F. Engels, p. 126.
2 *ibid.*, p. 238.

Horace Mann believed that "although by natural inclination they are adverse to the entertainment of religious sentiments, and fortified in their repugnance by the habits of their daily life, there still remains in them that vague sense of some tremendous want". His proposals for meeting the problem were akin to those of Thomas Arnold twenty years before. Both were sure that much was to be learned from Methodism with its creative use of laymen; the artisans' haunts should be "invaded by aggressive Christian agency" both clerical and lay, rooms should be set aside and licensed "exclusively their own", "Ragged churches" should be set up, though he recognized that the term was unfortunate, and large meetings on the Exeter Hall model with absence of all class distinction should be organized. Even "street preaching", under proper sanction and control, "would not be a too energetic measure for the terrible emergency"!

*   *   *

Self-criticism within the Churches

Whatever may have been the attitude of mind of the people to the churches, or the psychological barriers to their entry into them, it was of course a simple matter of arithmetic that new churches and great numbers of them were in fact necessary. The Church of England had realized this for many years. In Sheffield alone, between the building of the 'Million' churches and 1851, no fewer than eight new churches had been consecrated, and seven preaching rooms opened, that were early to be replaced with churches—more than any other denomination provided in the period, although the Established Church had much leeway to make up. In other parts of the country the building programme was immense, notably in London where the need was far greater than in Sheffield, because of the early tardiness of the Church and the far smaller provision made by Nonconformists. London was one of the blackest spots in the country from this point of view, in spite of the fact that Bishop Blomfield had consecrated 200 new churches. And Bishop Tait, who succeeded him in 1856, continued the building programme. But he did so with many wise words and much warning about the nature of the problem. "It is wrong," he said, "to mistake the erection of churches for the spread of the

Gospel throughout the land. . . . It will be necessary to place in the churches faithful ministers of God's Word . . . and we must be careful to use every means to bring in the poor. It is the upper and middle classes who form the churchgoers throughout this country, and a vast mass of the population are estranged not only from the Church of England, but from the Gospel itself . . . in our crowded cities and in our remote country districts there is a very numerous body of the poor who cannot, and another who will not enter the churches".[1]

Tait set a good example along the lines proposed in the 1851 survey, encouraging and leading open-air meetings, meetings with porters, omnibus drivers and postmen, and it was in his tenure of London that Exeter Hall was opened by Lord Shaftes-bury and keen evangelical clergymen, much of the Church being scandalized by "the Bishop's undignified and almost Methodist proceedings". It led to the opening on Sunday nights of the Abbey and St. Paul's, which for a winter were thronged with people, but the Chapter of St. Paul's unanimously de-clined the Bishop's wish to continue through the year! The Bishop's retort to his critics exposed their obtuseness as clearly as it did the situation: ". . . It would be well if those who feel so strongly against this movement would see that the churches we already had were thrown open to the poor as freely as possible. It might be very difficult to lure them in, but at present they were not lured in but locked out. No idea seemed to be more deeply ingrained in the minds of many officials in our parishes than that the abject poor had no right to accommo-dation in our churches."[2]

This devastating comment of Bishop Tait referred of course to the practice of pew rents, which were so general a feature of the new churches and indeed, as we have seen, of the older ones in the towns where they had been remodelled or en-larged. Unfortunately there was an acute dilemma that the Church at large had failed to see until the middle of the nineteenth century, by which time it was too late to reverse established practice. It was the dilemma of whether church rates or pew rents should be the means of providing money for the running expenses of the churches and the stipends of the ministers. The church rate had existed from time immemorial

---

[1] *Life of Archbishop Tait*, Randall Davidson, 1891 : vol. 1, p. 253.
[2] *ibid.*, p. 264.

8

as a means whereby the parish church and churchyard could be maintained, and it was associated with the common law that every man had rights in his parish church. It was an equitable custom in that the cost was borne by the parishioners in proportion to their wealth. It was self-levied by the parishioners at a meeting convened by the church-wardens, usually held in the church, and distraint of goods for non-payment was enforceable in the courts. But of course it implied a willing and conformist population. The Dissenters who had contracted out of the Established Church had built their own meeting houses, and introduced pew rents as the major means of supporting them—and indeed, the old parish churches had provided the precedent; the Church of England both for economic reasons and for the social satisfaction of her more affluent members had continued the practice in the new churches.

We have seen in detail how the system obtained in the Sheffield churches. Not unnaturally the Nonconformists felt a grievance that they should be taxed to support churches they neither worshipped in nor approved, and in some places they were strong enough to carry a vote against a rate at the parish meeting; we have seen how early and in how summary a way the rate had been ended in Sheffield by militant Dissenters. In theory the National Church had a strong case against the Dissenters, on the grounds that an adequate rate could ensure a church wholly at the free disposal of the parish, including its poorest members. And in fact the case was so argued by the Establishment when Dissenters countered the necessity of a rate, advising in its stead the use of pew rents, as they themselves did. The Established Church had the better case since pew rents in fact always tended to exclude the poor, if not wholly to exclude them, but the strength of the argument was completely lost by the Church's long established habit of allotting and letting pews. It is more the pity that the lack of any ecumenical perspective ruled out the possibility of a church rate, divided between the churches according to their strength; it is interesting if idle to speculate on what the consequences might have been. But whatever the rights and wrongs of the issue between churchmen and dissenters, the appropriation of pews and pew rents were material factors debarring the poorer people from any churches with such customs. There were no doubt other more imponderable factors of greater importance in the mood of the people, as Horace Mann believed; but a mood is harder to formulate and express, even by those possessed of it, and anyway the mood was nourished by material factors. To say the least, the practice prevented the poor from feeling that they 'belonged' to the worshipping communities.

Much light on the consequences of these customs, the attitudes of Churchmen and Nonconformists, and the habits of the poorer people is obtained from two voluminous reports on the national situation. There is the *Report of the Select Committee on Church Rates*, published in 1851, before the results of the religious census were known. And there is the huge *Report from the Select Committee of the House of Lords, appointed to inquire into the Deficiency of Means of Spiritual Instruction and Places of Divine Worship in the Metropolis, and other Populous Districts of England and Wales, especially in the Manufacturing Districts, and to consider the fittest means of meeting the difficulties of the case*, of 1857–8. Both cover a great deal of similar ground, and the mass of evidence adduced by question and answer of a great variety of persons, including many Dissenters, makes fascinating reading. There was no direct evidence given concerning Sheffield, but glimpses of other industrial towns are many. The Coroner of Manchester, for example, stated that "all the churches, with the exception of the Cathedral, are in general terms, diverted from the use of the poorer classes, by their private appropriation to the use of the higher and middle classes".[1] The Archdeacon of Liverpool, in answer to the question whether the free seats were generally well-filled in that town, replied "Not all—some are; but for this there is a special reason . . . in those churches which are not of a parochial character, the free sittings are put in the most uncomfortable positions, where the people feel degraded. . . . The reason why many of these churches have such a small number of free sittings, is that they were erected just to suit the wants of the respectable class of society, who lived in the district at the time when they were erected; but have now gone upwards into the environs of the town, and these places are deserted; the pews are not free, and they are not occupied."[2] The Vicar of Bradford on the other hand affirmed that a great many working men came on Sunday evenings to the parish

---

[1] Select Comm. of House of Lords, 1857–8: question 5590.
[2] *ibid.*, questions 5816, 5821.

church and gladly sat in the aisles, because they knew there were no pew rents in the church, whereas they were ashamed to sit in the aisles of the new district churches—"it hurts their feelings of independence to sit in the district churches where other people pay, and it is a very important element in the Yorkshire character, I assure you".[1]

The secretary of the London Diocesan Church Building Society showed that a great deal of the new church accommodation was not taken, which he ascribed to the fact that the adults, now heads of families, had grown up "in one of the deadest times of the English church", and were very hard to influence and bring in. And on being asked how it was that, though the Dissenting chapels had pew rents, there seemed a greater readiness to take them up, he gave as one interesting reason that "they have more offices, deaconships and visitors and tract distributors : and in these ways the chapels manage to employ their people very much better than the Church. This is an attraction to small shopkeepers and mechanics, who find they are looked upon as somebody in the congregation, and they are not an unheard-of unit as they are in the church congregations . . . they have more meetings, they bring their people together more, and are able to carry out the spirit of union more fully than we have yet the secret of doing in the church . . .".[2] These are all revealing comments from a mountain of evidence showing clearly that the appropriation and renting of seats worked against the best interests of the Church by excluding the working people, and destroying the proper influence of the incumbent over the people whom he could neither invite to church, nor blame for not coming. "The greater portion of the people," said one witness, "feeling that the greater part of the pews are the property of private individuals . . . seldom make any attempt to attend Divine worship, but either take themselves to Dissenting chapels or remain at home, perhaps unknown and uncared for", while up in the North "where the people are intensely commercial in their ideas" when a perpetual curate called on a home he was told that "he was looking after his pew rents" ![3]

It was not only the Church of England that gave specific

1 Select Comm. of House of Lords, 1857–8 : questions 5414, 5415.

2 *ibid.*, questions 837, 838, 874, 1286, 1288.

3 *ibid.*, Letter of Hon. C. Lindsay for use of the Committee.

consideration to the estrangement of the artisan class, around
the middle of the century. The 1848 Conference of the Congregational Union of the Independent Churches made the
subject its main study, with deep heart-searching and many
shrewd judgments. "Why is it," it was asked, "that the preaching of our ministers, except in very rare instances, is not attractive to them? Why have they no sympathy with our testimony,
or our struggles for religious liberty? Why do our new-built
chapels gather congregations of tradesmen, but never of
artificers? Why do not our schools either win the parents or
retain the children? Why has our literature no charms for
them? They are readers but we do not seem to write for their
taste. Why do not our domiciliary visits succeed in establishing
friendly relations and sympathies between our religion and
their affections?"[1] Particular thought was given to the skilled
artisans, as a crucially important group for the nation's present
and future, a group becoming politically and industrially alert,
eager and apt for technical education, whereby "they acquire
considerable surface of knowledge (but) the lower power of
knowing becomes far more developed in them than the higher
faculty of thinking. They become conscious of their mental
advancement, and presume upon it, quite unconscious of the
existence of wider fields of truth they have never explored"[2]
—a fascinating comment in the light of the present debate on
technical education. It is admitted that "their domestic life
need not be painted in dark colours, but it wants improvement
and elevation . . ."; some few are attached to evangelical
communities, but most are not, and "a serious belief in revelation is not their general characteristic"! These were shrewd
insights at a very early period, and the following sociological
analysis was on a level at which the missionary problem has been
rarely posed. Edw. Swaine lecturing to the assembly said that

> . . . If the ill-clad and woe-worn, or the over-worked and weary
> mechanic, is under strong conviction that the want of work, or the
> over-work, the deficiency of maintenance, or the hard struggle to
> secure, and the uncertainty respecting it, are the fruit of unjust
> political arrangements, he will scarcely feel at home with those
> more favoured, even if not at variance with them. Is there no
> distance between churchmen and dissenters, because of the
> inferior political position of the latter? Does not the political

[1] *Congregational Year Book*, 1848. Lecture by Rev. A. Wells.   [2] *ibid.*

affect the social? It is not in nature to trample on itself—however, under holy influence, men, for peace sake, may endure, and for Christ's sake, forgive. The wronged have ever clung together. There may be in many of the working classes, but little of conscious jealousy; but all wrongs, real or imagined, engender discontent—and it is well; or where would be redress . . .? Some apprehend the wrong; they declaim, or write—and lead. The rest follow. Thus we conceive it is with the operatives as a class . . .[1]

It is a pity that solutions did not measure up to analysis, but analysis itself was just beginning.

It was also out of Independency that there came in 1849 the most penetrating and trenchant critique of the churches in Edward Miall's *The British Churches in relation to the British People*. Unfair perhaps in parts, attributable to the strength of his passion, it is not really an ungenerous book, and it could have been wholesome salt in a more wounded church. It is hardly surprising that a timorous committee of Exeter Hall refused the use of the building for his lectures when it saw the prospectus! It is sufficient here to quote his words that "the bulk of our manufacturing population stands aloof from our Christian institutions . . . an immense majority of those who in childhood attend our Sabbath schools, neglect throughout the period of manhood all our ordinary appliances of spiritual instruction and culture . . ." and probably the two most important reasons he gives among many, are, on the one side that the class divisions in society have been carried into the house of God so that "The poor man is made to feel that he is a poor man, and the rich is reminded that he is rich" through the graduated scales of accommodation from the square, carpeted, cushioned and curtained pews to the hard, narrow and obscure benches for the poor, while on the other side is the mood in the heart of the working people: "There is a deep discontent of soul which a sense of social ostracism has engendered. The majority of our over-wrought labourers, whether manufacturing or agricultural, are thrust into a position that taxes their endurance to the utmost . . . all things go against them . . . what wonder, if a spirit of sullen resentment gradually rise within them—a temper prompting them to quarrel with, and defy all that is above them, human or divine!"[2]

[1] *Congregational Year Book*, 1848. Lecture by Edw. Swaine.
[2] *The British Churches in relation to the British People*, Edward Miall, 1849: chapter 4.

When Miall subjects the churches to his acid analysis, he refuses to countenance the thought that evangelistic techniques, buildings, missions and tracts can change the situation. Only deep spiritual renewal could be effective. He refers to the "aristocratic sentiment" of churches, the strong operation of class and caste, and the unregenerate value attached to "respectability—a term we employ with exclusive reference to whereabouts in the social scale", and to the "trade spirit of the times" which has subtly invaded the churches and the very concept of salvation "refining selfishness instead of destroying it". In fine words he insists that churches must recognize that they sow bad seed; they must understand what revival presupposes and implies, and "turn to the Gospel with a governing desire to know more of God—to get at His mind—to comprehend His excellence—to become conversant with the principles of His government and to gaze upon illustrations of His character and purpose". Not least will it require that opinions on trade and politics are scrupulously tested by religion.

*   *   *

The national religious picture

The national picture at the mid-century, painted as it must be with a large brush, is quite clear in outline—a return to the church on the part of the upper classes, not unrelated to the strict example in morality, social etiquette and evangelical piety set by the Queen and Court; continued religious habits of the growing middle classes, shared by the thickening social stratum of the lower middle classes with some of the superior, more respectable, and individualistic of the artisan class, although different denominations corresponded to different shades in this middling section of the social spectrum; and the labouring class, itself capable of cultural sub-division, generally outside all the religious institutions.

It is a generalized, large-scale view of course, subject to a variety of qualifications of locality and denomination, but it is supported by the Sheffield evidence in the 'forties, examined in the last chapter. And, of course, it is not a picture just for one point in time: points of time, even decades, are consecutive and conjoint. Men and their generations come and pass away, but their social habits, notwithstanding the reality of social change, are both inherited and bequeathed. And the more strongly does this happen where there is no sudden dislocation or fracture in the social body, but where, as in the nineteenth-century British society, social evolution is reasonably peaceful and continuous. Great social change took place in the century, but the pattern of religious habit in the second half of the century, certainly of the middling and labouring classes, is basically determined by the habits of the first half; so strong is the law of social habit, a 'law' to which churches have paid virtually no attention. Not that churches remained static or the mood of people unchanged—far from it! The boisterous gales of social aspiration were blowing hard; new denominations were born in the hurricane, and social and political changes around the mid-century showed how much of the old world had been blown away.

Liberal politics and Liberal Nonconformity

Of decisive importance were economic and political factors; after the terrible years of the early 'forties the Golden Age of British industry was ushered in with its growing material prosperity, in which every class shared, some to a greater and some to a lesser extent. Intimately related to the economic advance was the continued growth of fervent political Liberalism, in which, after the second Reform Act of 1868, the bulk of both the middle and the newly enfranchised working classes unitedly reposed their hopes.

Perhaps the most important single social consequence of these factors was the strengthening and expansion of that great middling group in urban society, ranging from the wealthy industrialists, merchants and inventors, to the little shopkeepers, tradesmen, clerks, working foremen, and superior working men economically secure in well-established crafts. While Britain was the workshop of the world, these were the men who kept the wheels running; politically, they were the great Liberal Party, and their strength was sufficient to impose changes not only on Whigs but also on Tories, and the outlook of both Liberal and Conservative parties and their leaders is coloured by the existence of this important national group. Traditionally the urban middle classes had been religious in habit, and largely Dissenting, as we have seen, and the appended social groups at the lower end took on their religious characteristic. All churches benefited from this thickening social group, but most of all the Dissenting churches and particularly Methodism that had always been more open to newcomers from lower strata of society. In the industrial towns it led to a striking 'boom' of religion from the mid-century, the history of which we shall trace. Everything combined to inflate it. The political dynamic of a fast-increasing, vigorous, industrial social group, including all the important middling shades of the social spectrum, was placed at the service of liberal Nonconformity, and the winds of religious fervour filled out the sails of political Liberalism.

It is in the combination of these economic, social and religious factors operating so powerfully on one another that the religious boom of the second half of the nineteenth century is to be sociologically explained. All denominations benefited, but it could not happen without immense and even catastrophic consequences for the churches most liable to the impact of the boom. The Independent congregational churches, with their long radical, liberal tradition and their homogeneity of class and outlook, became nakedly political, as their critics saw it, and all the objectives of Liberal politics became the demands of the Christian conscience and the Christian religion. The 'Nonconformist conscience' was not to be relegated to the sphere of private religion; it was a vitally important political factor that governments had to respect and even embody in legislation, while at the social level men outraged it at a cost of their own social ostracism. Wesleyan Methodism was most disturbed by the new social factors, not only because it was the denomination most swollen from the expanding lower middle-class group, but also because the nascent Liberalism of this middling group found itself in a denomination traditionally Tory, opposed to any mixing of politics and religion, and rigidly authoritarian in its system of government. The Conference was dominated at the time by a caucus of men, led by the great Jabez Bunting, "Pope of Methodism", famed for his view that "Methodism hates Democracy as much as it hates Sin"; they were determined to resist, at whatever cost in membership, the demands of a liberal-minded laity concerning the structural organization of the Connexion. So strong was the liberal pressure, and so rigid the Wesleyan mould, it is hardly surprising that it led to the greatest schism within Methodism.

Since the death of John Wesley the Connexion had been continually subject to division and secession, illustrating on the one hand the authoritarian paternalism of Conference, ministry and leading laymen, and the democratic liberalism in the ranks of its members on the other. At each secession the reformers had been inspired by 'radical', 'liberal' and 'democratic' ideals to challenge the spiritual tyranny of Conference; each time they claimed the scriptural support of the Primitive Church and the rights and privileges of English subjects. And on each occasion they were expelled for "unworthy, secular and political motives". It had been so in 1797 when the Kilhamites were accused of Jacobinism. It was so in 1827 when Methodists in Leeds, objecting to Bunting's high-handed treatment of their opposition to the installation of an organ, formed the 'Protestant Methodists'. And again in 1835 when Dr. Warren was expelled for contumacy in a dispute concerning the Methodist Theological Institution, the intransigence of Conference and the reform agitation were both in evidence. By 1839 the Wesleyan Methodist Association, formed of recent secessions, numbered 28,000 members with 600 chapels,[1] whose distinctive features were great circuit independence, free choice of either minister or layman as representative to conference, and a strong sense of independency in the congregations. And the birth of the Primitive Methodist Church in 1811, following the expulsion of Hugh Bourne and William Clowes on the issue of camp meetings, really illustrates the same tension. The fears and political suspicion of the Wesleyan Connexion were in evidence, and although the movement was the offspring of purely religious revival in different parts of the country, its lay emphasis, and unwillingness to submit to Conference, place it with the reforming secessions from the parent body.

In themselves the occasions of secession were not of great importance, but each in turn witnessed to the underlying reform agitation in the Connexion, finally expressed in the demands for lay representation in Conference, and a constitutional exercise of authority by district courts and particularly by Superintendents, who after 'the regulations of 1835' had absolute powers of expulsion from the Connexion. The actual occasions were like thunderstorms in an atmosphere highly charged with liberal, reformist electricity; with each storm came the light-

[1] *Methodism and Politics*, E. R. Taylor, 1933: p. 157.

ning of dissension and the thunder of secession, and then calm ... until the atmosphere was once again dangerously charged. The culminating storm broke in the mid-century, in 1849, with a head-on collision between the liberals and Conference on the issue of rights versus autocracy, in which the Conference was attacked for its inquisitorial actions and its un-English and illiberal expulsions.

The leaders of the agitation were the 'Three Expelled', reforming 'martyrs', the Rev. William Griffith, a most open advocate of Liberal politics from the pulpit, the Rev. Samuel Dunn, and the Rev. James Everett who had ministered in Sheffield and always retained a close association with the town. Their expulsion from the Connexion in 1849 led to further crisis; huge enthusiastic meetings to hear their case were held in London and in all the large industrial towns in the North, which became rallying centres for the liberal Methodists and created platforms and committees of their leading laymen. The losses by expulsion and secession were formidable; in the course of the year 1851, 56,000 society members were lost to the Wesleyans, and by 1856 the loss totalled over 100,000, apart from probably greater losses of adherents. In spite of such losses, and the persistence of the reformers with their "No Surrender! No Secession! No Supplies!" cry, Jabez Bunting and Conference refused any concession to reform, and it was in the light of this situation that negotiations took place for the unification of all the liberal Methodist churches. In fact the amalgamation of only two was secured; a large group of the Wesleyan reformers of 1849, and the Wesleyan Methodist Association, who in July 1857 at an Amalgamation Assembly in Rochdale formed the United Methodist Free Churches (each word of which is significant) with about 40,000 members, half from each group, and with James Everett as their first President.

It is only in the light of this story that the solid political liberalism of the Free Methodist churches can be understood. Their emergence on such issues, and their subsequent expansion greatly strengthened and increased the force of Liberal Nonconformity in the second half of the century, even influencing in due course the parent body from which they had all seceded. For after the death of Bunting, significantly enough called 'the Last Wesleyan', Conference could no longer continue as an oligarchy, nor any figure within it rule as 'Pope'. When next the atmosphere was charged with reform, it simply happened, and Wesleyan Methodism added her contribution to Liberal Nonconformity, even if she remained less politically monochrome than her offspring.

*   *   *

Enterprise and Liberalism in Sheffield

All the forces we have seen at work in the national picture, so important for the relationship of the churches and the community, are to be seen in Sheffield with clarity of detail and depth of colour. For "the 30 years 1843–1873 the industries and trade of Sheffield enjoyed a period of development uninterrupted by any severe or prolonged depression".[1] The number of men and boys employed in the older trades increased by over 50 per cent, in spite of periodic setbacks through foreign competition and financial crises. But the chief economic progress was due to the rapid growth of the heavy steel industry, as a consequence of new processes, new plant, new metallurgical discoveries and new demands in the engineering, railway and armament industries. The advance from the mid-century was breath-taking. A supreme example is seen in the enterprise of such a man as John Brown, who in 1837, his apprenticeship finished, set up as a factor of steel, files and cutlery. A few years later, on his own account, he began to manufacture files, steel, and conical spring buffers which he had invented and patented. By 1856 he employed 200 men at the 'Atlas Steel and Spring Works', and by 1864 he employed between 3,000 and 4,000 men with an annual turnover of close on £1,000,000. Similar possibilities were realized by the Firth family; the father, Thomas Firth, was head melter with Sanderson Bros. and Co., earning 70s. a week, where his two sons Mark and Thomas were also working for 20s. a week, after their training. The two lads took the initiative in 1842 by acquiring six pothole furnaces to make high grade steel on their own account, at which their father shortly joined them. By 1850 they had agents in America, Canada, Russia, Berlin, Brussels, Copenhagen and Melbourne; in 1851 they built the 'Norfolk Works'; by 1857 they employed 500 men, and by the 'eighties had over 2,000. Early in the present century the

[1] *Report on Unemployment in Sheffield*, A. D. K. Owen, 1932.

companies were amalgamated as Thos. Firth & John Brown Ltd.

In such meteoric ways did the large steel works develop, and their early history illustrates the economic expansion from the mid-century, as well as the character of the men that made modern Sheffield. They were independent, hard-working, enterprising men, philanthropic, public-spirited, religious without being otherworldly. In politics, rarely radical, they were generally Liberals of some hue, though by the 'sixties the ' Liberal-Conservative' and 'new Conservative' position was finding growing support among commercial interests. And of course they made fortunes. A story goes of surprise expressed to a Sheffield manufacturing factor that he should supply stilettoes to Spain, poignards to Italy, scalping knives to Red Indians, and bowie knives to Americans, when the reply was made: "We boast of free-trade here, and if the d——l himself were to send an order for pitchforks, and sent with it a strong remittance, we would let him have as many as he liked to order at 25 per cent. below Birmingham!" With men like John Brown and the Firths in Sheffield, the knives soon gave way to steel gun barrels, armour-piercing shells, and armour plate capable of resisting them! But the principles remained the same.

There were rumblings within the working class; periodic strikes for the advancement of wages or against arbitrary reductions of 5 and 10 per cent, lockouts, and disputes over new machinery and the limitation of apprentices, and there were the famous 'Sheffield Trades Union outrages', the 'rattenings' which led to the Government inquiry in 1867.[1] They concerned the long practice, though not widespread, that persisted in Sheffield of Union officials using force and victimization against workmen who refused to enter combinations. Some had been shot at, others had had their tools and machines damaged, and some had cans of gunpowder inserted into their wheels and even thrown into their houses and down their chimneys. The Sheffield outrages brought the town into national disrepute, and they were writers sympathetic to the working classes who wrote that

> . . . Trade outrages, which 30 years ago were to be looked for in al-
> most any trade, have become confined almost exclusively to the
> town of Sheffield. . . . It is well-known to those who have given
> any attention to the subject, that the artisans of Sheffield and its

---

[1] Trades Union Commission : Sheffield Outrages Inquiry, 1867.

immediate neighbourhood are marked by special characteristics, produced by peculiarities in the trade of the district, and just such as might be expected to lead to the crimes which have been proved against them. The trades whose office bearers have ordered and encouraged these outrages are . . . small bodies of men, with occupations purely local, sickle and reapinghook grinders, saw-grinders, edge-tool grinders, fork grinders, scythe makers—the men engaged in them know that their time in this world is short, disregard all life-saving precautions, plot for high wages, which they too frequently spend in brutal indulgence, and meet the inevitable end with as much indifference, as they seem to have manifested when plotting the destruction of others. . . .[1]

But serious though they were, they were survivals from a bad past, and it is fair to say that the Trade Societies themselves both asked for and welcomed the inquiry as a means of clearing the reputation of the many in their trades, and the fair name of their town, and that the numbers found to be guilty were infinitesimal compared with the numbers in the trades. The Golden Age of British industry, notwithstanding the general improvement in which all groups shared, was not without its ups and downs.

In the national picture we have noted the growth of the middling classes in society, the gale of liberal politics blowing through the industrial towns, the impact of the democratic mood on the churches and on Methodism in particular. We have also examined substantial evidence of the estrangement of the working classes from the churches. All these characteristics are conspicuously present in Sheffield in the period under review. We have seen in the last chapter how solidly liberal in politics were the middle classes enfranchised under the Reform Act of 1832; the first election in 1868 after the second Reform Act that enfranchised the working men as householders in the borough, showed the strengthening of the Liberal opinion. Four candidates contested the two seats, and the three Liberals polled between them 36,654 votes, the Conservative, standing for 'Church and State, and Protection', receiving 5,272. There were different emphases in the Liberal candidates that the working classes, solidly voting for Mundella, were not slow to notice—but the basic acceptance of Liberal policies by the constituency as a whole is clear.

[1] *Progress of the Working Classes*, J. M. Ludlow and Lloyd Jones, 1867.

The Boom in the Liberal Methodist Churches in Sheffield

From the mid-century and the 'reform' period, the growth of new Nonconformist churches is most striking, as a cursory glance at the building chart in the appendix will show. Of course, one would expect the huge population increases to be reflected in further expansion by all the denominations,[1] and this indeed happened, excepting the Wesleyans, who between 1834 and the late 'sixties built only one large chapel at Heeley— the others were small chapels in far outlying areas of the borough—which is to be explained by the acute disturbances caused by the reform agitation within that body, and the heavy loss of members that took place after 1850. The population increase warranted further churches of all denominations; the Church of England provided no fewer than 26 new parish churches between 1848 and 1883, a rate of building that has never been equalled either before or since. And the first large Roman Catholic church in the town was erected in 1850, from which time others slowly followed, well spaced out to meet the greatest convenience of members of that communion.

But the population increases alone do not explain the respective denominational contributions to the total provision after 1850. Other sociological factors must be taken into account. The greatest expansion was in the liberal Nonconformist churches, embracing a great part of the thickening, middling stratum of society, itself the consequence of rising standards of living, and finding in liberal Nonconformity a completely congenial vehicle for its social and political aspirations. One factor was the growth of the lower middle-class group in this stratum, that found in the scores of new chapels up and down the town, at every few corners, natural rallying-points for all who were disposed to take on the decorous habit of chapel-going. It conferred status and confirmed respectability; it provided a centre for like-minded people in an age when organized social facilities were few; it provided the opportunity to 'be someone', and it separated one from the rough lower element in society—

[1] The population increases from the mid-century are as follows:

1851	.	. 135,310
1861	.	. 185,172
1871	.	. 239,946
1881	.	. 284,408
1891	.	. 324,291

all this and Heaven too! The Independents, the denomination most classically liberal, received new life, and after more than half a century during which their building expansion had been negligible, between 1853 and 1880 they erected thirteen chapels.

Another factor, so intimately related to the growth of the lower middle classes, was of course the reform movement, violently at work in Sheffield Wesleyanism, and which in due course led to two new Methodist denominations. The 'reform martyrs', Everett, Dunn and Griffith, had been expelled from Conference and from any connexion therewith in August 1849 at the Manchester Conference, for alleged complicity in the publication of the notorious and anonymous 'Fly-Sheets', in which the abuses, as their authors saw them, had been bitterly attacked. The organization of giant meetings by reformers up and down the country began almost at once, and by the following year were well in hand in Sheffield, with a committee of 40 to 50 "many of whom were tradesmen and shopkeepers". They met to protest against "the absolute despotism, without law, control or responsibility" of Conference, that elected itself and impugned the characters of reformers "comparing them to the red republicans of France", and to demand reform and constitutional government in the Connexion, "even though some of their Tory Methodists might go over to the Church . . . [whom] they could spare rather than those evangelical, British and Christian principles which they advocated".[1] It was the language of Liberal political meetings, except that no Tory Government was attacked with such vehemence as the Wesleyan reformers attacked their Conference! The reaction of the local Conference-party leaders was prompt, sharp and high-handed. Figures at the middle of 1851 showed that the membership then stood at 9,168, a decrease in the previous year of no less than 4,734 actual members of society, apart from those who were not members of society.

The preachers' plans show something of the turmoil, and the way in which the secession took place. In the earlier plans of 1850, for the Sheffield East Circuit, 62 local preachers are listed. In the last plan of the year, 16 of them were simply removed, and a copy of this plan exists that bears handwritten information that of the 46 remaining, 8 are "known reformers",

---

[1] Report of meeting in Sheffield, Sheffield *Independent*, Sept. 14, 1850.

3 "marked for expulsion" and only 16 as "conference supporters".[1] A meeting of expelled preachers of the town was called, which simply produced a new plan for the first quarter of 1851, with 44 names of preachers for 27 preaching places in the district, not in chapels, but in halls, school rooms and in private houses. The new plan required that "when any of the expelled ministers are in Sheffield it is the understanding that the brethren planned at the Athenaeum resign the pulpit to them". It was like the birth of Methodism all over again, a new indigenous movement that rapidly produced a new crop of chapels, small ones at first, and later larger ones. One of the very first was at Grimesthorpe, in the East end of the town, where 1,000 attended the stone-laying ceremony of a new school room and preaching room in June 1851, and the inscription deposited under the stone shows the attitude of the reformers ". . . to record to future generations the convictions which have led the teachers of Grimesthorpe Wesleyan Methodist Sunday School and members of the Society to attempt the erection of a new school and preaching room . . . in the presence of an assembled multitude who have unjustly been deprived of church membership, simply because they could not conscientiously contribute their money to support a system of priestly intolerance and irresponsibility which has shaken our beloved Methodism to its centre, and bids fair, without the counteracting influence of the Great Head of the Church, to vie with the Apostate Church of Rome".[2]

Not until 1857 was the United Methodist Free Church formed as a national denomination, when the unwillingness of Conference to make any concessions to the reformers had become plain; but in Sheffield the reformers had long before accepted the position, and begun to build their reformed chapels. When the amalgamation with the Wesleyan Methodist Association took place, the Sheffield reformers were divided about the wisdom of joining it; those congregations approving duly joined, but the others, unwilling to bind themselves again to a connexional government, abstained, and a little later, in 1859, formed the Wesleyan Reform Union of Churches. The

---

[1] Wesleyan local preachers' plan, Nov., Dec., Jan. 1850–51 for Sheffield East Circuit. Copy in the possession of the Wesleyan Reform Church House, Sheffield, who graciously made their plans available to the writer.

[2] Sheffield *Independent*, June 21, 1851.

Wesleyan Reform Union was born in Yorkshire, with a Yorkshire spirit, Sheffield becoming its most prominent centre, as
indeed to-day it is the national headquarters of that small but
redoubtable denomination.

Both the new reform denominations rightly claimed descent
from the 1849 Secession, but there were differences between
them that illustrate the wide social range of liberal Methodism.
The United Methodist Free Church erected much larger
chapels, some of them on a level with the most imposing of the
Wesleyan chapels, with an educated ministry, and all the
accompaniments of the 'big chapel': organs, graded pews, and
substantial well-to-do congregations. The Wesleyan Reform
Union on the other hand had smaller, humbler buildings in
less fashionable areas, with plain wood varnished pews, a
majority of free seats, few professional ministers, but relying
almost entirely on local preachers to serve almost solid working-
class, though well-dressed, congregations. A contemporary
observer calls them "the very democrats and radicals of
religious society", and tells us that his visits to their chapels
discovered orchestras of the euphonium, trombone, fiddle,
flute, fife and cornet, with steel-melters preaching the sermons.
Very different from Hanover Street, where he found the finest
of the United Methodist chapels and "a large and respectable
congregation, chiefly of the middle ranks of life, flourishing
tradesmen, rising manufacturers, energetic shopkeepers and
the better sort of artisan. There are several who have made
money and a great many intend and expect to make it before
long. They are a pushing, active, restless, enterprising class of
people, intent on religion, and determined to make the best of
both worlds". That was in 1869, nine years after the chapel had
been built; in 1873 in the same chapel he saw "well-known local
legislators . . . gentlemen connected with coal, iron and steel . . .
and flourishing merchants . . .".[1]

But the contribution by both reform secessions to the religious
boom is clear. Between 1851 and 1881 the smaller Wesleyan
Reform Union erected seventeen chapels mostly in working-

[1] Articles by 'Criticus' appearing in the Sheffield *Post* between 1869 and 1874
describing visits to churches and chapels of the town. They are of particular interest
to this study since the writer was at pains to show the social level of the various
congregations and the kind of people that worshipped within them. (Sheffield City
Library.)

class areas of the town, the largest of which could seat 500 people, but most of them being much smaller, combinations of preaching room and school room; although after this date the advance was slow, almost drying up with the end of the century. No doubt the independence claimed by each congregation and the refusal to become integrated into a large national connexion explains in part the weakness of the denomination. From the same date, 1851 to 1889, the United Free Church acquired or erected fourteen chapels, half of which were large buildings seating between 500 and 1,500 people; although it is noteworthy that after this date, indeed after 1876, the expansion gradually slackens.

The boom in Primitive Methodism in Sheffield

An immense contribution, also evidencing the new habit of chapel-going on the part of superior working-class people, is seen too in the astonishing awakening and growth of Primitive Methodism, the more remarkable when set against its small contribution to the religious life of the town in the first half of the century. The Primitive Methodist secession had taken place in 1811, and it was in 1819 that they made their first public appearance in Sheffield, through a Wesleyan layman, who, being impressed by the fervour of a Primitive Methodist sweep he had met at Worksop, secured the visit to the town of an itinerant minister, the Rev. Jeremiah Gilbert. It led to a larger society, the acquisition of the small, old Independent chapel in Coalpit-Lane, the recruitment of a few local preachers, and a Preachers' Plan headed "The Sheffield Circuit of the People called Primitive Methodists, known also by the name of Ranters". It covered a very wide area, but showed no preaching place in the parish of Sheffield except in the township itself, although Jeremiah Gilbert did as much on his Sunday there as could be expected. His diary records that he "preached at 6 o'clock in Young Street; at 8 in Water Lane; half-past 10 in the chapel; the Lord's Supper at 2 o'clock; preached at the chapel at 6 o'clock, and in the Park at 8". They sold the little chapel and built a larger one for 900 people in 1835, the Bethel Chapel in Cambridge Street, in the centre of the town, and this remained their only building until 1855. Unlike all other Methodist churches, the Primitives, apart from growing within their one congregation, showed no expansion at all. And then suddenly, in 1855, there came vitality, and from that date until 1897 they erected no fewer than thirty-one chapels, some of them very small and some of them large, and mostly in the more working-class centres of the parish where new artisan terraced streets were being built. Altogether it was a quite phenomenal expansion, and the building rate, unlike the two 'reform' denominations, was maintained to the end of the century although it tailed off from that time.

The Primitive Methodists are the hardest of the Methodist groups to define sociologically, since the denomination was not born in the fury of political and social reform, yet neither was it marked by the Toryism of Wesleyanism, being born in a later age and traditionally located in quite distinct kinds of community. Their strength was largely in the rural and mining parts; in East Yorkshire and the Wolds, for example, they were 'the church of the people', as also in mining communities in North-East Derbyshire, South Yorkshire and Co. Durham. Wherever Primitive Methodism appears it seems to be born of purely religious revival, often amongst the poorest and most outcast from society. Probably this explains why the Connexion officially, like Wesleyan Methodism, discouraged strong political activity in its members, and particularly among its ministers. But because of the political liberalism after the mid-century of the social stratum in which it took root, inevitably it became one of the great liberal Nonconformist churches.

This fact, and the thickening of the social stratum that swelled the liberal churches, account for the remarkable expansion in Sheffield of Primitive Methodism from the mid-century. Dr. Wearmouth in his latest work adduces ample evidence of their political liberalism. . . . The journals of the Connexion are vociferous on liberal issues, and contributors averred that "by the Liberal Party we are regarded as amongst its most trusty and reliable forces. The Conservatives, on the other hand, have come to look upon us with suspicion, distrust and prejudice . . ." and "the Liberal Party is that natural political instrument for those who wish to promote the interests and establish the principles that Primitive Methodists have at heart". Dr. Wearmouth himself adds that "it was close association with Liberalism that made the editor view with regret the decision of the Labour Conference in 1906 to 'establish a distinct Labour Group in Parliament'".[1]

Nevertheless Primitive Methodism was the most chameleon-like of the Methodist churches; when the social group in which it was set became Liberal in politics, it became a great liberal Nonconformist church, and when later the working class embraced Labour politics, the Primitives gave many men into their front ranks. It is the reason too for the large contribution made to the trade union movement from Primitive Methodism, in those areas where it was the predominant Nonconformist denomination. Primitive Methodism reached further down into the lower social strata than any of the large denominations; and the denomination reflected more than any other the changes that have taken place in the working class. It accounts for the fact that the most pietistic, otherworldly, politically-passive working-class religion is to be discovered in that denomination, as also the proudest pages of Christian contribution to working-class leadership.

The picture in Sheffield is less simple, in a mixed community with a more complicated social structure than a mining or a rural village. The general political liberalism of the denomination in Sheffield we can no doubt infer, but in Sheffield the expansion of the Primitives is indicative not only of the religious habits of the lower middle classes, but also of the social elevation and newly-acquired religious habits of some part at least of the superior working class. But it is a mixed picture, and we must beware of assuming a completely monochrome working-class composition of the Primitive Methodists from what we know of the denomination in simpler social contexts. It is borne out by descriptions of their chapels in Sheffield.

In Petre Street Chapel in 1873 at the Anniversary the congregation included "horny-handed sons of toil with their wives and families . . . others whose hands were encased in kid gloves . . . all were respectably dressed . . . one or two persons gave vent to various ejaculations, and there was a considerable amount of enthusiasm and energy, and an utter absence of that chilling stateliness and constraint so frequently met with". At the Bethel Chapel in May that year were some 300 people ". . . the free seats were almost empty . . . there were very few

1 *Methodism and the Struggle of the Working Classes, 1850–1900*, R. F. Wearmouth, 1954: pp. 225–40.

of the well-to-do people present, the worshippers mainly belonging to the working classes, with a slight sprinkling of tradesmen, and a few little manufacturers . . .". A visit four years before showed the congregation "almost entirely of the poorer classes" although the free seats were almost unoccupied. In John Street Chapel in 1874 "the pews are roomy and comfortable, particularly those with hassocks and cushions . . . abundant provision is made for the poor who do not take advantage of the accommodation specially set apart for them . . . working men and their families chiefly composed the congregation with a sprinkling of tradespeople, clerks, and people of fair social position, and the galleries were well-filled with people who appeared to be of somewhat superior social position . . .". At Langsett Road, on the other hand, "the congregation was chiefly composed of artisans and their families, the very class for which the chapel was intended . . .".[1]

The Primitive Methodist picture in Sheffield is of a denomination largely made up of the most respectable of the working class, always appearing well-dressed, devout, enthusiastic, and even in places 'corybantic' in their worship, with an admixture of the lower middle group, small tradesmen and such people; not without a handful of wealthier families in some chapels, who had made money and retained their old associations. There can be no doubt that Primitive Methodism embraced more of the artisan class than any other church in the second half of the century; its Sunday schools, in this like all other churches in the poorer areas, would have influenced many thousands of the children of the working classes; it is equally certain that the great bulk of the poorer workmen and their wives were not thronging their chapels.

The Old Dissenters in Sheffield

The picture of the older Nonconformist churches from the mid-century, during the course of the religious boom, is easier to trace. And a very imposing scene it is. 'Criticus' in his visits in the late 'sixties and early 'seventies was himself extremely impressed and made some shrewd judgments, not without a degree of cynicism, on the subject of fashionable Victorian worship, more in keeping with the iconoclastic outlook of the

[1] 'Criticus' in the Sheffield *Post, op. cit.*

twentieth century upon the religious habits of that age. In fact, so cool and detached is our observer that one is forced to wonder whether he had any faith at all, and any personal allegiance to church or chapel; perhaps, however, his objectivity does no more than show him an excellent journalist! Some of his random comments are well worth republishing, and the consistency of his evidence helps us to get a reliable picture.

In the old Queen Street Chapel, seating 900, he found 200 downstairs and about the same number in the gallery "principally in the middle ranks of life with some professional and a few with claims to gentility. There were not many poor people present, and the free seats displayed frequent vacuity. Most of the people seemed to be long settled and deeply rooted in Queen Street Chapel. Not a few of the men were of the sturdy old Independent type, long-headed, keen-eyed, close-lipped, cool, calculating and not easily moved about with every wind of doctrine!" In the Nether Chapel, the first Congregational chapel in the town, "there was a numerous congregation . . . with more of Dives than of Lazarus in that place. All were well-dressed, married ladies comfortably enclosed in the costly luxuries of Cole's or Cockayne's, with their daughters equally elegantly attired . . . family pews are a feature at Nether as at other old-established chapels . . .". In the Broompark Congregational Chapel, erected in 1864 in fashionable suburbs of the town, "the congregation was of course highly respectable . . . an almost entire absence of anything which could be called impecuniosity . . . the pews were comfortably cushioned in crimson and carpeted . . . none were conspicuously labelled 'free'", and 'Criticus' sarcastically adds that "the people of Broompark are not afraid of entertaining angels unawares" since they put him in a pew uncarpeted, and destitute of hassocks! But at Burngreave Chapel, where the 600–700 sittings were all let, and the 200–300 people present were "principally middle-class respectable people, with a few of the superior orders" he was welcomed, and put into a pew without waiting for the psalms to commence "which is not always the case at some of the old-established churches and chapels where all the sittings are let". He adds that there are many advantages in going to a newly-opened chapel, when the officials are wanting tenants for the pews and contributions towards a debt on the building. The general middle-class social consistency of the

Congregational churches, especially the older ones drawing generation after generation of the same families from a growing radius as they moved out to better districts, and also of the newer chapels erected in suburban areas, is very clear indeed.

But there is some qualification to be made. In the more working-class areas the Independent congregations were more mixed, and drew some of the most intelligent and politically alert of the working class. So we find that on a Sunday morning at Garden Street Chapel, in a very poor district just off the town centre, "the congregation consisted principally of persons in the humbler walks of life, a great many working men and their families, respectably dressed . . . the middle classes were also represented, but not to any great extent". And the best example comes from Mount Zion Chapel in Attercliffe, a vigorous, rapidly expanding industrial part of Sheffield's East end; on a Sunday evening in 1873 the large chapel of 900 sittings "was exceedingly well-filled. The congregation was a thoroughly representative one . . . managers of various works, merchants, tradesmen and artisans. Some of them dressed in broadcloth and some in corduroy". He adds, "I was informed that the congregation was chiefly composed of working classes, and that it was a fair specimen of the evening congregation. The working classes of Attercliffe who wend their way to Zion must be a superior class. They looked intelligent and serious, with every indication of attending carefully their outer and inner man . . . on good terms with the butcher and baker . . . good trade and high wages must have been utilized to some purpose at Attercliffe of late years".

These two chapels are particularly interesting, showing how even a middle-class denomination, sensitive to the newly-awakened liberal aspirations of the working classes, with good leadership that engaged their interest, could be transformed by the winds that blew from the mid-century. Garden Street, for example, was led by a staunch publicly-political Liberal minister from 1865, the Rev. R. Stainton, who was deeply immersed in the social problems of the time and closely associated with the working-class leadership of the town. On the very closing day of the Trade Union Outrages Commission he convened a public meeting in Paradise Square, attended by 15,000 people mostly of the working classes, to pass a resolution expressing shame and abhorrence of the crimes, "that those who

have committed them are enemies of the best interests of
working men in general and to trades' unions in particular . . .
and to declare our readiness and determination to do all in
our power to redeem the character of our town . . .".[1] He even
interceded with the employer of Sam Crookes, one of the two
most guilty of the ratteners, but, true to colour, drew the line
at soliciting the return of a beerhouse licence for Wm. Broadhead, the other! The Tory local paper mocked at the "nice
gentlemen in fair white neckties dancing attendance" on such
company![1] It is hardly surprising that he had a congregation
of working men, and had had to rebuild the chapel in 1867.
John Calvert—he declined to adopt the title 'reverend'—
was also a strong Liberal; he had come to Zion Chapel
in Attercliffe in 1857, and found it in very low water; he
swept away the pew rents, and by 1863 had to rebuild
the Chapel with further schools and mission rooms to hold the
increased membership. He stayed until 1895, and when he
left there were still good congregations and the buildings
crammed every Sunday afternoon with 250 scholars over
fifteen years of age, and a 'Pleasant Sunday Afternoon' of over
900 members.

Such men and their ministries are the best evidence of the
way that the gales of liberal politics could fill the sails of
liberal churches, and how a church open to those new social
forces could benefit from the rising section of the artisan class.
The general middle-class consistency of Independency stands
notwithstanding such magnificent exceptions, and we may
assume that the Liberal political views of the better class congregations did not dissolve the social barriers. The ministers,
like the greatest of their laity, were probably more perspicacious than the general level of their congregations; Liberals
not merely by political interest or social convention, but by
moral and theological conviction.

The Baptists, never a strong body in Sheffield, seem to have
been of similar composition to the better class Congregational
chapels; middle-class people, merchants and tradespeople
with "very few if any very poor people", being a general picture of their congregations. And the Upper Chapel, Sheffield's
earliest Dissenting meeting house and centre of Unitarianism,
embraced the highest stratum of the middle classes; not a great

[1] Sheffield *Independent*, July 9, 1867.

congregation assembled in January 1870 for Sunday worship, but the "audience consisted principally of the upper classes . . . more than a fair proportion of Aldermen, Town Councillors, local 'literati', a number of highly educated intellectuals, and a sprinkling of miscellaneous orders of society."

The resurgence of Wesleyan Methodism in Sheffield

The Wesleyan Methodists, as would be expected after their catastrophic losses after 1849, made a late contribution to the religious boom. In 1851 they had fourteen chapels in the entire borough of Sheffield, and as we have seen, their slow recovery is seen in the paucity of additional provision from that time, when the Methodist reform denominations and the Primitives were soaring ahead. But Wesleyanism regained her momentum; the losses were stemmed in 1856, in which year there was a national increase of some 3,000 members. Most years after that showed accelerated increase, and by 1876, the very year in which Conference expressed a willingness to admit laymen to its deliberations, the pre-secession figure had been reached. The membership figures, especially in the towns of the North of England, continued to mount at a great rate. It is well seen in Sheffield; the Sheffield Wesleyans recommenced building in 1867 and erected twenty-eight chapels, mostly sizable ones, between that date and the end of the century; and even then the building extension did not tail off for a decade. It showed a remarkable recovery, and brought Wesleyanism again into the front of the picture. And it was a new Wesleyanism, freed from its old inhibitions and cautions, more mixed politically than its younger daughters, and in the 'new look' of the largest and most flourishing of the Nonconformist churches.

Such a plethora of chapel building all over the area could not fail to bring in all sorts and conditions of men, especially those that were built in largely working-class districts. Thus on a Sunday in January 1875, Bridgehouses Chapel, with 900 seats, had "a good congregation of 450 to 500 . . . exceedingly respectable and decent . . . there were several genteel families from the suburbs in that locality, with many artisans from the new streets in the neighbourhood, and an unusually large sprinkling of what looked like middle-class people . . . the congregation was well-dressed and they wore an air of comfort and respectability". But many of the largest chapels both in the town and better suburbs were thronged with the middle classes and the very élite of society. So the fine Carver Street Chapel, with 1,650 sittings, of which 400 were free, had "an excellent congregation, both in quality and quantity, particularly the former . . . last season it had the Mayor and Master Cutler within a few pews of each other. In the main the congregation consists of members of the middle classes, with merchants, manufacturers and professional gentlemen. There were 300 downstairs and 400 in the gallery . . . the comfortable pews were filled with 'haut ton' of Carver Street Methodism. . . . Several pews, very plain, are intended for the other extreme; they were well-filled. . . ." The large Brunswick Chapel on Sheffield Moor had "one of the largest I have seen anywhere. There would be at least 700 or 800 people that night I was present. There were many families of good name and position, with a sprinkling of professional people, and it struck me that Brunswick was more an assembly of the great middle classes than any I had seen. There was a considerable admixture of the working classes, and the poor were also present, although not in great numbers. I noticed several, uncushioned benches for the poor. There were very few in them and none at all in the free attic gallery".

Our observer has a significant word to say upon his visit to Norfolk Street Chapel, the oldest home of Sheffield Methodism; there were not above 550 present at a Sunday service in March 1874, in this large chapel with accommodation for 1,400 people, and he comments "of course all places of worship suffer from the westward tendency of wealthy people. It is the ambition of a tradesman to have his house at Ranmoor and he naturally seeks a church or chapel not far from his own vine and figtree". This was a trend that could have the most serious consequences for the most stable and vigorous chapel communities when the group that literally possessed them moved away to better areas, leaving them near derelict in a sea of poorer people who had never felt any sense of belonging. It could entail the complete pulling out by a chapel from a poor district with the loss of all the hitherto exerted influence. One of the arguments of the Church of England against the liberal Nonconformist clamour for Disestablishment was based precisely on this point.

We see a striking and a sad illustration of the process in the history of the Park Wesleyan Chapel. There had been Methodist preaching in houses in the Park area of the parish, just off the south-east edge of the township, from as early as 1770; in 1814 a school and preaching room had been built. In 1831 a chapel was erected that had 400 members within a few years, and the demand for places in the new chapel had been so great that the original estimate of free seats had to be greatly reduced. It had a huge congregation, huge Sunday schools, day schools, and every possible kind of social organization connected with the chapel. Many were lost in the reform period, but, as with other chapels, there came strong recovery, and economic prosperity to many of its members. By 1866 the chapel was full again, and new applicants for seats had to wait three to six months for a vacancy, in spite of wealthier members continually moving from the Park district, now a teeming working-class area. "They were made in the Park, and they moved out of it" it was said. But the boom and prosperity continued, until 1901, when the wealthier members who lived further out in the Park area, in solid Victorian suburban villas, decided on a new chapel in their area, further up the Park hill. Many elected to worship in the fine new Victoria Chapel, and the Park Chapel shrank to half its number, bereft of its most prosperous members, and now in one of the poorest downtown areas of the whole town. With the decline in the present century, the old Park Chapel was closed—but the masses of people are still living there. There is much indeed to be learned by all churches from such rise and decline.[1]

The boom in the Church of England in Sheffield

For many reasons the Church of England in the large industrial towns is the hardest to define sociologically in the second half of the nineteenth century. Though traditionally Tory in its leadership and expressed opinions (and however estimable and laudable in the eyes of later generations the exceptions but prove the rule) the Church of England was never the religious expression of a single social group, however dangerously near to becoming so in some epochs and places. To say the least, she remained the Church to which everybody with no other allegiance nominally belonged. She was 't' owd church', as aged Sheffielders still call the Cathedral, in more

1 *History of Wesleyan Methodism in Sheffield Park*, J. J. Graham, 1914.

than date, where generation after generation of Sheffielders
had been christened, married and buried, from nobility to
paupers. Its abuses were public scandals on which anybody
could expatiate, and yet some of the same abuses obtaining in
other denominations received little obloquy. And as the old-
established Church from which men dissented in the name of
reform and liberty, and whose historic privileges men contested in the name of equity, it was inevitably prone to censure
in such a boisterous, liberal age as the second half of the
century. It is inconceivable that it could have been otherwise,
without the history of England having been quite other than
it was. But its recognition as 'the Church' was unique; people
'went to it', or dissented from it, or found excuses for not
going to it—and they were not hard to find, and had the
masses known more about it they could have advanced better
reasons than in fact they did.

The very existence of a Parish Church, whatever the restrictions to its common use, imposed within and conceived
without, brought the bulk of the parishioners into periodic
touch; and, with the great expansion of religious habit, the
Church of England also received a great increase of worshippers. From 1851 to 1881, which saw the continuous upward
curve of the boom though probably not the highest point
reached, during which the population of Sheffield doubled,
from 135,310 to 284,410, the Church of England increased
from twenty-three churches, some of which were only mission
rooms, to fifty buildings; and religious-census figures disclose
an increase in Sunday attendances from 14,881 to 33,835,
showing that she not only held her proportion of the population
but actually increased it. It was no mean accomplishment,
and showed a rate of increase slightly greater even than the
combined Methodist churches. Inevitably the increase was
from all social groups, particularly from the middle and
lower-middle groups, but also of the poor, where provision
was made, and where they could probably worship with less
inhibition than in a large predominantly middle-class chapel;
not least because the Church was not a body one joined in the
more deliberate sense in which one joined a Nonconformist
society, and because there was less social community in the
church than the chapel, and so less to feel excluded from. To
the church one 'went', the chapel one 'joined'; a distinction

not to be pressed, since the Church herself produced a large variety of social agencies and societies, and as the chapels, especially the Methodists, took on the open public character of a 'great church'. Yet the distinction indicates an important if subtle emphasis. It is probable that the more working-class Nonconformist denominations, as we have seen, had more of the superior, respectable, politically-minded working men than the parish churches, and that the latter had more of the indiscriminate poor.

There were factors making the parish churches more available to all and sundry, although the process was slow. The Oxford Movement, though it influenced few Sheffield churches until the twentieth century, was set against pew rents in its religious concern for the poor, if not their political advancement; and Thomas A. Ward, the cutler of Sheffield, who both rented a pew in the Unitarian Chapel and sub-let his freehold one in the Parish Church, makes a comment in his diary for 1843 that "Puseyism is progressing; the pews are swept away from Chesterfield Church"![1] In many other quarters they were condemned; lawyers proclaimed their illegality, and a plaintiff seeking arrears of rent for his 'freehold' pew let in the Parish Church of Sheffield lost his case on this very point at the County Court.[2] Sections of the Church press attacked the practice, and a typical comment is in the *Record* of 1856:

> . . . Examine the provision made for the largest class of all, the working men and their families. A few benches up the middle aisle, or at the back of the galleries, constitutes almost the whole of the accommodation set apart for those, whose numbers in the vicinity must be told in thousands. What wonder if the mechanic, entering such a church and feeling himself regarded almost as an intruder, resolves to go there no more? . . . The simple remedy is repentance, and immediate restitution. . . .[3]

The Select Committee of the House of Lords on the deficiency of the means of worship in 1858 ventilated the question of rented and appropriated seats, and the relation of the custom to the estrangement of the poor; many church leaders, as Bishop Tait, were concerned; and, not without interest, the Bampton Lectures for 1862, delivered by the Archdeacon of

---

1 *The Diary of Thomas Asline Ward*, pub. 1909, p. 307.
2 Broomhead v. Oakes, 1856. Sheffield *Independent*, Feb. 9, 1856.
3 *The Mission and Extension of the Church at Home*, J. Sandford, 1862: p. 341.

Coventry on the home mission work of the Church, dealt very largely with the subject. He was very forthright, insisting that the custom "stultifies the claim of the Church to be the Church of the poor, and almost invalidates its credentials as an institution of Christ, for it is in direct contravention of the principles and precepts of the Gospels".[1] But the effects were slow, congregations were very conservative, and people disliked the loss of their places, and of course the rents were often required towards the stipend of the minister. A few Sheffield churches abolished the rents, although there is no evidence that they were thronged with the poor as a result. In 1865 the Sheffield Church Extension Society was formed, which planned to build seven new churches in the following five years, all the seats of which were to be free; although the question of appropriation, that is, the allocation of particular places to particular people, was left an open question. Clearly large changes were taking place. Canon Sale, who was Vicar of Sheffield from 1851 to 1873, tried to do something about the practice in the Parish Church, but apparently without much effect, and some of his comments are revealing—the Scripture readers, he said, "when visiting the poor, and asking why they do not come to Church, were often met by the reply that the pews in the church were owned or let, so that there was no room to sit in them". He spoke of the illegality of selling or buying the pews, and alleged that "some had purchased pews believing that it was the best investment for their money, and when they died left them to their wives or children as a source of income". To his knowledge there were some ladies in the town, almost the whole of whose income was derived from the rent of pews their fathers had left them![2] Not until 1880, when the popular Canon Blakeney was Vicar and extensive alterations were made to the fabric of the building, were the pews replaced with oak benches for 1,600 people, all of which were to be free, one half to be assigned to the old seat-holders and the other half unappropriated.

Some glimpses through the eyes of 'Criticus' between the years 1869 and 1875, in the booming years of religion, show a less socially monochrome picture than any other denomination.

[1] *The Mission and Extension of the Church at Home*, J. Sandford, 1862: p. 326.
[2] Sheffield *Independent*, Report of speech on the pew system in the Parish Church, Jan. 23, 1867.

Many factors contributed to the composition of the congregations, but it is clear that a wide cross-section was to be found in the Church of England as a whole. But it is also clear that the attendance is heavily weighted from the middle-class section of society.

So in 1869, on a Sunday at the Parish Church, he found about 600 people besides children; ". . . the congregation was highly respectable and comprised many of the best families in the neighbourhood, a large number of middle-class people, and better sorts of tradesmen . . . there was also a sprinkling of the working classes . . .". At St. Paul's, in the centre of the town, there were 800 present in the morning, and 1,200 at night, almost solidly middle class, and a large number of them men, certainly not attracted, he suggests, by "sensational services, midnight missions, or religious novelties, home or imported"! Of course these were 'city churches' that had always drawn the élite. In the new suburban areas of middle-class villas, the congregations, as would be expected, were solidly made up of that class. So the new St. Mark's Church, in Broomhill: "the congregation is a 'good' one in a commercial as well as a religious sense . . . mayors, aldermen, and councillors who expected to be aldermen, merchants and manufacturers, with a considerable sprinkling of gentlemen learned in the law, and gentlemen learned in all the luxuries that wealth can supply . . ."; the thirty-five seats set apart for the poor were probably all that were ever required.

In many of the more mixed parishes the general picture seems to be of good congregations, largely middle class but also with some of the lower orders, and in some, as St. George's and St. Mary's, both very flourishing churches, the benches for the poor were completely filled. On the other hand there were parishes less mixed and almost solidly working class, perhaps with new industrial housing, yet where the congregations seem to have been exclusively middle class and even very fashionable. Thus at St. Silas', in 1873, where all the seats were "free and appropriated", the church was "exceedingly well-filled, scarcely an empty pew to be seen . . . several manufacturers, solicitors, commercial travellers, managers, accountants, and a sprinkling of working-class people". And at St. Stephen's, where "the district is inhabited principally by working people and the poorer classes", he is led to ruminate that "this is not the only occasion on which I have noticed the predilection of fashionable congregations for unfashionable neighbourhoods. . . . The congregation in the morning was not as numerous as I had expected. Evening is the time at St. Stephen's. Then it is always crowded and frequently it is impossible to gain admittance . . . men and women, boys and girls waited patiently while the stream of fashion and respectability flowed past them. The arrangement could not have been stricter if each pew had been a seat at a high-class concert, charged half-a-sovereign, reserved and numbered".

The Church of England has been greatly at the mercy of personal factors that complicate the analysis, more so perhaps than any other church. Thus in 1869 on a stormy November Sunday morning 'Criticus' went to "full Cathedral service" at St. Philip's, one of the four huge churches put up after the Napoleonic wars, and capable of holding 1,800 people. Old John Livesey was still vicar; not more than a hundred adults were present and "each in the gallery had 25 pews a-piece", and in the free seats were about ten people. "They were all decidedly respectable; the very fact of anyone going to church or chapel makes him or her respectable, in the best sense of the word." But when he went in the same month four years later he found a new vicar, and a congregation not short of a thousand!

These personal factors have always been of particular importance in the Church of England, where the very minimal demands made by the Church as an institution have given great scope to men of calibre, often producing a remarkable response from quarters least expected. Comparisons between men no doubt are odious, but some examples of very different kinds can be cited. There was John Edward Blakeney, who was Vicar of St. Paul's, and later Vicar and Archdeacon of Sheffield, who in 1868 organized a meeting of nearly a thousand working men to put their criticisms to the Archbishop of York, and who was 'put in the chair' in 1887, when he appeared at a large meeting of unemployed workmen in Paradise Square, in the bad year of 1887. A very different kind of man was Father Ommanney, who became vicar of St. Matthew's in 1882, and in the face of opposition and rioting turned that church into a lively centre of 'Anglo-Catholicism', as well as a vigorous community for the poor of the district. Certainly it had not been one of the

10

vigorous churches when 'Criticus' had visited it in earlier days, to find "a not very numerous congregation, 120 people, of whom 30 were the Sunday school children, though several respectable families and a number of the working classes", including none other than the notorious William Broadhead of the Trades 'Outrages' infamy, who had settled there to make his peace with God, after a brief sojourn in the United States!

The astounding results that could follow when the boom in church-going found a man of singular ability to give lead and direction are superbly exemplified by the case of St. Mary's, Bramall Lane, one of the 'Million' churches. In 1874 'Criticus' observed that "in the body of the church would be fully 900 people, and over 400 in the galleries. The benches in the centre aisle were occupied by the poor. The bulk of the congregation looked comfortable and well-to-do, evidently belonging to the upper and middle classes, with a large sprinkling of the wealthy and influential families from Sharrow, Nether Edge, Brincliffe, Kenwood . . . (i.e. new better-class suburban areas, beyond the parish on the south-west side of the town) . . . there were county and borough magistrates, professional gentlemen (particularly solicitors) in profusion, doctors, brewers, Aldermen, Councillors, public officials, merchants, manufacturers, and wholesale dealers, and many ladies and gentlemen of independent means—several who build churches all out of their own pockets. . . ." Such a congregation was set in what would have been a better working-class area of Sheffield, with a certain number of wealthier people still living within it, although clearly many had already moved further out in the same direction, but continued to attend. The large congregation was maintained, and twenty years later received an able incumbent, the Rev. R. H. Hammond, who was in demand all over the country as a mission preacher. His energies, and those of the congregation he harnessed, produced a mountain of work in the parish. It was in 1893 he became vicar. In a few years there was a Bible class of 270 for women, and one for men that rose to 700; clergy and lay-people between them maintained 145 open-air services a year, and 50 workers were organizing cottage-meetings during the winter. The Sunday schools numbered 1,500 with 135 teachers. And 109 factories in the parish were visited each year by the clergy and readers to address the workpeople. The Watch-Night service would pack the church with over 2,500 people.[1] And all of this was work in the parish, with the parishioners, in which many of the wealthier of the congregation found a field of social and religious work.

Such immense Bible classes were by no means confined to St. Mary's. We know that they existed at the Parish Church, where in 1885 there were also 600 women in the Mothers' Meetings, and also at All Saints, Brightside, which had been erected by Sir John Brown to serve the needs of many of his employees at the Atlas Works who lived in that locality. In 1859 John Brown had found a group of men meeting at work for prayer and Bible study in their mealtimes, and had placed a room at their disposal, and appointed a Scripture Reader to help them. It led to a Sunday school of more than a thousand, and to evening services at the works, and in 1869 to the fine new church in the area, attended by huge congregations, many of them John Brown's own workmen and officials, and to further expansion of Sunday schools and Bible classes for adult men and women. Nor would these have been the only cases by any means. They are all illustrative in their different ways of the 'boom', and they also explain the different social level invariably existing between the normal worshipping congregation and the Bible class meeting on the Sunday afternoon, and indeed their considerable independence one of the other; a feature that debilitated the church life at the end of the century in Sheffield as in many industrial towns of the North of England.

The 1881 Sheffield census of church attendance

We have looked at a wide selection of vignettes illustrating the relation of the different denominations to the people during the palmy years of the second half of the century. More statistical evidence is given in a local census, made throughout the whole borough in 1881 by the initiative of the *Sheffield & Rotherham Independent* newspaper, the politically Liberal paper of the area. It took the form of a count of all who attended the morning, afternoon and evening services in every place of worship, on Sunday, November 20 of that year; and the paper informs us that the figures should be regarded as 'maximum' ones, in that the day was beautifully fine, the heads of the churches knew it was to take place, so that it was not done in

[1] *Through the Power of Christ; Memoir of Rev. R. H. Hammond*, C. J. Hammond.

secrecy, and that another local paper—the Tory one—
"announced publicly that the census was to be taken and in-
cited the clergy to drum up their people by the fiction that the
Dissenters had, by hocus pocus, got the start". These were the
days of genuine competition, in which the churches were by no
means backward! The total population of Sheffield at that time
was 284,410, and the following figures of attendances do not
include Sunday scholars.

Denomination	No. of places of Worship	Sittings	Present Morn.	Present After.	Present Even.	Total for Day
Church of England .	50	32,751	13,385	1,778	18,672	33,835
Independent . .	22	10,900	3,010	123	4,714	7,847
Baptist . . .	6	3,200	1,205	—	2,001	3,206
Unitarian . .	2	1,100	421	—	767	1,188
Wesleyan Methodist .	29	14,917	5,065	—	6,783	11,848
Meth. New Connexion	12	5,342	1,034	—	1,692	2,726
Primitive Methodist .	25	8,904	1,676	82	3,644	5,402
United Meth. Free Ch.	15	8,178	2,850	—	4,296	7,146
Wesleyan Reform. .	15	3,720	776	102	1,648	2,526
Salvation Army . .	4	2,800	579	1,320	2,155	4,054
Presbyterian . .	2	540	230	—	253	483
Various minor . .	8	1,730	832	—	1,190	2,022
Roman Catholic .	6	2,715	3,602	—	1,871	5,473
Totals . .	196	96,797	34,665	3,405	49,686	87,756

The details should be compared with those of the 1851
Religious Census.[1] It will be seen that the population slightly
more than doubled itself in the period of thirty years, and the
total number of attendances is also just more than doubled.
Altogether it showed a valiant effort on the part of the churches
to cope with the great increase of population. Horace Mann,
working on the earlier census, had estimated that one-third of
those attending in the evening were not present in the morning,
and that 58 per cent. of the population could have been able to
attend worship had they wished to do so; on this estimate,
however questionable it may be, one in three who could do so
attended a place of worship on an average Sunday. On the
same basis of calculation in 1881, the same percentage was
maintained. But, of course, the much larger percentage of the
population who did not attend was also doubled. The *Independent* deplored this "sad deficiency of attendance" in Sheffield,

[1] See p. 109, and Appendix I.

and took little comfort in the fact that it was worse in Newcastle and Liverpool.

Many comments could be made on the 1881 figures and on their comparison with the earlier census. We notice the strides of the Church of England despite the advances of the liberal Nonconformist churches. We notice, too, the lesser advance of the 'old Dissenters' compared with other churches, which the Tory *Daily Telegraph* seized on to prove that "politics don't pay in the pulpit"! The relative weakness of the Wesleyan body is due to the effect of the reform secessions, although they were in process of mending the situation and engaged in huge building expansions, whereas the initial velocity of the liberal Methodist reform churches was slowing down by 1881. Also we see the appearance of the Presbyterians, and also the Salvation Army with four citadels embracing working class and poor people exclusively.

Whatever may be said of the 1881 figures relatively, and some denominations will have reached even higher figures before the end of the century, they do in fact represent a vast body of church- and chapel-goers that, with the tens of thousands of Sunday school children of all denominations, add up to a substantial proportion of the population in the churches. The personal and public influence inevitably exerted must have been immense. And judged by modern standards and expectations, the figures are quite extraordinarily high; in 1951 the population of the City, its boundaries much increased in this century, was 512,834, something less than double the 1881 figure, yet the total attendances to-day will be far less than in 1881. It is almost certain we have near doubled the population, and more than halved the actual numbers of attendants, and this is probably true for every denomination except the Roman Catholics, whose advance, if at a slower rate than might have been expected, has throughout been steady and unremitting.

Certainly the great building extensions by all the denominations, the emergence of new and successful denominations, and, above all, the capacity of the churches to hold their proportion of the great population increase between 1851 and 1881 justify the description of the progress in these years as one of 'boom' and 'inflation'. Nor was 1881 necessarily the high-water mark. That year happens to provide a statistical reading and a point for comparison, and the Wesleyans certainly continued to advance with great strides at least until the early years of the twentieth century. But the high mark for the aggregate of the churches was probably between 1881 and the end of the century, and, although we have no exact figures to demonstrate it, we have some pointers. From the mid-eighties, the building extension of the Church of England and the Congregational churches show a marked slackening, while the liberal Methodist churches show a quite sudden cessation of building from the end of the century. And we know too from the national membership figures of the liberal Methodist churches that the rate of growth was falling, although in Sheffield probably less so than the national figures suggest. Sheffield Methodism was peculiarly strong during the years of inflation, as we have seen, and its members were a very stable section of the community whose social habits would persist long after the denominations as such had ceased to expand.

*   *   *

The approach of the Churches to the working classes

One social group remains to be considered. However impressive the years of growth, and however imposing the congregations of those days as we picture them in the imagination and compare them with the reduced numbers now worshipping in those same buildings, in respect to the working-class population the churches had made negligible gain. We have seen that from 1851 to 1881 both the population of the town and the aggregate of attendances had almost exactly doubled. It was a great achievement, making worship and membership of the church or chapel a propriety of respectable life for the large and almost entire social groups in the middling strata of society, the consequences of which indelibly marked the Victorian era. But the even greater number not included in this number was also doubled in the period, and substantially it comprised the entire working class. It is a generalization of course, and subject to all the qualifications properly made for the different denominations; but when the work of the Church in the poorer parishes is taken into account and the solid working-class composition of the Salvation Army, and the contribution of the Primitive Methodists and the Wesleyan Reformers, neither of whom were uniformly composed of the poor, the generalization stands substantially true. And it is supported by comments from a variety of quarters during the period, and demonstrated by the specialized agencies set up to deal with the problem.

Much thought was clearly given to the problem by the Rev. Samuel Earnshaw, who was assistant minister at the Parish Church from 1847 to his death in 1888; certainly one of the most distinguished ministers that ever adorned the pulpit of the parish, not only as a theologian of broad views, stoutly defending the humanities over against his narrow Evangelical brethren, but as a mathematician who could write on such abstruse subjects as the Sine and Cosine of an Infinite Angle, the Mathematical Theory of Sound, and the Molecular Forces of the Luminiferous Ether! One wonders which is the more impressive, his scientific capabilities or his length of service as assistant minister in Sheffield. But in 1861 he preached on the subject of the Church and the Artisan, and the sermon, subsequently printed, maintained that "the Christian religion has almost entirely lost its hold upon the artisans of this country", and that "great numbers are godless, both because they do not believe in God, and because they never intentionally acknowledge His existence either by word or deed . . .". He was probably less than just concerning the totality and universality of their infidelity, but it is hard to believe he was not correct in his main thesis. His proposals are of interest in that he derided the new fashionable evangelistic methods, calling instead for more ministers, smaller parishes of not more than 400 houses, and smaller churches. It was a shrewd judgment, and he could have claimed the support not only of Thomas Arnold, and John Livesey, but of the Methodist pattern of humble buildings multiplied over the town. Modern evangelists should be interested in his comments:

. . . Great efforts are now being made to win back the masses. We hear of sermons preached by Bishops and popular Divines in unusual places, in theatres and worksheds, in beer houses and in the streets; we read in the newspapers of monster congregations assembling in St. Paul's, and in Westminster Abbey, in Exeter Hall, and in other places, and monster organs and monster choirs to allure. We are told of agents employed to read the sacred Scriptures in the public streets, aloud, on the chance of catching the ear of some casual passer by, and to scatter amid the noise of carts, and the confused din of business, the holy words of everlasting life. All honour to the good *intentions*. . . . But when I hear of these things, my only wonder is that any man, of ordinary experience and knowledge of the world, should ever for a moment suppose, that they will or can succeed in winning back to the Christian religion the wandering masses of the people. Working men will not go to these monster meetings, and people cannot now be converted on a monster scale, and by thousands at a time, as on the day of Pentecost. . . . And as long as we have only monster parishes there will be apathy and standing aloof of the people. They will not be visited by their parochial minister, because he cannot personally visit so many; they may be absent from Church too, but he does not know who is absent because his church is a monster church; and they may in their hearts desire to receive counsel and comfort from him, but he cannot know the state of their minds, neither if he did, could he comply with their wishes, because his parish is a monster parish. . . . In the meantime the evil will spread from the workers to the shopkeepers, and the middle classes generally.

It showed a convinced view on the subject, still worthy of consideration, and by no means least important is his final barb that glaring inconsistencies in the lives of Christians must be done away, in such things as tricks of the trade, short-weights, deceptive advertisements, oppression of workmen on Mondays and depreciation of their wages on Saturdays. Otherwise, he concludes, religion "will be set down as an imposition, and an invention of the higher classes for keeping the lower classes quiet and submissive"![1]

Earnshaw clearly had his ear to the ground, as we should say, and he was also sensitive to working-class outlook in his condemnation of the excessive narrowness of evangelical religion, which he insisted kept many people away, and made many others into hypocrites. In a sermon in 1860 on Mark 7:2-3 he attacked the "traditions of the elders" on the grounds that "God, who made man, is the best judge of what his creature can bear with advantage in the form of religious restraint. And though by pushing religious obligations to extremes, and by inventing new forms of religious duty, and multiplying moral and religious restraints, the cause of religion seems at first to be advantaged, the ultimate and permanent effect will not be good . . . there are floating in the popular mind certain traditions of the elders by which certain things are stigmatized as

[1] *The Church and The Artizan:* Sermon at the Parish Church of Sheffield, Feb. 10, 1861, by Rev. S. Earnshaw, M.A. (Sheffield Library.)

irreligious and ungodly, about which Scripture is silent . . .".
And he instances such things as games, sports, the theatre,
cards, billiards, games of chance, hunting, shooting, and
fishing, "though it will of course be understood that every
form of *gambling* is an abuse, as is every excessive indulgence . . .".[1]

No wonder a Sheffield theatre published extracts on its
hoardings, to the dismay of the religious-minded of the town.
And we can only guess his relations with his neighbour, the
Rev. Thomas Best, not a hundred yards away at St. James's,
who preached everlasting punishment to "all those who can
seek and find pleasure in the impure scenes and ungodly
sentiments of our existing theatres" in a sermon touching on the
Shakespeare Tercentenary proceedings, which he described as
"one enormous act of inconsistency and hypocrisy, when so
large and influential a part of this so-called Christian nation
paid *almost idolatrous* honour to the memory of a man who wrote
so much that would not be tolerated in any decent domestic or
social circle, and whose works, taken as a whole, whatever
amount of genius and talent may be manifested in them—
whatever literary beauties they may exhibit—notwithstanding
the moral sentiments interspersed in them—and however
esteemed among men, yet are, I doubt not, an abomination in
the sight of God".[2] It is improbable that the workmen of
Sheffield were guilty of this adulation of Shakespeare; it is
more certain that they liked fishing, as they still do, and it is
still more certain that they liked "games of chance", since the
same Mr. Best alleged in a sermon in 1864, that "at the last
Doncaster races, no fewer than 10,148 railroad tickets were
issued in our town, and that on one day more than a thousand
persons are calculated to have gone on foot to these notorious
occasions of vice, peril and profligacy".[3] These pulpit revela-
tions at least suggest the world of difference between the
working people and the outlook of the evangelical churches,
even if the estrangement of the people is to be ascribed to
profounder reasons.

As we should expect, the continued estrangement of the

---

[1] *The Tradition of the Elders.* Sermon by Rev. S. Earnshaw, Aug. 1860. (Sheffield Library.)

[2] Sermon by Rev. T. Best, Incumbent of St. James', Sheffield; Nov. 6, 1864. (Sheffield Library Local Pamphlets, vol. 1.)

[3] *ibid.*

growing artisan class was a subject of comment when the 1881
religious census figures were published. Indeed, the press itself
had been responsible for the census, and comments upon it
filled the papers for weeks afterwards, at a time when the
opinions of churches were esteemed worthy of serious reporting.
Many sermons appeared verbatim, and although they feature
much cavilling about particular aspects of the great count,
there is general agreement that the masses outside the churches
are largely the working classes. It is indisputable evidence from
the churches themselves, and though there was much charity
expressed—more than Samuel Earnshaw evinced—there was
little self-criticism, and none of his positive proposals to cope
with the problem. Perhaps the churches had grown more
sentimental since his day. But Canon Blakeney, the Vicar of
Sheffield, insisted that the masses should not be regarded as
infidel; they are poor, often lack decent clothes, and family
demands are heavy upon them, but in times of sickness, adversity and at death they are seen to be sincere and to have faith.
Certainly, he maintained, they should not be denied the
appellation 'Christian'.

Evangelistic agencies

It should not be thought of course that the churches, all of
them so deeply rooted in the evangelical tradition, had done
nothing to convert the masses. Long before the mid-century,
when 'evangelism' began to be as fashionable as the conversion
of the heathen overseas half a century before, there had been
agencies at work among the poor, predominantly aimed at their
spiritual salvation. The most important without doubt was the
great Sunday school movement reaching back in Sheffield to
the late eighteenth century, with its day school development,
itself an evangelistic agency catering for the children of the
alienated poor, which cannot be overlooked in calculating the
influence of the churches upon the masses even where they
were not brought into the worshipping congregation as a
consequence.

An early report of the famous Wesleyan Red Hill Sunday
School in Sheffield speaks of the depravity of the younger
people "particularly on the Sabbath day, when the wild
creatures are let loose from the drudgery of the week and have
the opportunity of herding together, corrupting each other and

disturbing the public peace".[1] This was in 1818, and surely
not limited to that year. Wherever the Sunday schools were at
work, young people were being brought under a civilizing
influence, and where so many young people were touched at
some time or other, the influence upon them and their adult
attitudes, though impossible to calculate, should not be ignored.
In fact the turnover in the schools was high, and proves the
strong pull of the world, and the failure of the churches to
integrate their scholars into the adult congregations. The
Wesleyan Red Hill School report of 1832 showed 512 boys and
530 girls in the Sunday schools, but admits that the admissions
and departures produce "as an average, an entire change of
boys in less than two years".[2] It was the same in the Church of
England. In 1839 the Church of England Instruction Society
was set up, since in the Mechanics' Institute, "the only
Institution accessible to the working classes, where literary and
scientific instruction is afforded . . . all allusion to the fundamental doctrines of Christianity is most carefully excluded".
The inaugural meeting went on to lament the chasm between
the schools and the Church, and that although "there are
7–9,000 children receiving instruction in the schools connected
with the Established Church in this town, hundreds of the
elder scholars are leaving every year, turned into the world,
and it is feared that the majority of them . . . contract bad
habits, and with very few exceptions are all lost to the Church,
and eternity only will discover how many are lost to heaven".[3]

It is easy to decry the Sunday schools, but it would be a
grave misjudgment. As means of converting the masses to full
Christian faith and practice, clearly they were inadequate, but
as the forerunners of schools for the masses, and as habitual
places where the poor sent their children for such moral and
religious instruction as many of them ever got, they constitute
a major working-class institution in the nineteenth century,
and the source of an indefinable, no doubt slight, but pervasive
influence upon the people at large. And many other agencies
sprang from them: an army of Sunday school teachers, and
district visitors, and later in the century the adult classes, Bands
of Hope, Libraries, Penny Banks, week-night classes and so on.

---

[1] Third Annual Report Red Hill Sunday Schools, 1818. (Sheffield Library.)
[2] Fifteenth Annual Report Red Hill Sunday Schools, 1832. (Sheffield Library.)
[3] Sheffield *Mercury*, Oct. 26, 1839.

By the middle of the century there was considerable recognition of the enormous home missionary task, and voices insisting
that if the denizens of the large towns were in some distant
island of the Pacific, there would be no stint of money or effort
to Christianize them! And certainly a variety of specialized
evangelistic agencies appear from this time, designed to win the
artisan class. We have seen Samuel Earnshaw's scathing
strictures upon them, and no doubt many ministers and congregations occupied with their own religious affairs took no
cognizance, either positive or negative, of new efforts that were
being made. But efforts there were. Thus in 1850 a Town
Mission was set up in Sheffield, at a time when the Manchester
Town Mission employed seventy agents. At its annual meeting
in 1855 a speaker described the position of the artisans in
Sheffield as "peculiarly demoralizing, since they were almost at
liberty to work at what times they please, and a self-reliant
spirit was the consequence. These circumstances were favourable to the formation of the highest type of character . . . but
terrible temptations were involved", and he besought the
meeting "to look at the turbulent flood of vice pouring down
the streets, and at the myriads of working men over whose
heads a frightful doom was gathering".[1] In the summer of 1854
the Vicar of Sheffield and other clergymen are found preaching
in the open air; something, it was claimed, unknown in Sheffield before.[2] In 1860 there were special religious services for
working men in the theatre, and a further series in 1866
organized by the Rev. R. Stainton, the popular minister of
Garden Street Independent Chapel. Moody and Sankey
troubled the waters apparently in 1874, and made 526 con-
versions.

More important than these spasmodic efforts was the advent
of the Salvation Army in Sheffield in 1878 where the '32nd
Blood & Fire Corps' was established with the initial assistance
of Gypsy Smith. And in spite of hooligan ribaldry and even
attack, as they processed through the streets of the town, they
gathered to themselves a remarkable number of the outcast.
An early article on their work in the Sheffield press speaks of
their "scouring the gutters" and "netting the sewers", and
"gaining many recruits from that class of people nobody seems
to care about, the occupiers of our courts and alleys who have

[1] Sheffield *Independent*, Nov. 17, 1855.   [2] *ibid.*, July 9, 1854.

hitherto known more about drink and dirt than religion. . . .
As we passed from Westbar on Sunday to the Temperance
Hall, for the night service, the Army was joined by many
strange recruits, out at the elbows, smelling of thick twist,
miserable looking wretches, led either by curiosity or repent-
ance, or perhaps a bit of both . . . men in whose minds the
truth was probably dawning that it is not absolutely necessary
to wear patent leather boots and a broadcloth coat to enter the
Kingdom of Heaven".[1] By 1881 they had four halls, with a
Sunday attendance of no less than 4,000, predominantly of the
working class and the poor.

Another permanent agency, the Workmen's Mission to
Workmen, was set up in 1880 through the action and with the
leadership over many years of Mr. A. S. O. Birch, F.S.A. He
writes that he had a Bible Class of 400 men, but found the
greatest difficulty in getting men not religiously-inclined to
attend, whereupon he advertised in the papers that "100,000
men in Sheffield go to no place of worship. Christian working
men of all denominations are requested to attend a meeting at
the Albert Hall . . . and if thought desirable to elect a Committee to carry out a scheme to reach some of our fellow-men".
Sixty or seventy men attended, but Birch adds that they were
"not quite the class of people who were invited . . . the bait
was too strong for several gentlemen of Sheffield who have the
weal of their fellow-men at heart". At the meeting he made
the point that the vast proportion of the men of the town never
attended a place of worship, and that working men should try
to influence their fellows where the regular ministry had
failed. Plans were duly laid for Sunday meetings in the Circus
in Tudor Street, where working men could come in their
working clothes to hear addresses by working men. Thousands
of handbills were distributed, and within a month nearly
3,000 were in attendance, sitting with their hats on, smoking
pipes, and calling across to each other in the "odoriferous
circus", until the brass band struck up the Sankey hymns. The
Workmen's Mission continued many years, finding a later
home in the Montgomery Hall, where in 1893 it claimed the
largest congregation in the city, "over 2,000 workmen and their
families every Sabbath", and in 1898 there were still 1,500
attending. Such, in Sheffield, was the beginning of what

[1] Sheffield *Independent*, Aug. 14, 1879.

became the Pleasant Sunday Afternoon Movement, some of whose meetings were enormous, such as that at Zion Congregational Chapel, in Attercliffe, which in 1894 had over 900 members.

How dated these evangelistic efforts amongst the poor strike us to-day, and how harsh the modern theological judgment upon them; but how much they speak to us of the alienation of working men from conventional religion, of the possibilities in those days where the churches broke out of their formalized patterns, and of a social revolution since accomplished. Clearly there was a situation and a mood in which striking things could be done outside the normal congregational setting, in neutral places and amongst the disinherited. There can be little doubt that curiosity, and the lack of other amenities, contributed to the attendances; and that the later developments, though working class in composition, were more decorous than the original assemblies. The wariness of the working men is apparent from Birch's comments on the early meetings. "I have noticed," he writes, "how men hover about the Circus, and then quietly glide in . . . and dart off before anyone could get a word with them. We were compelled to hold our meetings in the Temperance Hall one winter, but for some reason not quite clear, we got a class of people who dressed better, the general opinion being that the broad daylight acted prejudicially against that class attending which we were striving to reach."[1]

The pattern of working-class life

The very existence of these endeavours, courageous in concept, pathetic in their disclosures, and pathetic perhaps in themselves, is evidence enough of the failure of the churches to embrace the poorer people, and they witness to the cultural isolation of the masses. And with this picture we are able to set the social range of the churches up against the class stratification. We see that either the religious bodies were restricted to a single social stratum, embracing a lower percentage of the population as they approached the working class, or they reached down and embraced groups of all classes but with smaller percentages the lower they went, and in so doing pro-

[1] For the Workmen's Mission see *Christian Work in the Grand Circus, Sheffield*, A. S. O. Birch, Pamphlet in Sheffield City Library, and *The Hammer*, Nov. 11, 1893.

duced religious groups of different social levels that seemed incapable of merging. Thus the Bible classes were distinct from the congregations, the frequenters of the Workmen's Mission would not go to the classes. Beyond them all was the ocean of the masses and the submerged who would not go to anything. And if in the second half of the century the sociological winds were blowing hard into the denominational sails, beneath them the ocean was becoming broader and deeper at an even faster rate, and new currents running fast! If only to hold the general picture in focus, we must remember the qualifications to be made in this picture of the working classes. There was that fraction of the poor in the parish churches, respectable and socially conservative; that fraction of the skilled craftsmen and superior mechanics at home in the liberal Nonconformist chapels, amongst whom would be men active in the world of the Unions, the Benefit Societies, and political affairs, and there were the reclaimed poor in the Salvation Army and the Workmen's Missions.

There would be greater numbers of active trade unionists critical of all the religious bodies, and the masses without any serious social interests, preoccupied with the job of living from day to day, from week to week, and with their sport, drinking, racing and gambling. The women would lead a narrower life—more of them in the religious bodies—immersed in the family, the life of the court, the old people, the daily battle with poverty, soot and dirt, the annual event of turning out the children in white muslin and ribbons for the 'Whit-walk' and the 'Sing'. And all of them at the mercy of the slightest dislocation of trade, a strike, a lockout, or an arbitrary wage depreciation. And economic dislocations and subsequent increased industrial and social tension were characteristic after 1875 and provide the background to the changing political mood of the working classes from that time. From 1843 to 1873 was the so-called 'Golden Age' of British industry; from then until the end of the century were the years of 'chequered progress', with severe slumps in 1876–9, 1885–6, and 1892–3, due to a combination of causes; the inflation of production in alliance with new processes in steel making, the tailing-off of railway development, and increasingly to foreign competition and tariff barriers. The consequences for Sheffield, so largely dependent on export trade, and reliant on increasing demands of British industry in general for engineering products, were grim. In the first of the crises for example, the wages of colliers, puddlers, and engineers were reduced even where men were not employed on short time, and the Sheffield *Telegraph* in December 1877 declared that "within 18 months the wages of iron-workers have been decreased by nearly 50 per cent", and at the end of 1878 the *Independent* declared that the year had been one of the worst experienced that generation, and that prices and wages were still declining. Revival set in by the end of 1879 and was maintained for several years, but in 1884 trade was "the worst of the present decade", and 1885 was worse.[1] So the town staggered on, population increasing, industry increasing, and wealth increasing, but from 1877 subject to severe recurrent crises: a feature that was to persist until the great depression of the inter-war years of the present century.

It is impossible to give adequate description of the social consequences of these crises, their cost in human life, happiness and social relationships, in a society visibly advancing in wealth, invention and amenity, yet visibly also in the midst of mass poverty. Nor is it possible to do justice to the variegated pattern of working-class life accommodating itself to such conditioning, or to its remarkable capacity of living for the day, its resilience in the face of permanent insecurity, shot through with evanescent gaiety, and family calamity. Such was the ocean in which new currents and swell were running.

Re-orientation of working class

The changing temperature in the working class, and the new currents of thought, organization and action flowing from the 'eighties, belong to the history of the British Labour movement and need not be treated here with any detail. But it is of crucial importance in our study in so far as it marks a gradual though decisive change in the attitude of working-class leadership to the existing organization of society, and a loss of deference to the political instruments, and social ideals forged by the middle classes. It marked a change of orientation. Not that in itself it led the working classes away from the churches— we have studied in great detail their general historic estrangement—but it certainly led many of the very cream and élite

[1] See *A Report on Unemployment in Sheffield*, A. D. K. Owen, 1932.

of the working-class leadership away from the churches, or, to be more precise, from the chapels. It led the *formative* elements in the working class to look in a different direction, away from dependence on liberal political machinery and away from the middle class and lower middle class way of life as standards of social decorum. The significance of this re-orientation for the future crystallizing-out of a positive working-class pattern of life cannot be overestimated. It was evidence of a social cleavage and a subsequent social revolution, hardly realized because of its gradualism; but it was none the less indicative of a fracture in society, in which the churches were found almost wholly on one side of the break. On the one hand it led to a massive working-class society, neither submerged, nor an appendage to middle-class society; and on the other hand to the increasing 'sociological imprisonment' of the churches.

It is, of course, a commonplace to note the remarkable social cohesion in English society in the late eighteenth and the nineteenth centuries, in comparison with the turbulent social revolutions of less fortunate Continental nations. Many reasons have been given, including Halévy's famous if questionable dictum on Methodism. There were surely many factors at work, but one at least was that, in spite of periodic tensions and flare-ups, the bulk of society looked in the same direction for social amelioration, including those in the working-class leadership whose attitudes ultimately triumphed over those of more revolutionary outlook. Thus, the Chartists regarded the first Reform Bill as a sham, and their more revolutionary element proposed "commencing action on their own account" to use the phrase of a Sheffield Chartist. Yet, as we have seen, the leaders of the workmen expressing themselves through the trades unions refused 'direct action' and placed their reliance on Free Trade, and, later, on extension of the franchise through constitutional action through the Liberal Party. The trades unions through their officials constituted working-class leadership, and they were in fact both a progressive and a conservative stabilizing force in the industrial towns, and their members had a stake in society as it was, and as it could be through radical liberal measures. No wonder that in 1842 Dr. G. C. Holland, a convert to the value of combination, could challenge his industrialist critics to disprove that where men were in union, the higher their pay, the less fluctuation in their trade, the more sober, intelligent, moral and thrifty the workmen, and the fewer in the gaols and on the parish.[1]

Had the Liberal industrialists not regarded laissez-faire as written in the very structure of the universe, they could have seen that their own political leadership was being accepted by the working-class leadership—that they were all looking in the same direction. Of course men labouring under some grievance could put the master 'uppo't shelf'—and this could happen where men were in union or not—but there is no evidence that the unions in any general sense engaged in wild-cat action, whatever was said by the religious devotees of 'freedom' to the contrary. The attitude of the unions in Sheffield to the 'ratteners' is good evidence on this point. Again, after the second Reform Act in 1868 the newly enfranchised workmen accepted the Liberal candidates, not blindly, at least in Sheffield where they were well able to distinguish an 'advanced Liberal' from a Whig! Of course, participation at all in the democratic process entailed accepting the existing machinery and candidates put forward; but the fact remains, it was accepted, and for many years.

Yet despite this willing acceptance by working-class leadership of the existent definition of the political arena, more and more after 1868 Liberal candidates of all hues had to direct their words to the ears of workmen, and it was dictated by the growing political self-consciousness of working-class leadership, as well as by the size of the new electorate. In 1874, at the second General Election after the Reform Act, Joseph Chamberlain was accepted as a candidate, and although he was defeated he made the frankest appeal to working-class interest on a programme of "free schools, free labour, free land, and a free church", and as "an advanced Liberal".[2] He was sponsored by the chairman of the Trades' Council. Chamberlain was standing on a programme by no means accepted by Liberals at large, but the incident shows both the continued working-class support for a radical liberal programme, and also the growing sense in the working class that they had their own particular political interests. The concession of a few safe Parliamentary seats to trade unionists by the Liberal Party

[1] *Mortality, sufferings, and disorders of grinders*, Dr. G. C. Holland, 1842. (Sheffield City Library.)
[2] See Speech of Joseph Chamberlain in Sheffield, Jan. 1, 1874.

from 1885, and the 'Lib-Labs' are further indications on a national level of the recognition of developing self-consciousness in the working class.

The decisive re-orientation is seen in the birth of new working-class political agencies from the 'eighties—The Social Democratic Federation in 1881, the Independent Labour Party in 1893, born of the 'New Unionism', and the Labour Representation Committee of 1900 which begat the Labour Party in 1906.

In Sheffield the new direction of the working-class political outlook was not achieved smoothly or suddenly, and a few straws may show the direction of the wind. From the 'eighties Sheffield had its propagandists, both at home and as visitors, for Socialist views. In 1887 the Socialist Club was opened in Scotland Street under the distinguished leadership of Edward Carpenter, who lived just outside the town in Derbyshire, and it was no doubt through him that no less a person than Prince Kropotkin lectured in Sheffield in that year. H. M. Hyndman, the founder of the S.D.F., lectured at the Temperance Hall in 1888, to a hall half-full, and told the meeting that Socialism now existed in England, and had done so for the past six years, and that "Whig, Tory and Radical, when they represented capital, all meant the same thing", and that "it was difficult to tell the alligator from the crocodile in the same river"![1]

But there seems no evidence that the trade union leaders were moved from their traditional political position. Political self-consciousness there was, but political re-orientation was still ahead. In fact in 1888 a conference was held of trades' delegates under the chairmanship of Councillor C. Hobson, the president of the Federated Trades' Council, on the trade depression at that time. The main speech was devoted to the evils of drink, and the vast sums spent in 'booze' as the major cause of the bad days they were living in. Speaker after speaker apparently concurred and only one "contended that the social system required altering, and that many persons who got thrown out of employment and ultimately found their way to the workhouse had become reduced through no habits of intemperance, but through the bad social system".[2] Even less would they have been influenced by the wild voices off stage, from the Sheffield group of Communist-Anarchists, which was

<hr>

[1] Sheffield *Independent*, Feb. 28, 1888.   [2] *ibid.*, Apr. 9, 1888.

formed in 1891 under the leadership of Comrade Dr. J. Creaghe, who through their journal the Sheffield *Anarchist*, with the motto 'Neither God or Master', advocated pillage and dynamite.[1] Though 600 copies of the first issue were sold in the town, it seems to have run for only a few months! They were a long long way to the 'left', if the term should even be permitted, of Edward Carpenter and William Morris, and were opposed to the S.D.F., the I.L.P., and the Fabians. At least the little group enable Sheffield to claim further colourful testimony to a radical tradition!

But the currents were running faster. An I.L.P. candidate put up for Attercliffe in the Parliamentary elections of 1894, and received 1,249 votes of the 9,230 polled—it was the first expression of the break from the Liberal Party—but still the trades' delegates showed no official departure from their Liberal support. But more acceptable advocates were at hand. Keir Hardie became a regular visitor to Sheffield, setting Socialism in a wide ethical context, "not merely a bread and butter movement, but aimed at brotherhood and fraternity".[2] And Tom Mann in 1897, with the assistance of the Clarion Glee Club singing, carried with him a large and enthusiastic gathering when he told them why he was a member of the I.L.P., that the Liberal-Labour advocates had no grasp of the fundamental issues at stake, and that neither Liberals nor Tories, "chapel-goers or churchgoers" believed in righteousness or fairness.[3]

Only gradually and piecemeal was the Trade Union shift made. There were two delegate trades' bodies in Sheffield, the Federated Trades' Council, and the Sheffield Trades' Council. The latter body moved more quickly. In November 1902, by a unanimous vote, the Sheffield Trades' Council entered into affiliation with the national Labour Representation Committee, whose direct object was to get a distinct Labour group into Parliament, and into other administrative bodies, with their own whips. It showed a final break with the Liberal and the Lib-Lab position, and the local logic of this move created much consternation. At the following municipal election the Liberals criticized "20,000 trade unionists" for not supporting a Lib-Lab candidate, for engaging in 'cut-throat' business,

1 The Sheffield *Anarchist*. (Sheffield City Library.)
2 Sheffield *Independent*, Feb. 24, 1896. 3 *ibid.*, Apr. 28, 1897.

whereby only the Tories, the Established Church, and the beer and betting interests could benefit. The delegates felt obliged to make a public repudiation that they had been influenced either by Tory gold, Tory beer or Tory religious bigotry![1]

In 1903 a conference was called of the entire organized labour of Sheffield by the Federated Trades' Council, as a result of which a Labour Representation Committee was set up in the town under the name of the Sheffield Trades' Council and Labour Representation Committee, which was to be the only authorized body to promote Labour candidates for municipal or parliamentary elections. While not carrying all the unionists or all the working-class voters from the Liberal position—and indeed, it was regularly affirmed by Liberals that the "bottom stratum of society" voted Tory—it marked the official political re-orientation of working-class leadership in the town. It constituted the most significant symbol of the overt social re-orientation of the formative leaders of the working class, away from mere acceptance of or deference to the established ordering of society, the significance of which for the churches we have already noted.

[1] Sheffield *Independent*, Nov. 29, 1902.

Chapter 5

CHURCH AND PEOPLE IN THE YEARS OF 'DECLINE AND FALL', 1900 TO THE PRESENT

THERE ARE THOSE who delight in ecclesiastical hypochondria, but there are few themes so tiresome and profitless as bewailing the decline of the churches. Apart from its futility, it rarely lays bare the facts of the case or points intelligent lessons that might be learned. We are merely depressed. But sound and dispassionate analysis of the decline and fall is nonetheless important, if only to deliver us from nostalgia, from the dead hand of the past, and to set us free for positive mission into a new future.

There certainly has been a large-scale collapse of membership in the past two generations, both in absolute figures and relatively to the size of the population. From the 'eighties to the present time, in the industrial and urbanized areas of the country the sequence has been a slackening of what we have called the 'boom' in church-going (that is to say, a failure of the churches to maintain their proportion of the ever-increasing population, as they had succeeded in doing in Sheffield in the preceding generation), a steady 'deflation', and an eventual 'recession'. The pattern is not identical for all denominations, and only the Roman Catholic Church shows absolute increase. All the other churches show absolute losses over the period. From the end of the century the over-all curve of aggregate attendances would show a gradual fall to the inter-war years, when a steepening downward trend takes place. The relative curve, of course, in view of the population increases, would show a steeper fall.

National and local statistics of recession

Unfortunately there are no later census figures for Sheffield comparable to those of 1851 and 1881, which would have permitted the charting of a graph, but though a census to-day would show the extent of the collapse it would not enable us to trace the pattern of decline. The best we can do is to assemble a variety of known facts from different parts of the country, piece them together and form a general view of what has happened. The only instance of measurement roughly falling within the period of decline is that provided by Seebohm Rowntree for the City of York, where the adult population had risen from 48,000 in 1901 to 78,500 in 1948, while the adult attendances at churches of all denominations on an average Sunday had fallen from 17,060 to 10,220, representing a fall in the proportion of the adult population from 35.5 per cent to 13 per cent.[1] We can assume that in the larger industrial cities, such as Sheffield, the fall has been greater and from a lower initial percentage.

The *British Weekly* in 1955 published articles on the Decline of Nonconformity,[2] and showed that though the membership of the major Free Churches of England and Wales had continued to increase from 1900 to 1910, from that time, before the commencement of the First World War, a gradual fall in total membership has taken place; in 1935 membership was almost equal to that of 1901. But the decline of the Free Churches is more serious than the loss of membership suggests. At the beginning of the century, says the *British Weekly*, the Free Churches had as many 'adherents' as they had members, but "by 1935 the situation had become similar to that of the present, in which it is rare to find a Free Church congregation that is larger than the membership of the church". The loss of adherents therefore is much larger than that of members, and points to the weakened habit of worship on the part of those who may not have been fully committed, as it also points to the greatly diminished influence of Nonconformity on the public at large. Nor even is this the whole picture. From the 'thirties the decline has steepened sharply. Thus in the Methodist Church since 1932, the year of union, the membership in Great Britain has fallen from 838,019 to 740,872 in 1948, with losses in every single year, since when there have been some slight accessions that may show a staunching of the loss. Again, the membership of the Congregational Churches of England and Wales has fallen from 299,906 in 1935, to 221,370 in 1955, a

1 *English Life and Leisure*, B. Seebohm Rowntree and G. R. Lavers, 1951.
2 *British Weekly*, Mar. 10, 17, 1955.

loss of 26 per cent, though the losses in recent years have been fewer than in the earlier ones.

There are some figures for Sheffield that illustrate the decline, and all of them show a more serious recession than the national picture. Thus the Congregational Church shows a complete tailing-off of building extension after the first decade of the century in spite of the huge area expansion of the City after that date, a static membership of 3,643 in 1904 and 3,841 in 1930, and then a drop to 3,345 in 1938, and 2,037 in 1955. The Baptist membership of the City fell by much the same percentage, from 1,709 in 1931 to 1,070 in 1954. Again in the same period there are losses from the Methodist Church, but as the national figures would suggest, they are less heavy than the other Free Churches. Thus in the eight 'districts' that fall in the City boundary (though they also include some areas outside the City), the membership in 1932 was 15,960, and had fallen to 12,528 in 1954. It is interesting to note however that the Methodist recession, as the other Free Churches, is considerably greater in Sheffield than the national fall, and suggests the greater losses in the industrial towns from the 'thirties.

One of the most striking ways of grasping the decline is to look at the building chart.[1] Free Church denominations which were building at a feverish rate in the years of the 'boom' quite suddenly terminate their expansion in the early years of the century, notwithstanding the continuing increase in the population, from 380,793 in 1901 to 512,834 in 1951, during which time the boundaries of the City were enlarged, and in which after the First World War vast new housing estates were erected on the perimeter. The Wesleyans alone of the Free Churches continued to plant new buildings in the extending areas, and the Methodist Church has continued to do so since 1932, the year of union between the Wesleyan, the Primitive Methodist and the United Methodist Churches. But the two latter Methodist denominations had virtually ceased to build twenty years before the union took place. It showed the greatest decline for the most liberal of the Nonconformist churches.

The decline in the strength of the Established Church is harder to measure since there are no 'membership' figures. Technically its numbers are always increasing with the population advance, but clearly this gives no indication of real

[1] Appendix V.

strength. But we have some comparative figures for Sheffield that demonstrate the losses since the 'eighties. Thus the 1881 census of worship gave total attendances at adult services of the Church of England on an average Sunday of 33,835, at a time when the population of the City was 284,410. In 1956, with the population slightly over half a million, the comparable figure of total attendances is between 12,000 and 13,000.[1] It should be noted that the 1881 figure does not represent the high-water mark, but a point of comparison. Again there are figures of Easter communicants, which were rising until after the First World War: 11,901 in 1910, and 13,456 in 1916. In 1950 the total of Easter communicants was about 11,000. This shows a degree of stability in communicant membership, but it should be borne in mind that the centrality of the Holy Communion has been greatly stressed in the present century, and in many churches is now the only Sunday morning service, while at the same time the age of admission to Communion has fallen. The near maintenance therefore of communicant figures, good though it is, should be set in the context of changed pattern in the worshipping habits of the Church.[2] There is however one other broad qualification to be remembered in making any statistical comparison between Victorian and modern habits. To-day great numbers of practising Christians attend church only once on a Sunday, and many of them not every Sunday—so changed has become our social pattern of life into which worship is to find its place. Undoubtedly it means that the present number of worshipping Christians is higher than a count on any average Sunday would suggest.

Nonetheless, with all the favourable qualifications that could be adduced, the statistical evidence, not to mention the evidence of our eyes, is sufficient to prove the deflation of the religious habits of the people. A rough but graphic indication of the change is to mark how church extension in the twentieth century provides smaller buildings than earlier periods, housing congregations that would have been considered diminutive half a century ago, and yet set in the midst of larger parishes

[1] Based on Articles of Enquiry to the Church-wardens at the Archdeacon's Visitation.

[2] The number of Easter communicants in the Church of England as a whole was rising steadily from 1891 (the first year in which figures were collected), until the mid-twenties. But this does not refute the over-all loss of worshippers in the period.

and districts. And some denominations have not even made this reduced provision to the expanded city. But there is more to be said on the pattern of decline throughout the nation during this modern period, and sociological aspects of it deserve examination.

The recession nation-wide

When did the 'boom' tail off, and deflation commence? And why did it happen? These are questions we seek to answer in this chapter. Neither of them can be answered simply, and the latter question is particularly complex, despite the facile and varied reasons that are customarily given. Both questions will take us from Sheffield, partly through the absence of local data, but it is also dictated by the nature of the problem. The origins and growth of churches in relation to social groups is better studied in a single area, as we have done—without this treatment, the necessary generalization would obscure all the finer points and issues and invalidate the local documentation. But in studying the decline of nineteenth-century religious institutions, the over-riding factors are to be found in the eroding acids and positive leavens at work in society as a whole. The causes are to be found in the impacts of events, ideas, new moods and aspirations that are nation-wide, and indeed far wider than this, penetrating every part of the modern world. It is of course the outstanding characteristic of the modern era, though one that has been developing through the generations of industrialism, that the local community, be it village or town, no longer lives to itself. The local, at a certain stage, becomes integrally related to the nation and the world beyond, and subject consciously or otherwise to the impact of inventions, events, and ideas of that world beyond. Unless we are woefully parochial, or wilfully blind, we are forced to think in large-scale general terms, and to set the affairs of the parish pump in a broad context. For good or ill, extending horizons, with whatever appears upon them, are part of growing into the modern world. There is good reason then for setting the problem of man's fidelity and infidelity into the large context.

The date of deflation and the beginning of the recession of the churches cannot be given with exactness. And naturally enough. Social customs do not change overnight, nor do they change uniformly over a nation, city, class, or identically within the various denominations which we have already seen to be related to a class structure of the nation, which is itself in process of change. At the same period it may be possible to trace both advance and decline. In Sheffield we have already noted that the 1881 figure of church attendance does not necessarily represent the high-water line; it shows a point of high participation, and certainly the Wesleyans continued to advance well beyond this date, as their membership figures and extensive building programme testify. Nor is there any reason to believe that the Church of England did not continue far beyond this date to maintain her proportion of the population. Certainly it is a matter of legitimate argument when decline begins in any particular area, as also the pattern of decline. What is more certain is that between 1881 and 1900 the peak was reached, passed, and slow deflation had commenced. Speaking broadly, it is probably true to say that the general over-all decline of church-going in the nation begins in the late years of the nineteenth century.

Evidence of recession in London

The clearest available evidence of changing social habit in the matter of worship during this period relates to London, though, let it hastily be said, London is not Sheffield! But none-theless there is striking evidence from the Capital. A census of religious attendance was taken in 1886 by the *British Weekly* newspaper, by a count on one particular Sunday, and again by the *Daily News* in 1903 by a count spread over that year. The figures are subject to all the criticisms and qualifications that can be made of such compilations, but they provide means of comparison between the two dates. In 1886 the population of Smaller London was 3,816,483, and by 1900 it had risen to slightly more than 4,500,000. At the earlier date the total attendance at all the churches on a Sunday was calculated to be 1,167,312, of which 535,715 were for the Church of England, and 369,349 were Nonconformist (excluding the Salvation Army figures). In 1903 the *Daily News* computed the total attendances to be 1,003,361,[1] of which 429,822 were Church of England and 416,977 Nonconformist (including the Salvation Army figure of 22,402). The voluminous analysis of the figures for the latter census are published in Mudie-Smith's *Religious*

[1] Including children at church services, but excluding Sunday school figures.

Life of London; they enable the Londoner to know the exact number of people at his church or chapel at the beginning of the century. Mudie-Smith also provides a chapter on the comparison between the figures for 1886 and 1903. While the population had increased by over half a million, the total attendances had fallen by something like 150,000. The decrease in attendance was almost wholly confined to the Church of England "and fairly uniform all over London, affecting rich, middle class and poor districts", while the Free Churches as a body were holding their numbers, but not significantly expanding with the increased population.

The reasons for the erosion of the Established Church in comparison to the Free Churches are many, but most important would be the sustained and greater momentum of Nonconformity in the middle-class and lower middle-class groups, their greater affinity with the social and political aspirations of those sectors of society, the undoubted superiority of the immense social organization of the Nonconformist churches, and possibly the development of the 'weekend habit' that would play greater havoc with churches not imbued with the Nonconformist conscience. All of which is to say that if there were forces at work weakening all churches, there were social and centripetal forces at work in Nonconformist congregations that were lacking or far less strong in the parish churches.

Would Sheffield and other large industrial areas have shown a similar trend in these years? It is a pretty question, and the probable answer is that the boom continued later in Sheffield, even if the pattern of deflation was the same. The greater social stability of the industrial North and the absence of anything comparable to the Greater London hinterland, into which Londoners were spreading, would give greater persistence to established social habits anyway. And if it was a general characteristic of urban areas that the Free Churches maintained their hold longer than the Church of England, this would have been an added reason for persistence, since Sheffield was more strongly Nonconformist than London, in 1881 with 46,441 attendances as against 33,835 of the Church of England. But on the *timing* of the deflation we are not on firm ground. Sheffield in due course has probably caught up with London, if it has not even surpassed it in this matter!

Before departing from the London scene we may profitably

examine some of the comments made on the 1903 figures, analysing the causes of deflation. As with every census available from 1851, the point is made for every section of London that the poor and the working classes are substantially estranged from the churches, even though some denominations are more successful than others. It may be noted, too, that the commentators were shocked by the paucity of attendances, alleged to be, after deduction for 'twicers', only one in five of the population, that "four persons out of every five in London and Greater London are either careless or hostile as regards public worship", though *we* may add, as with all the census figures examined, how large the attendances appear to the modern eye. This stands out even more in the figures for Greater London, where the borough with the highest attendance, High Barnet, registered attendances of one in 1.66 of the population, and the lowest borough, of Tottenham, showed one in 6.06. A few of the many comments throw light on the general picture. Thus Charles F. G. Masterman, Fellow of Christ's College, Cambridge, had the task of interpreting the figures of South London; he deserves to be quoted as one continuously pre-occupied with the burden of this study:

... In South London one man out of every six, and one woman out of every five, attends some place of worship at least once every Sunday . . . the poor (except the Roman Catholic poor) do not attend service on Sunday, though there are a few churches and missions which gather some, and forlorn groups can be collected by a liberal granting of relief. . . . The working man does not come to church. A few communities of Primitive Methodists, Baptists and Salvationists, and similar bodies, as a general rule represent his contribution to the religious life of the nation. . . . The tradesmen and middle class of the poorer boroughs exhibit an active religious life, mainly gathered in the larger Nonconformist bodies, especially the Baptists. . . .

On the side of the working people this is a period of unusual difficulty. The uprooting from the country and the transference to the town had caused a general confusion and disorder . . . dumped down in some casual street, unknown to his neighbours, unconnected with a corporate body or fellowship, he goes through life in a kind of confused twilight, dimly wondering what it all means. Material comfort and security is inevitably under these conditions his main interest; the memories of a life which is independent of the hard, visible, tangible boundaries become daily dimmer, as he clangs the hammer, or heaves merchandise, or manipulates hard material things . . . the failure is considerable from the side of the churches. The Anglican Church represents the ideals of the upper classes, of the universities . . . the large Nonconformist bodies represent the ideals of the middle classes, the strenuous self-help and energy which have stamped their ideas upon the whole of Imperial Britain. Each lives in poor districts, in them, not of them; each totally fails to apprehend a vision of life as reared in a mean street, and now confronting existence on a hazardous weekly wage from a block-dwelling or the half of a two-storied cottage. . . . We are recognised as meaning well, but our aims and ideals never become clearly intelligible. "What is he after?" "What does he get?" "What is behind it all?" are questions I have frequently heard as some church has bourgeoned out into fresh and ingenious enterprise. . . . We appear and we vanish. After a few months of this perplexing enthusiasm the curate or minister is called to another sphere of work, and disappears from the universe of those who had just, perhaps, commenced to realise that he possesses some traits of ordinary humanity. If we could only apprehend how entirely baffling and irrational all this must appear to those who are looking out of, instead of into, the abyss, our surprise would be less at the vastness of our failure than at the magnitude even of our poor success. Connected with this divergence we must recognise how scantily up to the present the Churches have identified themselves with those demands of Labour, which from the bottom of his heart the working man knows to be just. The battles of the past for social amelioration . . . have been fought apart from, and often with the open opposition of the larger religious organisations. . . .[1]

The passing of time has reinforced some of his caustic observations—that gigantic successful preaching centres merely draw from the local churches, and weaken them—"the water is not increased in quantity, but merely decanted from bottle to bottle . . .", that "the morning and evening services of the Church of England, as normally performed, with their complicated and mysterious variations of canticles, prayers, and irrelevant readings of Scripture, are altogether bewildering to those not intimately familiar with the books from which they are compiled . . .", and that "Sunday Schools conducted by mild-mannered and generous Buddhists would draw large and appreciative audiences". One further feature of London should be noted—the movement of population, first of the better-

1 *The Religious Life of London*, ed. R. Mudie-Smith, 1904; ch. VII.

class people into the growing suburbs of Greater London, leaving solid masses of the poorer and less enterprising of the population, duly followed by the outward movement of the working classes into the suburbs, and the further emigration of the better classes. Nowhere did this happen on such a scale as in London of course, but London provides an acute illustration of what was happening in all the large towns of the country, and visibly in the city of Sheffield. Thus of London, George Haw, another man, almost obsessed it might be said with the problem of the working classes and their relationship to the churches, writes of the problem of Greater London:

> . . . all the strong and prosperous people are running away from the inner belt of London as fast as they can; forgetting it, owning no responsibility for it, leaving it to the weaker, poorer, more weary ones. The manufacturers, their managers, and all the staff who take salaries as distinct from wages, come in the mornings, and go away in the evenings, and admit no responsibility, social or religious, for the crowded districts where their workplaces lie, and their workpeople live. The chronic poor and the small wage earners are left stranded, a class by themselves. It is a terrible thing the way London is separating itself into harsh divisions of class, into cities of the poor and cities of the rich. . . .
>
> Of churchgoers in Greater London you might say they consist of two classes only—the upper middle class and the lower middle class. That is simply because suburban London in the main consists of these two classes. You get the same all the kingdom over. The residential suburbs of all cities fill the churches. It is in the nature of things therefore to find a higher proportion of churchgoers in Greater London than in London itself. The thing that calls for serious thought is that where the wage-earning class is pouring into Greater London, the church attendance declines. . .
>
> . . . Observe that where the working classes are crowding into Greater London, and the middle classes deserting them as they deserted them before, the church attendance is at the lowest. It stands at about the same proportion as in the working-class quarters of Inner London. If anything it shows a tendency to be lower. Willesden is now as poor in its church attendances as Stepney, Southwark or St. Pancras. . . . Willesden is becoming another St. Pancras; in its church life it has already become so.
>
> . . . It may seem fairly satisfactory that in a big industrial borough like West Ham 1 in 4.80 of the inhabitants goes to a place of worship. But how many of the worshippers are working people? West Ham has still a large number of middle-class residents—

that is, the class that makes up the majority of the churchgoers. . . .
Take a church census of West Ham ten years hence, when the
middle classes, who are now running away from it as fast as they
can, will have almost entirely disappeared, and you will find the
number of worshippers shrunken like a plant stricken with
blight. Far quicker than in London itself, this decay of church
life is spreading among the working-class districts of Greater
London.[1]

Mudie-Smith's composite volume is thus a treasury of information on the religious condition of London at the beginning
of the century, and in the largest urbanized area of the country
it enables us to date the slackening of the 'boom' and the
beginning of the 'deflation', though for reasons we have
considered it should be used with caution in judging the
situation elsewhere. It also supplies impressive evidence of the
estrangement of the working classes.

The statistical survey should be used as a companion volume
to Charles Booth's monumental social survey of *Life and Labour
of the People of London*, which was carried out between the
years 1890 and 1900, of which seven volumes are devoted to a
study of the religious life of the Capital. As so often with surveys
uncongenial in their disclosures, it was not received with
universal approbation, but beyond dispute he too showed the
remarkable influence of class on religious observance, and that
"wherever the regular working class is found, and in whatever
proportion to the rest of the inhabitants, it seems equally
impervious to the claims of religion . . . while those who do join
any church become almost indistinguishable from the class with
which they then mix, the change that has really come about is
not so much *of* as *out of* the class to which they have belonged".
With all the proper qualifications to be made for some denominations and within denominations, with due recognition of the
widespread attendance at Sunday schools, and of the multi-
farious agencies of mission and charity whereby tracts of London, he averred, were "sodden with religion and unsaved",
this estrangement of the adult working classes stands out from
Booth's survey. And he puts his finger on the intractable
sociological aspect of the mission problem. ['Elaborate doctrinal
teaching may be inculcated in childhood, but its influence is not
likely to last unless maintained by the atmosphere of the home

[1] *ibid*, ch. XVII.

or unless supported by social usage. It is to social usage that the upper classes trust, and it is in the union of home and church that we find the strength of the Nonconformists. . . . Thus with regard to the working classes (and the poor) we seem to arrive at a deadlock. There is no hope of social usage, and to create religious homes a new generation of religious-minded parents must arise; while until we have the social usage or the religious homes all advance is stopped." The acute implications for the Church's mission posed by this sociological statement of the dilemma still await discovery.

Two factors in the nation 'unchurched'

We have strayed somewhat from the matter under particular consideration—the decline of the churches in the late nineteenth and early twentieth century. From this point two factors stand out, and both must be borne in mind. The one is the continued estrangement of the working classes, still enlarging, more and more colouring the urban and industrial areas, flooding into suburban areas. We have traced it at length, generation by generation, in the City of Sheffield. Their history, in this respect, is one of general continuity of habit, but with the decline of the denominations that had been more effective in reaching the working classes, with the political re-orientation of their leadership, and the solidification of their own pattern of life, and with the general weakening of religious faith in the whole nation, they were even more wholly outside the religious institutions as the twentieth century advanced. The other factor is the erosion within the churches themselves—a weakening adherence and progressive loss from the churches of their traditional supporters, whether upper, middle, or lower middle class, or even of the working classes where in small proportion to their numbers they were held.

These are the two factors that have found the churches so denuded in the course of the twentieth century; they are the two factors that in conjunction have left England so widely 'unchurched'. The two distinct histories coalesce in the twentieth century to form the mission problem of the nation; but, without an understanding that both have operated, we easily fall into a false analysis that ignores the persistent alienation of the urban industrial masses from the time of their very emergence

in the new towns. That is to say, the losses in the twentieth
century and the passing of time have obscured the more
deepseated and historic problem of the alienation of the working
classes. And the two factors still need not only separate analysis
but separate treatment, since whatever changes may have taken
place in standards of life and in the structure and outlook of the
social classes—and great changes have taken place—the
inherited attitudes and patterns of life of the working class, and
those of the continuing very mixed middle classes, are very
different. If Disraeli's 'two nations' are now less sharply defined
in economic terms, they are hardly less divided in cultural
terms, with different attitudes towards religion and the churches
even where non-membership is common to both. On this rock
many well-intentioned evangelistic hopes have foundered.

The weakening religious habits of the middle classes

There is a mountain of material to be sifted for anything
like an exhaustive tracing of the decline of the churches in
general, and of the decay of the religious habits of the middling
classes in particular. For the distant past, the researcher builds
a picture from all the facts he can discover; but approaching
the present, he can only consider the over-all change of mood
and habit, and give illustrations. It would be brash indeed to
assume that the entirety of the middling classes were faithfully
religious throughout the period of the religious inflation, and
even more erroneous to suppose that all were lost in the years
of recession. Still to-day they provide the backbone of English
church life, even though they are markedly different from their
Victorian and Edwardian forebears. Nor should it be thought
that the middle-class attitude to religion and the churches was
monochrome. How could it be in so vast and variegated a social
group, including in itself a whole group of colours in the social
spectrum ranging from the philosophical sceptic to the newly-
rich tradesman, and in a group that held individualism and
freedom as cherished dogmas? But with these wide qualifications, to make room for, let us say . . . the rationalist, the
speculative agnostic of a higher class, the cynical, and of course
the worldling, the disillusioned, the shallow, and even the
crank, the generalization concerning the religiousness of the
Victorian middle classes holds good. And indeed because
'convention' seemingly could hold some of these types as well,

to the horror of our more antiseptic age, we have further evidence of the strong religious conformity of Victorian England. Such was the strength of what Charles Booth called 'social usage' in the middle-class culture pattern which substantially held the class to its religious habits even where fidelity was low —which was precisely what was lacking in the working classes, where social usage was at a minimum, and the culture pattern operated to keep the excluded workman outside.

Certainly the fidelity of the English middle classes was a *stupor mundi* to rationalist Continental observers. And yet the decline came, in a long drawn-out recession, in which faith weakened long before habits were broken. As late as 1891, Matthew Arnold, a keen if not impartial observer of the changing intellectual mood in the country, could note the "grave beliefs of the religious middle class, serious and steady, with its bounded horizons", compared with the scepticism of the more educated class above it, and the more free, raw and secular class below it.[1] Yet where faith was weakening, conformity could persist of which literature affords many examples; and again we note a difference to the working class. To the cultured man "doubt may come through a hundred channels, till the strenuous faith of the past seems only a series of childlike illusions; but he may so feel the inconvenience both for himself and others of disturbing the established order that he will prefer to act as if what he knew to be illusions he believed to be realities. The workman, on the other hand, lives in a world of well-marked lines and clear-cut realities; his thinking has always the merit of directness and simplicity . . . he simply cannot understand how it can be an honest thing to join in professions you have ceased to believe . . .".[2]

But by 1909, C. F. G. Masterman, whose comments on South London we have already examined, could write that "It is the middle class which is losing its religion; which is slowly or suddenly discovering that it no longer believes in the existence of the God of its fathers, or a life beyond the grave. . . . Among the Middle Classes—the centre and historical support of England's Protestant creed—the drift away is acknowledged by all to be conspicuous—by friend as well as by enemy . . . it continues without violence, continuously, steadily, as a kind

1 See Preface to *God and the Bible*, M. Arnold, 1891.
2 *The Church and the Working Classes*, A. M. Fairbairn, 1895.

of impersonal motion of secular change. It is the passing of a whole civilization away from the faith in which it was founded, and out of which it has been fashioned. . . . It is not becoming atheist. It is ceasing to believe, without being conscious of the process, until it suddenly wakes up to the fact that the process is complete."[1] And Masterman sees that, though the solid religious habits of the middle classes are particularly affected, it is expressive of a changed mood throughout the entire community. "The tide is ebbing within and without the churches. The drift is towards a non-dogmatic affirmation of general kindliness and good fellowship, with an emphasis rather on the service of men than on the fulfilment of the will of God. . . . The children are everywhere persuaded to attend the centres of religious teaching, everywhere, as they struggle to manhood and womanhood in a world of such doubtful certainties, they exhibit a large falling away. . . ."

What was the nature of the change of mood and consciousness that infected the entire society, both those within and those without the churches, and that wrought such havoc with the religious habits of so large a social group of the nation? From what regions blew the raw winds which not only carried away the perspective and habits of the Victorian and Edwardian era, but continue, in a very different age, to produce the modern secular climate of thought? This is to ask a more profound question than why people deserted the churches. Numbers no doubt did leave, and as many immediate causes would operate, but social habits change slowly, and the immediate causes rarely throw light on the deeper sociological causes and more rarefied but all-pervasive atmospheric pressures at work. And great numbers no doubt did not 'leave the churches'. No— more significant than 'leaving the churches', would be the neglect of those to adhere who would have done so a generation before, and the looser membership of many within, and who were accordingly more easily detachable by all the immediate causes, excuses and rationalizations that human beings can discover.

We may note in passing that few men, and those never typical, can analyse the air they breathe, and it is still true that the explicit reasons people give either for leaving or for failing to adhere to the churches are singularly naïve, and from the point of view of deep analysis often quite inaccurate. Even if the

1 *The Condition of England*, C. F. G. Masterman, 1909: pp. 14, 268, 269.

reasons given should be seriously heard and weighed, at best they are found to show an inherited group attitude which may or may not still be justified—and it is crucial for the Church's mission to know—but not infrequently they are sheer excuse or obtuse rationalization. On the other hand it is of interest and of much value to the Christian mission in Britain that in general people still feel obliged to justify their failure to participate in the worship of the churches. Historically too related to feel the churches completely foreign to themselves, and finding the churches at periodic times, and solemn ones, the appropriate agents of their needs, and yet disassociated for historical and sociological reasons unknown to them, they feel obliged to proffer their pathetic reasons, when the fact is—they do not really know.

It is tempting to seek a basic cause for this widespread retreat from Christian faith and religious practice, and the Marxist, the scientific humanist, and the Christian historian have adduced in each case their basic causes; but they appear grievously over-simplified. Perhaps it is that any deep analysis of the recession and the change of mood is not free from the same bewilderment that the man in the street has. Deep-rooted causes no doubt produce their effects, but these in turn become strong and more immediate causes which run concurrently and interact on one another, and in the course of time new social patterns are created, that become the actual causes for contemporary alienation. Certainly ultimate causes are peculiarly elusive, and in the last resort the analyst shows more of his own philosophy than the undisputed facts of the case! But with this caution, it is of use to separate out some of the different elements in the atmosphere men were breathing in the nineteenth century, and still to-day in greater intensity, even though we cannot know precisely how and whence the new winds arose, nor exactly what is current and what is eddy.

*   *   *

The scientific spirit

Without tracing the origin to a Francis Bacon, a Roger Bacon, or the primitive anthropoid using the hand as a tool, it is to the scientific tradition and its extravagant flowering from the late eighteenth century that we look for the birth of those ideas and material possibilities that made the modern world. The wealth of new invention applied to industrial processes lies behind the industrial society; and in the new way of life, based on new modes of production and association, new assumptions were deeply embedded and more and more assumed, albeit unconsciously by the typical members of society. The new axioms, the new assumptions are of decisive importance in understanding how modern men think, as well as a means of understanding the erosion of ideas and institutions foreign to those new assumptions. Inherent in them is the notion that by empirical knowledge men have power to do what they will, and that knowledge or science is available to men to the extent that they have explored the physical universe, learned its laws and harnessed them to their purposes. This has always been implicit in the genuine scientific tradition, but new in the nineteenth century was the widespread currency of such ideas and even their erection into philosophical theory; and, most important, new also was the practical possibility of their use as a basis of the material and social organization of society. They made possible a new form of society, whether paleotechnic, neotechnic, or in due course biotechnic, to use the terms of Geddes and Mumford to describe the successive phases of the industrial revolution. And no study of nineteenth century ideas, even where those ideas seem in conflict, can overlook the matrix of Science.

Numerically, scientists were few, and philosophers of science even fewer. For the many the simplest expression of the influence of Science is seen in that liberal cornucopia of invention and industry wholeheartedly grasped by the industrial and industrious middle classes in the towns. It provided the material for a transformation of life, and opened vistas of unending possibility that were filled by a justifiable faith in Progress. It is a familiar theme and its symbol, of course, is the Great Exhibition of 1851, for which a Sheffield poet sang that

> "The Spirit of the Age is ministrant
> In thrice ten thousand ways . . ."

and of

> "Knowledge and Industry—gigantic twins!
> Born of true Freedom, in a temperate clime,
> And nurs'd by Prudence and brave Enterprize . . ."[1]

[1] *The Great Exhibition*, John Holland, 1851.

Less well known than the lines of Tennyson who
  "Saw the heavens filled with commerce, argosies of magic
      sails,
  Pilots of the purple twilight, dropping down with costly
      bales

  . . . .

  Till the war drums throbbed no longer, and the battle
      flags were furled
  In the Parliament of man, the federation of the world",[1]

they epitomize a view of life made possible through scientific
Progress, that despite cynics and moralists is still with us, even
if much scarred, and though the handmaids of its chariot—
Reason, Freedom and Liberalism, not to speak of Commerce,
Empire and Peace—have hardly maintained the pace! And
this appropriation of the fruits of science and industry went
hand in hand, as we have seen, with a vigorous religious life,
in which if not Science at least its handmaids were in the
pantheon. Indeed, one of the marvels of the religious life of the
industrial middle classes is the way in which a narrow, ascetic
and pessimistic evangelicalism merged with an unbounded
optimism in man's sublunar possibilities. Perhaps the tensions
were too easily resolved, the 'trade spirit' inducing a shallow-
ness of spirit too easily eroded by the strong acids at the end of
the century. We remember Calvert Holland's devastating comment that "the love of the world grows with the contemplation
of things above".
  But the class that most benefited, and in many ways was most
conditioned, by the industrial possibilities of applied science
was the least influenced by other ideas that stemmed from the
same source. More subtle forces were also at work in the realm
of thought, even if the social pressures and limited intellectual
horizons of the middle classes gave protection from their
influence. The spirit of inquiry, the notion of reliable natural
laws of cause and effect, a closed if a vaster universe in which
Lelande's telescope could sweep the heavens and find no God—
these too stemmed from the scientific tradition of the eighteenth
century and were powerfully at work in the nineteenth and in
the thinking of intellectuals, and not solely intellectuals, but in

[1] *Locksley Hall.*

the minds of any who were free and willing to expose themselves. The pre-evangelical church of the eighteenth century had found at least some of these views not uncongenial, and capable of tenure with the inherited Biblical view of reality. Thus, to cite an eighteenth-century Sheffield illustration, the first Vicar of St. Paul's, the second church in the township, who was no evangelical enthusiast but a man of his century and a sober admirer of the laws of nature, could nonetheless accept the historicity of Jonah in the whale's belly as "extraordinary Providence" without which "we would unmiracle everything that is miraculous".[1] But by 1847, years before the *Origin of Species*, it was observed that "science has banished belief in the exercise by the Deity of special acts of supernatural power as a means of influencing human affairs, and has presented a systematic order of nature, which man may study, comprehend and obey, as a guide to his practical conduct . . . the old belief has died away and our churches scowl at the new belief, but it is no longer felt to be a reality by modern enlightened Christians".[2]

The number of "enlightened Christians" was probably small, and the enlightened Christians of to-day may be as disconcerted by the latter statement as the former. But the change of mood is significant as one gaining ground and repute. At first it was restricted to those seminal thinkers of the century, "the devout sceptic, the sage who rejects traditional religion, not because he is shallow or immoral, but because he is too earnest to accept it", as Basil Willey describes them in his fine study.[3] We might call it the intellectual impact of science on evangelical religion, leaving in the mind a strenuous moral sense and a religious devotion to truth and humanity, combined with a wistful nostalgia for the robust faith of the past, and a "faint trust in the larger hope". It was the reaction more typical of poets and philosophers. That of natural scientists was more precise; on one hand it could produce the extreme intellectual crisis and scientific retreat that Edmund Gosse describes so powerfully in the life of his father.[4] More commonly it led to the agnostic outlook of Huxley.

Certainly it was not atheistic in intent, but whatever the

---

1 *Sermons* by the Rev. John Downes, 1761.
2 *On the relation of Religion to Science*, Geo. Combe, 1847. (Sheffield City Library.)
3 *Nineteenth Century Studies*, Basil Willey, 1948.
4 *Father and Son*, Edmund Gosse, 1907.

reaction, there was an inability to reconcile the traditional Biblical view of Providence with scientific discovery and method; and, with the exception of a few courageous and enlightened individuals, the churches neither catholic nor evangelical would make any concession or attempt any theological re-interpretation. Indeed, the over-conversion of the churches to evangelicalism intensified the head-on collision. It left religion less seriously esteemed where it was respected, more conventional where it was practised, and more scorned where it was hated. But no part of society could remain permanently insulated from the new ideas at work, whether they came with refinement and scholarship, a blatant crudity, or as bowdlerized pseudo-science. In some way or other they became part of the *Zeit-Geist*, and before the end of the century even the stolid, uncritical middle classes, suburban and industrialized, the 'Philistines' as Matthew Arnold naughtily called them, were under its influence.

An associated factor, less profound though not less powerful, is seen in the intense pre-occupation with the material affairs of living, which has become such an accepted feature of modern society. Inevitably, to the extent that religious seriousness declined, and a simple faith in the personal Providence of God —always the keystone in genuine religion—receded, the material affairs of the here-and-now would loom larger, but the secular mood was positively and mightily enforced by the way of life exacted by industrialization. An invincible combination of factors was at work seemingly—the drive in work, industry and business, all becoming more and more complex, for the entrepreneur class the pressures of competition and technological advance, and for the masses, the sheer endeavour to survive in a world where the capacity to work meant salvation. And, at the same time, the gifts and spoils were ever increasing in range and allure, and the claimants on time ever more pressing. We have hardly as yet begun to count the cost of the technological society on the spirits of men. When we add to this the growing pre-occupation with the social problem, not as disorder to be endured, but to be changed by man's own efforts, the shallower religious faith of the *fin de siècle* as well as the mood of the twentieth century is not hard to understand. It is a mood shared by all classes, whatever their different inherited attitudes to religion.

Secularism

It is clear enough that the reactions to new ideas in a new form of society were very varied; different in different social groups and intellectual levels, and yet related in some way, directly or indirectly, to a common origin. In turn the reactions themselves became causes of new effects, and subtle changes were made in the composition and direction of the Spirit of the Age. And it was into a more 'secular' mood. Here we have the connexion between the agnostic thinking at the rarefied level of scientists, philosophers and poets, and the unconscious, implicit attitude of ordinary workmen. It is to be found in the concept of 'secularism'. It was a new word in 1850, and in 1856, at the consecration of Bishop Tait, the preacher apologized for using a word "just coming into use", but which he accepted as a definition of the major characteristic of the great towns and which dwarfed disputation on any lesser issue. It was selected and popularized by G. J. Holyoake, the free-thinker and co-operator, not to denote atheism or infidelity—a matter on which he continuously clashed with the famous Bradlaugh—but more devastatingly and literally to indicate a positive and exclusive concern with this life as the only possible province of human action and interest. From 1853 there were free-thinking societies and secular societies up and down the country, fore-runners of the National Secular Society. In themselves they were not important, any more than the intellectual Positivist churches of Frederick Harrison and the Comtians. The import-ance of the secularist movement is that it was indicative of a widespread attitude on the part of masses who had never heard the word, as Horace Mann shrewdly remarked comment-ing on the 1851 religious census:

> ... There is a sect, originated recently, adherents to a system called
> 'Secularism'; the principal tenet being that, as the fact of a future
> life (in their view) is at all events susceptible of *some* degree of doubt,
> while the fact and the necessities of a present life are matters of
> direct sensation, it is therefore prudent to attend exclusively to the
> concerns of that existence which is certain and immediate—not
> wasting energies required for present duties by a preparation for
> remote and merely possible contingencies. This is the creed which
> probably with most exactness indicates the faith which virtually,
> though not professedly, is entertained by the masses of our
> working population, by skilled and unskilled labourer alike ...

they are unconscious Secularists, engrossed by the demands, the
trials or the pleasures of the passing hour, ignorant or careless of a
future. . . .

It could not have been better expressed by Holyoake himself. Shocking though such views were to the religious-minded
in 1851, they are understandable enough to us surely, and how
natural to those outside the churches, immersed in the hard
job of keeping alive in the industrial town. How much more
congenial to those antipathetic to the churches, rebelling against
their social condition and demanding a changed world here and
now, as indeed Holyoake himself who laboured in the Radical
movement on behalf of Co-operatives, free education, trade
unions, cheap travel, Sunday facilities, the rights of women,
the abolition of public executions, and many other worthy
causes. Towards the end of the century Holyoake defined the
three broad principles of Secularism: the improvement of this
life is by material means; Science is the available Providence
for men, and, in answer to those who denied morality without
religion, "it is good to do good". In no fewer words could the
axioms of scientific agnosticism and secularism be stated—
man's hope is in the advance of science, an arbitrary Providence
is ruled out, and we have enough to do in this world to keep us
busy. Holyoake's tenets are indeed a mighty creed, reinforced
as they are by the material basis of modern life. At first sight
they rule out the Christian Credo, as Holyoake assumed they
would, and as vast numbers unconsciously subscribing to his
tenets have also assumed. And yet on further thought they
enshrine positive, if partial, human experience at a certain stage
of history, and to the extent that they are true, must reflect that
ultimate truth that is the proper concern of Christianity. Certainly their reconciliation and the interpretation of the one in
the light of the other is the major theological task of our time,
and without it the traditional religious understanding of reality
must grow dim, and decay through disuse, or become restricted
to a minority who can remain psychologically immune to the
dichotomy.

To counter an obvious criticism, it should be emphasized
that Secularism as a philosophy, allied to Rationalism and
falling easily into dogmatic Atheism, was never widespread, and
was on the decline before the end of the century. So far as a

philosophy survived, it was in the gentler Agnosticism of Huxley. There were of course influential voices, such as Winwood Reade, preaching the perfectibility of man through martyrdom and Science, and prophesying the day when nurses would recount the legends of Christian mythology to children, as fairy tales. And his influence must have been very great on an entire generation of reading and thinking people. There was the more popular and strident voice of Robert Blatchford, mightily influential on the reading working class, proclaiming the proven falsehood of the Christian religion; but even this robust and endearing infidel confessed to his loss of faith in materialism at the end of his useful life, and fell into an 'agnosticism-plus', while to the precepts of the Litany he had always claimed to be faithful. The fact is that England has been singularly unfavourable ground for dogmatic atheism, as also perhaps for dogmatic religion. But on the other hand, and this cannot be said too strongly, the secular mode of thought, that almost total preoccupation with immediate and temporal affairs—always a characteristic of the bulk of the working classes—became more and more widespread in the second half of the century, and deeply pervaded the traditionally religious middle classes, even where their religious practice was maintained. Sharp lines between fidelity and infidelity cannot be drawn in English society, and one way of stating this is to say that the secular-minded outside the churches have a Christian colouration, and that the practising Christians inside have marked secular characteristics. It still persists, a baffling feature of English life.

Scepticism

The secular mood was undoubtedly fed by the changing attitude to the Bible as an inerrant source of revelation, for however vigorously the churches defended literalism against the scientists and the higher critics, the scientific assumptions slowly and inexorably worked themselves into widespread acceptance. "Clergymen and ministers of religion are full of lamentation," said Matthew Arnold, "over what they call the spread of scepticism, and because of the little hold that religion has on the masses of the people—the lapsed masses as some call them. Practical hold on them it never perhaps had very much, but they did not question its truth, and they held it in considerable awe . . . now they seem to have hardly any awe of it

at all, and freely question its truth."[1] It showed an undoubted
change, and the churches were too occupied with their own
interests and prejudices to give much attention to the changing
mode of thinking in the nation. They fought a defensive rearguard action, when a complete change of strategy was required,
which required the entire Church to be more consciously
exposed to the external forces of the age.

The Church was neither able to equip men with a faith that
bore with the modern spirit, nor prevent the development of its
only alternatives, a conventional unreality or an irrelevant
pietism. There were some who could reconstruct a noble faith
of the remnants—a George Eliot, a Tennyson, a Matthew
Arnold, but it was not for ordinary mortals, and the precious
blooms of their solutions required an uncommon soil and hot-
house. When Seeley published his more matter-of-fact *Natural
Religion* in 1882, he showed how easy it was for undogmatic
liberal Christianity, reconciled to Science, to become sheer
naturalism, that rescued the unmiraculous values of the Bible
from the blaze of supernaturalism only by identifying God with
Nature and Christ with Humanity. The more common result
at the end of the century was the progressive loss of the 'Philistines' from the churches, and at a time when there was a
slackening spiritual energy in the middle classes and vastly
enhanced material amenities of life. All too often the consequence was seen in a pre-occupation with trivialities, amusements, pleasure and sensation, which have become so major a
feature of the twentieth century. The passage from stolid
Victorian religion to the agnostic, hedonist, suburban life of
the twentieth century is well epitomized in the astonishing
vogue of Omar Khayyam with its emphasis on the sentient,
the pleasurable, the meaninglessness of the perpetual flux and
the emptiness of "that inverted Bowl we call the sky":

". . . Unborn TOMORROW and dead YESTERDAY,
Why fret about them if TODAY be sweet!
. . . .

One thing is certain, and the Rest is lies;
The Flower that once has blown for ever dies.
. . . .

[1] *Literature and Dogma*, M. Arnold, 1873.

Ah, Make the most of what we yet may spend,
Before we too into the Dust descend;
Dust into Dust, and under Dust, to lie,
Sans Wine, sans Song, sans Singer, and—sans End!"

It is a small and odd pointer, but one taken by many incisive
critics right up to the First World War to illustrate a widespread
mood of the sophisticated if less intellectual and less heroic.
It showed the discredit of a cold rationalism, but it also
measured the departure from orthodoxy; and it pointed to that
exaltation of life and vitalism of the early years of the century,
which promised so much and produced so little.

The bankruptcy of prophecy in the Churches

Gathering up the several strands, we see a convergence of
outlook among the intellectuals, the middle classes and the
working classes, into a 'materialist' direction, a mental absorp-
tion with immediate practical affairs, even though the journeys
of the different social groups had taken such dissimilar routes.
Hitherto in considering the changing direction of thought we
have been concerned with the impact of ideas and of a changing
form of society upon the assumptions of society and upon the
institutions of the churches. Something should be said on the
character of the religious outlook itself, which was also making
its contribution and impact, directly on those in the churches,
and indirectly, very indirectly, on those outside, in all those
devious ways that religion in England has seeped out of the
churches into the mind of the public at large. A few sentences
cannot do justice to the variety of English religious life, with the
different churchmanship in the Church of England, and the
multiplicity of denominations, such as we have tried to portray
in detail in the City of Sheffield. The influence of the Christian
Churches on English life right up to the present cannot be
statistically assessed, of course; down the centuries, on generations of individuals, families, communities and the nation at
large, the Christian religion has left its mark, and that mark is
ultimately traceable to the Church in the land. In some ways
any criticism of an institution that has so moulded the nation is
indecent—as criticizing the mother that bare us. But it is just
because the role of the Church has been so significant in our
history, just because Protestantism has given such distinctive

features to the English people—not to speak of the Scots and the Welsh—that a critique and, more precisely, a criticism is required, where that influence has weakened. The failures of the Church in the nineteenth century cannot be ignored in any study of the decline of religion in the period, from any study of the estrangement of the people or from any consideration of the present mission task.

Just as a subtle complex of causes weakened the Church from without (though of course they were also at work within), so a complex of causes have debilitated English Christianity within the churches. Sin in the camp there always has been, from apostolic times; worldliness and pride, division and faithlessness—and how indeed could it be otherwise in the Church of God that is the Mother of us all? But these were not the major defects of the churches in the nineteenth century. Superstition and idolatry were at their lowest ebb, the grosser scandals of the Established Church were removed early in the century, and where political power was exercised it was done openly and within the constitutional framework of the country, while morality was never so firmly rooted in the churches at all levels. Evangelicalism had done a thorough job. No, the major defect of the nineteenth-century Church, as indeed the twentieth too, was a failure of prophecy, a failure to understand and interpret the phase of history into which the age had come. Not all ages demand of the Church the same degree of prophetic interpretation, but in an age of revolution it becomes the one thing needful. Prophecy means understanding the signs of the times. It can be clear to us looking at the contemporary world, and casting our eyes back, that the two basic factors, intimately related to one another and together making the explosive character of the modern world, were on the one hand the scientific revolution making possible the technological and secular-minded society of our day, and, on the other hand, the social revolution throwing up a massive working class determined to secure its own place in the sun, and destined to make its own preponderant culture. Lenin's dictum that Communism is the harnessing of electrification to the social revolution epitomizes the powerful significance of these two formative elements in conjunction with one another.

There were men who sensed the providential character of one or other of these factors; there were some who saw both, and that long thin line, whose greatest names are those of Kingsley, Maurice, Henry Drummond, Washington Gladden and Rauschenbusch, Hugh Price Hughes, Gore, Tawney, Temple . . . is evidence enough that prophecy was heard. But it is astonishing how little the general thinking and the official leadership within the churches was influenced by them. Partly they were tolerated as great but erratic men; partly the religious enterprise of their day was too massive and successful to be disturbed, and not least, the churches have always relished a limited degree of prophetic titillation, garnishing the tombs of dead prophets when their contributions were too 'dated' to be exactly relevant.

This is not to say that the profound changes in human thinking, social organization and world upheaval would have seen a different course had the Church's witness been other than it was. It ill befits humans to play the role of the Lord of History. But had Christian perception been greater it is fair to believe that there would have been less reason for the heathen to blaspheme—and perhaps even fewer heathen. The modern debate is not concluded on the extent that men make history or that history makes men, but the significance, for example, of Independency in the radical tradition, and the significance of that tradition in the evolution of our institutions of self-government, allows us to believe that perceptions and convictions on other subjects on the part of influential Christian men would not have been wholly without impact. The alternative is to believe that at any time this is the best possible of worlds, and that there is a ruthless dialectic working to some final synthesis on which the will of men has no bearing whatsoever. The 'givenness' of history is acceptable enough to Christians, but it does not absolve men from seeking to understand it and mould it. Not that the churches made no contribution of this kind. Indeed, a supreme illustration is seen in the alliance of liberal Nonconformity with Liberal politics—as we have seen, at first a strong liberal current, Nonconformity then rode the waves and indelibly marked the history of the country. But the example also serves to illustrate the point we are making; after riding the waves, she was driven by the waves, waves that were themselves receding, and in a turbulent sea whose deeper currents were not understood.

The supreme weakness then was a failure to understand the

signs of the times, a failure of vision and perception, stemming from theological error that narrowed the claims of God and the concern of the Church from the dimension of the Kingdom to the dimension of 'religion'. Inevitably it meant that the churches were pre-occupied with their own affairs rather than with the affairs of the world; witness the tumultuous clamour on establishment and disestablishment, ritualism and Romanism, the controversies on education, burial acts and deceased wife's sisters! A failure of prophecy always spells a failure of sensitivity. There was the lack of creative tension with contemporary thought, and the strong emphasis on personal morality that either ruled out the issues of social morality altogether or restricted that concern to such social evils as patently issued in the most glaring personal vice. Albeit unconsciously, it was all calculated to produce a spirituality within the churches that was pathologically religious or highly conventional, lacking in understanding, sympathy and sensitive encounter with the estranged world, within which the most unfortunate reactions were induced that obscured the very nature of the Christian faith.

Many illustrations could be given, small in themselves and even ludicrous, but explaining how an attitude to the churches was formed which has been passed down over the generations, persisting even when the causes of those reactions have disappeared. Still to-day they obscure the meaning of the Gospel in the eyes of the world. And how could it be otherwise? For the estranged world could only react to the impressions it received; it could not be expected to perceive theological error or a failure of prophecy. The churches were good but not good enough, penitent without understanding the complexity of sin, pious without a relevant spirituality, individualist without being fully personalist, and corporate-minded without being sufficiently community-minded. And by contrast, the prophets were precisely those who evinced what was generally lacking— a wide interest in social morality and an understanding of its conditioned character, a theological interest in new knowledge and its reconciliation with Christian truth, and the concern of Almighty God with His whole creation. The continuous clashes of F. D. Maurice with conservative elements in the Church afford superb example. All of them were intimately related to his theological understanding of the Kingdom of God, which made him at once sensitive to the world of men, and impatient of obtuseness within the Church. Both characteristics are present in every controversy in which he centred, whether on Biblical criticism, Revelation, Christian Socialism, the universality of Christ's Kingdom or the future state of sinners. On every point he touched, he 'earthed' the Gospel, and related it to the entirety of mankind and to the secular world in which men live—and met with opposition from all wings of the Church.

The moralism of the Churches

A serious aspect of the lack of sensitivity to the secular world, and ultimately traceable to theological narrowness, was the tendency of the churches to reduce complex social problems to a matter of personal morality. It still persists, a dangerous heresy amongst Christians. Inevitably the social habits of the working class, as the massive group outside all the churches in which the social problems were most glaring, were the easiest targets for the darts of evangelical moralism. There was of course a good side to this moralistic zeal that must never be overlooked. It produced organized opposition to vice, strengthened legislation making for virtue and produced a wide variety of social, temperance and educational agencies, deeply scarred though many were by denominational feud that obscured the meaning of Christian service. But on the other hand the moralistic context in which the social problem was invariably set obscured the very nature of the Gospel itself, inducing the wrong kind of reaction both inside and outside the churches, and giving men the opportunity of attacking Christianity for the wrong reasons. Take for example the noisy issues of Sunday Observance and the Drink Question. Admittedly, they were both legitimate interests of the churches, and yet the way in which the problems were approached and handled served to alienate even further the estranged population, and have left in their wake a legacy of misunderstanding that is still a great impediment to the Church's mission. In fact the churches had a better case than they generally presented, that could have embraced a profound analysis that went to the roots of the social problem. Instead, both issues became moral crusades in which the social aspect of the questions was lost in the passionate warfare with sin and with sinners, and Parliaments, even Liberal ones maintained by Nonconformist votes, had to defend the proper rights of citizens from the reforming excesses of Evangelicals and Nonconformists.

So we see the widespread opposition to any legislation making for freer Sundays, to any extension of social facilities or travel on Sundays, and the attempt to close the public-houses on that day. F. D. Maurice, who was no Latitudinarian, had a word for it when he expressed his distaste for the Lord's Day Society literature, in which "every quotation from Scripture which they contained . . . was used . . . with reckless and profane indifference to its original meaning and application, as if the divine oracles, instead of being authorities to which we must bow, were mere instruments which we may compel to secure any temporary purpose that we consider holy".[1] The Sheffield newspapers ring with the fury of the combat. One interesting example[2] is the memorial of the Sheffield Sunday League signed by 350 working men requesting the opening on Sunday of the Free Library, on the grounds that it was the only day the regular workman had for self-improvement, that he was exhausted after work on the other days, that important books of study like 'Loudon's *Gardening*' required hours of attention and could not be taken out of the library, and so on. The Rev. Brewin Grant replied with a lecture and a pamphlet, maintaining that to open the library would be "only the first act in opening the floodgates of dissipation, irreligion, and open profanity", and one by one he demolished every argument put forward by the petitioners, that "men who have no opportunity to read on other days, are not capable of gaining advantage from books of reference on Sunday . . . that men exhausted by six days' labour are incompetent to benefit by the general class of reference books . . . and that one would think these Sheffield memorialists were the competitors of Paxton and the Duke of Devonshire, and that instead of growing a few patches of cabbages and a few rows of celery, they were the owners of large conservatories and the most beautiful gardens in the world". The lecturer was sound enough in drawing the conclusion that a better solution was the reducing of working

---

1 *Life of F. D. Maurice*, vol. 2, p. 280.
2 *Shall we open the Free Library on Sundays? No!* A lecture by Rev. Brewin Grant, 1858. Sheffield Library Local Pamphlets.

hours, but this does not conceal his heavy sarcasm and want of sensitivity towards the workmen.

The second half of the century resounded with the Temperance Battlecry in increasing crescendo. Though confused with the political and denominational cross-currents, it was understandable enough, for although the eighteenth rather than the nineteenth was the century of debauchery and drunkenness, it would seem that in the eighteenth century men drank more in conviviality than in gloom; it was in the nineteenth century that "drink became the shortest way out of Manchester"! And not Manchester alone apparently! In 1853 the Town Council of Sheffield set up a committee to inquire into the drunkenness of the borough, apparently far in excess of most places. In that year one in a hundred of the Sheffield population was taken up and prosecuted, a far higher incidence than any town of the kingdom except Liverpool. Again we find reference to the greater freedom of the Sheffield workmen, "who for the most part are their own masters . . . much more than the labouring classes of other towns and are not compelled to attend large factories and mills and work for stated hours as in Manchester (one taken up in 432), Leeds (one in 440) and Bradford (one in 963), and therefore having more time on their hands. . . . Yet in Sheffield there is not a single moral or healthy amusement open to the working classes, who are driven to the public-house or beershop, to obtain that relaxation all men naturally seek, after great bodily fatigue."[1] The drinking habits could be set within a social context, stemming from the eighteenth-century habits of work where the cutler

"Like his anvil, he's steady, to labour he's ready,
He drinks, then he works, boys, again and again,"[2]

often with his ale pot on the idle anvil. There were all the occasions by custom to be 'wetted', foot-ales, loosing-ales, birthday ales, wedding ales, and payment of wages on Saturday nights in the beershops. Nor in the late eighteenth century had the customs been confined to workmen,

[1] Report of Committee appointed by the Town Council to inquire into the apparent excess of Drunkenness in the Borough of Sheffield, 1853. (Sheffield City Library.)
[2] *The Cutler's Song*, Sheffield Songs, 1862: p. 92.

"For all ranks and conditions,
Commence politicians
While sat at the alehouse on Saturday night."[1]

The churches flew in the face of this tradition, and at the same time were blind to the social and economic aspects of the problem. In fact the incidence of drunkenness in Sheffield fell from one in 100 in 1853 to one in 260 by 1867 due to legislation, better surveillance and education, and no doubt also to the churches' temperance campaigns. They made their steady contribution to the reduction of social evil, though the Temperance clamour seems to have mounted as the nation became more sober. But because the churches had reduced the social problem to one of personal morality, to be met by social restrictions, abstinence and pledge-signing, they had shown a lack of sensitivity to a population already estranged, and widened the gulf between them.

Nor is this conjecture, for within the churches there were men who proved by their exception the inadequacy of restriction and negative moralization. We have seen how Samuel Earnshaw of the Parish Church of Sheffield regarded the excessive religious and moral restraints of his time as one of the factors that put the outsiders even further beyond the pale. There stands the fine national example of Henry Solly, the Unitarian minister who became one of the founders of the Working Men's Club and Institute Movement, of which he became secretary precisely because he felt the mood of something more effectual for Temperance Reform than holding temperance meetings and administering the pledge—whatever its inadequacies, the Movement owes its origin to men who genuinely sought the means of good social intercourse for working men. Certainly too, one church in Sheffield made a positive contribution to the problem. In 1877, in St. Mary's parish, a workman's cocoa house was opened, and in seventeen months oceans of non-alcoholic drinks had been consumed, no less than 29,420 pints of cocoa and 175,720 halfpints, 25,116 pints of coffee and 96,024 halfpints, and 30,064 cups of tea, apart from ginger beer, lemonade, and milk![2] If these remedies were not based on profound social and economic analysis at

---

[1] *Saturday Night in Sheffield*, Sheffield Songs, 1862: p. 88.
[2] Report of the Church Congress, Sheffield, 1878: p. 181.

least they showed sensitivity and creativity, and the Church can rejoice that Christian initiative was shown. But the exceptions prove the rule. In general the Christian contribution was negative, moralistic and unsympathetic. The prevailing attitude is seen at the Church Congress held in Sheffield in 1878, at which a session was devoted to the problem of Intemperance. One member, Canon Harper, the Vicar of Selby, ventured the point that the Church had got the drink question out of focus, that for himself he found Bass's beer the most refreshing of beverages, and that he thought abstinence, as distinct from self-governing moderation, a form of slavery. There was unseemly interruption as no other subject, unless perhaps ritualism, could have evoked, and the Archbishop had to call for order.

But the simpler and sadder reaction of thousands of typical Sheffield workmen is well expressed in words put into their own dialect—"O don't believe t' Boible, becos it says we're to be sober, not to be drunken; an whooa can help it, when we get into some reit good jovial company?"[1]

Irrelevance of the Churches to the economic question

Important though these illustrations are in showing the moralistic mood widely prevalent in the churches, the deep division between that mood and the pattern of working-class life estranged from the churches, and that working-class culture as the obvious target of attack, they are but pinpricks compared with the insensitivity of the churches to the economic problem, the social problem par excellence. There were many reasons. The men of the churches had their own vested interests and they were not those of the working class. The political composition of the churches towards the end of the nineteenth century whether Tory or Liberal, whether they had been deeply implicated in politics or whether they had not, precluded any sympathy towards the new working-class political organizations that were being born. And there was that theological error, common in all the churches after Nonconformity had lost its zeal for Liberal politics, that reduced the social problem to issues of personal morality, and shunned technical and controversial issues as improper for open consideration within the churches. It is important that reliable contemporary evidence

---

[1] *Shevvild Chap's Annual*, 1852.

should be adduced to substantiate such a charge, from Christian men, exceptions and prophets even, who prove the point.

From Sheffield there is a word both critical and positive from Councillor Charles Hobson, J.P., President of the Federated Trades' Council:

> ... Modern religion is speculative, sensational, emotional, idealistic, and fails to satisfy the cravings of the human soul. Many of our religious teachers have missed their proper vocation. They should have been novelists, writers of fairy tales, as their main object seems to be to play upon the imagination of the people. They depict with exquisite imagery, heaven, rest, joy, peace and an eternal song, while they forget the humanity of man. Christianity is a great social system, designed to redress the wrongs of society, as well as to save men's souls. No system, social, political or religious will find favour with the masses which countenances the inequalities which exist among men. The Church of the future is that which identifies itself with the cause of the masses. . . .[1]

Elsewhere he maintains that Christianity is the dynamic of all true social reform, and lists some of the principles to be taken into account—

(a) That there is no difference between men (Acts 17:26).
(b) That life, with the means to support it, are the proper rights of all men.
(c) That the distinction between things secular and sacred is a confusion and not a contrast, and it is only because the secular, so-called, is so intensely sacred, that so many eyes are blind before it (1 Cor. 10:31).
(d) That the self-sacrificing care of Christ for the weak is to characterize His followers.
(e) That the wide social differences between men shall cease.[2]

Massive evidence is provided by George Haw, whose comments on the religious life of London we have already examined. In 1906 he edited a symposium entitled *Christianity and the Working Classes*, in which leaders of Labour and of the Churches gave their views. A typical Labour view is that of Mr. Arthur Henderson, M.P.:

> ... There are those that deny the estrangement of work-people from organized Christianity, but the more thoughtful members of the churches are realising that not only does this alienation exist, but that it is growing. I have had favourable opportunities owing to

[1] *The Hammer*, Dec. 9, 1893: "How to reach the masses".
[2] *ibid.*, Jan. 6, 1894: "The Duty of the Church in relation to Labour".

my close association with the workers in different parts of the
country to learn the true position, and I am forced to the conclusion that the vast majority of our wage-earners are at present
outside the various branches of the Christian Church . . . they
feel there is so much associated with the churches that acts as a
constant reminder of the social distinctions between them and the
ordinary church-goer. Some of our churches are little better than
religious hot-houses for the preservation of the interests of middle-
class society. . . . And the want of sympathy on the part of the
churches with the new aspirations and ideals dominating the
workers has been one of the leading causes of the alienation . . .
the churches have not appreciated the real meaning and true
inwardness of many of the movements which the workers have
themselves initiated and developed for their social and industrial
amelioration. Hence these movements have been treated with
critical aloofness or active opposition. . . . The attitude of the
churches towards social questions has been a powerful element in
creating the present situation. We know of nothing in the
Churches' history which is so difficult to comprehend as its unwillingness to take its rightful position, and accept full responsibility for dealing with the deep social wounds from which the
masses of the people suffer. That they possess knowledge of the
existence of these social sores is evident from the efforts, more or
less spasmodic, that they have made to give relief by way of
opening soup-kitchens, or doling out coal or blankets, instead of
using their vast resources and magnificent opportunities, and
going to the root of the evil by attacking the system which makes
misery and wretchedness possible in the richest country of the
world. It appears to me a strange conception of the purpose of
Christianity which moves the churches to become concerned with
saving the people from future hell of their wrong-doing, but allows
them to remain unconcerned regarding those social anomalies
which largely contribute to the making of the present hell of the
people's environment.

As powerful a theological exposition of the proper social
concern of the Gospel as exists is that of Dr. P. T. Forsyth,
delivered as chairman of the Congregational Union in 1905
under the title *A Holy Church the Moral Guide of Society*. It was
published in a denominational journal, and deserves to be
quoted at some length for its intrinsic value, and as evidence of
blind-spots in the vision of the churches.

. . . How are we to think of Christian Love? It is a real social and
political principle . . . it moves us both to private concern for

souls, and to a general concern for the state of the race . . . en-
larges charity to the dimensions of justice, and confirms mercy
with the assurance of righteousness and peace. . . . God's love
has given us a settled and political society. Then surely both
the care and conversion of that social order is a true service to
God, and a true work of love that is not merely kind. . . .

Our Lord did not come to save souls, or to gather devout
groups, or even to found churches, but so to save souls and found
churches as to make Christian nations and thus change society
to the Kingdom of God. . . .

There is a new interest in the largest social questions. There is a
desire to re-examine our social and industrial conditions in the
light of the Christian ethics. The result is disquieting. The Church
has been widely moved by Christian compassion, but it begins to
be moved by Christian compunction. . . .

. . . We have the ethical *note*—that is well. It is fashionable.
But have we the moral *word*, the sound and relevant moral word
for the age? . . . The Cross is the foundation of the Kingdom. . . .

It was captured first by the jurists of old, and now by the
sentimentalists and mere moralists of today. It has been either
neglected or individualized out of all public ethical authority. . . .

. . . Either salvage has ousted salvation and the cross has been
treated as a mere life-saving apparatus for personal escape, or it
has been made the servant of human needs instead of the agent
of God's glory. . . .

There are many that cannot believe that a moral society could
be a mere mosaic of free egoisms tempered by charity or patriot-
ism. They say, with Christianity, that society then becomes a
field of hostilities, desolated by a war of classes and even nations.
The sight of huge capital alongside huge misery, of over-produc-
tion on the one side and starvation on the other has its slow moral
effect on the public, and many, like Bishop Gore, are driven into
sympathy with Labour, not so much perhaps from faith in the
labourers, as from a desire to protest and balance the social perils
of immense private wealth in non-moral hands . . . old Liberalism
and even old Radicalism, which was based on individual rights,
issued in unqualified competition. . . .

Let us be clear what the question is. It is not one of individual
ethics—not Can a Christian be a capitalist? Of course he can. . . .
The question is about a certain economical stage or institution in
the light of a final moral power . . . it is not a question as to the
abolition of Capitalism, but its disestablishment. . . .

We need guiding principles for the larger scale of business and for
high finance. And we need a skilled and duly informed application

of them . . . it is not enough to say that the love and faith of Christ will keep a man right. They will not give individual men moral insight on the scale of a whole civilization. They will enable a man to make the Christian best of the current system individually, but . . . simple personal faith will not of itself give the power and the insight to apply the Christian moral principle to the accepted standards of the age. As a matter of fact such faith has had more effect on the disposal of wealth than on the moral making of it. Some of the truest believers are harassed by the way they are involved in an egoist system of accumulation. And how many more are mammonised by it! . . . Christian love must give up some cooing and go to business. . . .

We must move by economic methods and on constitutional lines, and with a moral basis, and the Church must do more to guide and inspire that movement than she has done. . . . It is easy to secure public interest in religion and public help for charity, but it is not easy to get the religious world to educate its agents, to fit them to face the moral issues of our time, or to elicit the ulterior moral resources of its own creed. No grace of piety will save a Church without the grace of moral judgment and public sagacity. But the pious function of the Church is very apt to impede the righteous. . . . It seems that we are near the end of what is morally possible for our magnificent philanthropy to do, and that the situation demands a more searching enquiry as to Christian justice. Philanthropy can deal with symptoms and effects, and we ought to get at causes. . . .

The Church's numbers can only be increased by thinking little about numbers, and more than we do about the Gospel. We need a better Gospel more than we need more gospelling.[1]

No one more clearly than Forsyth saw the social and theological error of reducing the social problem to one of individual moral and spiritual regeneration. Elsewhere he writes trenchantly that "It is not enough to say, Make every man a true Christian and the social question will be solved; therefore let us be satisfied to preach conversion and promote missions and philanthropies, and institutional churches. No. We cannot do without these, but to stop there shows some lack of insight into the complex nature of a great public problem. It would show that the speaker has not realized how dependent the individual soul is on the moral state of the public mind, how impossible it is for any man to be at his best except in a society looking toward its best. Let nobody say, To depend on new legislation is to fall

[1] *The Examiner*, May 11, 1905.

back from trust in grace to trust in the law. Laws have a moral and educative effect. They can be agents of grace as they may flow from the action of grace."[1]

Forsyth was a great rock in which a prophetic school could have quarried, bringing them into sensitive relation with the working-class movement, whose leaders had also discovered the hard truth that men are powerfully and subtly conditioned in body, mind and spirit by their material environment. But it was not a shaft that could penetrate the churches, pre-occupied as they were with religion, with an individualist morality, and a sentimental gospel that knew nothing of the 'law' and therefore could not go the mile beyond it. Not that the working masses were able to perceive this grave defect; they were more likely to resent the comparative trivialities—class consciousness in the churches, the stipends of bishops or the opposition to their tastes for beer and betting. But there were leaders of the Labour Movement who saw it, and expressed it clearly, as there were men within the churches to whom it was crystal clear. But in neither case were their views able to inform the inert masses within which and out of which they spoke. A great number come to mind—Stewart Headlam who formed the Guild of St. Matthew in 1877, "the first Socialist Society in England" and preaching a positive "Christian Secularism"; there were the pillars of the less radical Christian Social Union, Bishop Westcott, Gore, Scott Holland, and E. S. Talbot; there were Free Churchmen like the Rev. Hugh Price Hughes, the Rev. R. J. Campbell, and Christian laymen in the van of the Labour Movement, like Will Crooks, Arthur Henderson, George Lansbury. There were parish priests from slum areas, men like F. L. Donaldson of St. Mark's, Leicester, who led unemployment marches to London, Canon Barnett of Toynbee Hall, writers like James Adderley and Reginald Bray insisting that the churches and the Labour Movement were in desperate need of one another. And every industrial town had its Methodist laymen who had rolled up their sleeves and jumped into the fray of the Labour Movement, sometimes holding the tension and staying in the churches, sometimes ostracized and moving out of the churches, to reinforce that strong English sense that "you can be a Christian without going to Church".

[1] *Socialism, the Church and the Poor*, P. T. Forsyth, 1908.

The crises of the twentieth century

If, among other factors, theological imperceptibility rendered the churches insensitive to the nature of the secular problems, it is hardly surprising that they were impotent to withstand the shocks of the twentieth century. War and economic depressions were not new, but the scale of both in the present century, and the social mood in which they occurred and which they fostered, made them qualitatively different from any previous crises of their kind. Both the First World War and the Great Depression of the inter-war years further eroded the churches, and as we have seen, from a date as recent as the 'thirties, the collapse has been nothing less than catastrophic. Again the causes are complex, inter-related—a continuation of processes and trends already at work, fortified by new factors, all of them contributing to the solidification of a culture pattern excluding the practice of worship, that in turn becomes the dominant factor further militating against the habit. And within this complex of causes are the theological defects we have already traced in the pre-war years, ruling out the possibility of prophetic leadership by the churches, leaving the world unimpressed and indifferent, and a Christian laity unsustained morally and intellectually in the face of the crises, turmoil and seductions of the age.

We must not underestimate the importance of adequate theological perception in the face of those crises. The First World War raised the question of Providence, of the relation of God to History and of His character and very existence, in perhaps the most acute way that has ever happened, and certainly in the most public way. Not merely with religious men and serious thinkers, but quite literally with every Tom, Dick and Harry. Questions were wrung out of people that only a prophetic Christianity at close grips with the secular problems of the age had the slightest chance of meeting. And the word was not forthcoming. And the same events and crises emphasized with their brute material force the hard, material needs of men. The aftermath of war, social revolution, and the Great Depression brought the whole of Europe, and in due course the world beyond, into the age of politics with a vengeance. Men and nations were by no means agreed on the political remedies, as the Second World War and subsequent events were to demonstrate so tragically, but one thing was assumed from Soviet Russia to the United States, as later from Peking round the world to Indonesia, namely, that men's hopes were reposed in social engineering of some kind, and—to use Holyoake's words of a century before—the improvement of this life is by material means and Science is the available Providence for men. It was as implicit in the thinking of Keynes as of Lenin, in the British Welfare State as in New China. However differently men construed the means to be employed, the ends to be realized, or the dangers to be avoided, these assumptions are axiomatic to modern men throughout the world, and as we have seen they have a long history woven of the scientific and technological advance of the nineteenth century, and the growing self-consciousness of the common peoples. The change that had come about in men's assumptions was so great that it is valid to speak of the emergence of a new type of man, with a new structure of thought and a new mode of apprehending reality.

The First World War

The First World War put religion, as much else, into the crucible; it terminated one era and introduced another, and mightily consolidated forces and trends already at work. It is hard to get an objective view of the effect of the war on the religious life of the nation, as indeed on the thinking of the nation in general; little has been recorded on the subject that is not itself the expression of intellectual and spiritual upheaval, much understandably is bathed in sentiment, and the evidence is often contradictory. But some things stand out. Certainly a confident rationalism was at its lowest ebb—as out of touch, says an acute observer, "as the Gladstonian Liberal is in the political field". Indeed, the same writer[1] analysing the effects of the war on men's thinking makes the point that Reason itself was further discredited, having belied the hopes of a century of Progress, while the new authoritative criterion was that of Life, the truth of which was to be discovered by intuition, instinct and experience. And if a robust rationalism was out of favour on the one hand, so on the other was strict orthodoxy, whether in politics, science or religion. Such a mood, associated with a material upheaval without precedent, led the nation to a break

[1] *The War and Men's Minds*, Victoria de Bunsen, 1919.

with formality, with convention and with much deference to
traditionalism whether in social habit, morality or religion, and
social customs and stereotyped attitudes that had long ceased to
reflect conviction simply disintegrated. Inevitably the effect on
the churches was catastrophic and even more so in the years
following the war, when attitudes and habits fostered by the
accident of war became permanent norms.

The war had its own devastating effects on the religious life
of the nation. For the few, the more serious-minded, it increased
scepticism at the same time that it fostered more serious occupation with the foundations of faith. And for these, as for the
many, a reaction set in against 'organized religion'. A new set
of questions emerged—not concerned with Science and Religion,
Miracles and the Truth of the Bible, but asking Why God allows
War? Why do the innocent suffer? and What does religion say
about Political Questions? Clearly such questions had their
nineteenth-century ancestry, but they were posed in a new
and dreadful urgency within the context of a nation sobered by
a wholly new and tragic experience, and, as we have seen, the
churches were not enmeshed in secular life and sensitive to the
secular mind as was undoubtedly required if such questions
were to be answered either intellectually or existentially. There
is much evidence that the easy degeneration of the Almighty
into the God of Battles and the British cause, though a reflection
of the national struggle and in keeping with the national mood
during the war, proved a further stone of stumbling and a
further occasion for contempt, once the passions of war had
cooled. But the lack of a clear and relevant word from the
churches, even assuming that any word would have been
received with appreciation or assent, undoubtedly weakened
the status of the religious bodies in the eyes of the nation, and
men and women who were bound to the churches were
tempted to say, "It doesn't make any difference". Only a
faith for crisis could have met the crisis of faith that the war
precipitated, only a religion steeped in the tragedy of the world
could make sense of the human extremity of 1914 to 1918, and
only a theology that understood the judgments of God in history
could have interpreted the significance of the upheavals of
Europe. Again, the profoundest theological insights of the
time were those of P. T. Forsyth, who recognized the falsity of
an easy, complacent, confident faith.

... Very much faith is only possible through ignorance of one's self,
banality of standard, or lack of experience of the world. It is the
confidence of those who have never had their self-confidence
severely shaken. It is a faith which plain souls immune from wrong
or innocent of guilt take for a hermitage. It was acquired by no
taste of life's last tragedy, no real experience that challenged the
judgment of God. It may be the faith of people who take much
culture, but never grow up, never pass beyond a pietist or an
aesthetic religion. It is due to a sheltered existence, a happy
temperament, a limited knowledge of life's bitterness and
wickedness, and no knowledge at all of our own damnability. . . .
The weakness of the more idyllic type comes to light in the great
crisis. When a sudden crash brings such people face to face with
tragedy in its ghastliest and most inhuman forms, a faith that was
only humane or serene in its note is apt to give way. . . . The war
is a staggering blow to a faith that grew up in a long peace, a high
culture, a shallow notion of history, society or morality, and a
view of religion as but a divine blessing upon life instead of a
fundamental judgment and regeneration of it. It is fatal to the
piety of pony carriage, shaven lawn or aesthetic tea.[1]

And again he ascribes the inadequacy of faith to theological
error that narrows the concern of the Kingdom of God to
personal religion and morality:

... The Kingdom of God is treated as an interest which does not
concern nations, but only missions and philanthropies. Policy
may remain pagan if religion stands by with ambulance, lenitives,
opiates. The Cross has for the heart a securing and consoling
power, but it is not in the same position for active life. It belongs
to personal religion only, and chiefly to what might be called the
night side of that. It has the vespertinal note. It is not for political
or business affairs. It has not the dimensions of history. . . .[2]

It is clear enough, reading Forsyth's words written in 1916,
that the war would make havoc of the religious conventions of
the age, and that the post-war collapse of the churches, as the
brave optimistic hopes engendered in war gave way to dis-
illusion, should have taken place. The kind of religion purveyed
was responsible for the ignoring of religion—it could not
establish itself in command of the minds of men coloured by the
world since 1914.

Nonetheless the war was the occasion of much heart-
searching in the churches, and clergy and ministers, certainly

[1] *The Justification of God*, P. T. Forsyth, 1916: pp. 98–9.   [2] *ibid.*, p. 106.

those in the Forces, had opportunity to gauge the religious sensibilities of the nation under arms. A survey[1] was conducted on the matter towards the end of the war, through an inter-denominational committee, among them some of the ablest churchmen of their day and in the inter-war years. A mass of heterogeneous opinion was collected from the army, much of it contradictory and confused, but its general sense is clear, and it provides the reverse side of the coin to that of Forsyth.

From a volume of human documents there stand out the facts of the appalling religious ignorance and confusion of the nation, the estrangement of the bulk of the male population, and widespread criticisms of the churches. It would appear that the first impact of the war awakened the religious consciousness of great numbers of men, but only to be dulled by the impossibility of the questions that came to the mind, basic to which was the contradiction between the fact of the war itself and the being of a Living God, who had either never been real, or the object of the kind of faith that Forsyth exposes. And continuous mental wrestling was hardly conducive to survival. Men adapted themselves to the situation with the same kind of resilience that had been so long customary in adverse social conditions at home. There came resignation, cynicism, the condition of 'happy-go-lucky', 'carrying-on', and 'trench fatalism', all mightily enforced by the hardening material strain, and a compensatory mechanism that "lowered consciousness on all planes", as the report has it. And men discovered values which they never associated with religion or morality—again a characteristic evidenced in a thousand ways in working-class life back home, and throughout the years before—that comradeship and solidarity were the essence of life, that the damning sins were not 'wangling', drunkenness, impurity or profanity, but cowardice, selfishness, snobbishness and tyranny. As one typical comment from a Major of Artillery goes:

> ... I saw half a dozen of my boys, about 6 a.m. in winter, taking charge of two infantrymen at their last gasp from wet, mud, fatigue and exposure. The poor fellows had actually lain down to die on the roadside by our battery. My men gave them breakfast (we were short of rations in those days), their socks (we were

[1] *The Army and Religion. An Enquiry and its bearing upon the Religious Life of the Nation,* 1919.

short of these), shirts and everything; and rubbed them and lit
fires and sweated over them and got them to hospital. They would
be utterly surprised to hear that any of this had got to do with
morality or religion. Morality has to do with not breaking laws.[1]

The report showed the public mind to be in a state of utter
chaos on the matter of religion, and any attempt to define it
must be quite defective. There is the vague subscription, when
pressed, to belief in a distant Supreme Power which manifestly
does not act, the ethical Christ of nineteen centuries before,
good, respected, anaemic and impractical, and the Church, an
institution identified with clergymen, the object of every
criticism under the sun, and yet paradoxically expected to be
'there' and to give leadership. But the whole subject was one
that any man could judge and every man claimed his right to
do so; there was no sense that men themselves might be under
judgment by elements within it. None of it should be allowed to
make one serious or morbid, or to interfere with one's chosen
habits and the free play of humour and chaff—which is yet
another characteristic of long-developed resilience that finds
good expression in the comment of a steelworker—"You come
into this world crying, you go out crying, don't cry in between!"
The confusion is understandable enough, but was worse con-
founded when the image of the Church, itself distorted from
within, was subject to the free range of criticism by minds that
were the repository of Scriptural oddities, religious jumble,
childhood memories and inherited antipathies. The conclusions
could hardly be those of a Forsyth! In passing we may recognize
that this religious confusion still reigns, understandably, even in
part justifiably, a most grievous obstacle to any true understanding of the Christian faith. Only the most radical simpli-
fication of Christianity could begin to dispel the confusion; it
would be a primary task in a thorough-going reformation to
provide a simpler and profounder statement of the meaning of
Christianity that could shear through the chaos like a knife.

The collapse of the Churches in the inter-war years

If the shock of war raised the questions of Providence and
theodicy in the sharpest and widest way—though the words

[1] *The Army and Religion. An Enquiry and its bearing upon the Religious Life of the
Nation*, 1919, p. 68.

were not used—the long grey inter-war years relegated them to the interest of theologians, or restricted them to the perennial realm of personal grief. Compared with the pre-war days, religion and the churches simply dropped out of the public interest. Men came back from the war with high expectations, and the Church on her side expected religious revival and had fondly imagined its beginnings in the army. In neither case were the hopes realized, and after a few years of dislocation and uncertainty the nation settled down to the dull years between the wars. History already sees those inter-war years, above all others, as the unnecessary and the wasted years, the years without excuse throughout all of which the open cracks in society and the writing on the wall were visible. They were the years of drift and timidity, of vanity and wishful thinking in which cold reason, clear thinking and courage were at their lowest ebb. The pre-war social trends continued unabated, and after a few years of unsettled industrial activity the deterioration, leading to the Great Depression, set in. Sheffield, so largely dependent on a basic industry that was itself dependent upon the prosperity of British industry as a whole, was severely hit. Throughout the years of depression the unemployment incidence was among the four highest towns in the country, and after 1931 was the highest by a considerable margin, with 34 per cent of the insured population out of work representing a figure of over 60,000, of whom 50,000 were men. At no time between 1920 and 1937 was the unemployed total less than 20,000, an "apparently irreducible post-war minimum",[1] and only in a few 'bright' years did it approach this figure. Little imagination is required to see that, with so large an unemployment figure, poverty and insecurity were widespread, reaching far beyond those actually without work.

It was in these inter-war years that the decay of the churches was most rapidly advanced, and the curve of recession drops so steeply in the 'thirties that it is tempting to look for unique factors accounting for it, either in the war itself, or in the depression, or in the rapid growth of 'attractions' in those years. But there is no evidence that any of these factors were peculiarly decisive, apart from the obvious temporary losses during the fighting years, though many indeed of the losses in those years were not temporary. And although there is evidence

[1] *A Report of Unemployment in Sheffield*, A. D. K. Owen, 1932.

in the later years of the nineteenth century that denominations more largely supported by working-class people lost membership in years of sharp depression, the collapse of the churches in the inter-war years is too general and widespread to be attributed to this cause. Rather should we say that those eroding forces at work in human thinking and social habit that we have seen at work years before the war continued their inexorable influence, only consolidated by the great catastrophes after 1914. Religion as a public influence was continuously weakening, the secular culture pattern was continuously crystallizing harder, and to any who gave the matter thought it was clear that religion as generally understood had no bearing on the hard realities of the period. But within this continuing, unbroken process, successive steps and subsidiary causes can undoubtedly be traced in the passage of decline.

Many of the social habits whose continuance was calculated to sustain religious conventions, even where personal fidelity was weak, were quite suddenly destroyed by the war. There was the sudden fluidity of the nation, invading every home, as men left home for army life and the Front. Great numbers of women entered industry on a scale without precedent. The habitual became humdrum, and there were all the new pressures on leisure time and the traditionally quiet Sunday— the patriotic duty of digging on Sundays, the extension of shift work and Sunday work, the necessary increase in Sunday travel and so on. The Second World War of course made similar and even greater demands on the entire population—but there was one difference in the total effect; whereas in 1939 there was little of the English Sunday convention to erode, in 1914 there was a very great deal to erode, and with its erosion went family customs and social decorum that held many in the churches who would not otherwise have been there. Certainly the change of social pattern that bewildered the middle-aged and shocked the aged of that period became an accepted commonplace and a welcome liberation to the younger generation that fought the war—the generation, where it survived, that was lost to the churches in such vast numbers, and which grew up to say: "We were forced to go to church three times on a Sunday; we shan't force our children." It was the middle-aged generation at the time of the First World War, retaining its membership of the churches, whose inevitable passing around the 'thirties accounts for the steep fall in membership in that decade. *Their* sons and daughters, in general, deserted the churches; the churches lost the bulk of that generation that fought the war, even in social groups that had been traditionally conformist. And *their* children have certainly not reacted against their parents ! These are generalizations necessarily, but they explain the downward trend and the steepening fall towards the more recent period.

There was no return to the pre-war years; the social conventions and disciplines of those days were openly accounted 'old-fashioned' after the war even where they persisted, and the new freedoms were fed by popular social amenities on a scale without precedent—in the new vogue of the dance-halls, the cinemas, motor-cars, organized sport, transport facilities, the wireless and so on—all those material things to which facile analysis ascribes the emptying of the churches in the past generation. The weakening hold of religion is much earlier, for the deep reasons we have sought to trace; the war demolished social habits that were already dissolving; the post-war generation found the natural thing *not* to worship, and nature, abhorring a vacuum, was amply served by the fascinating distractions that a great amusement industry has given to the modern world. There were subsidiary factors, and of course the 'attractions' should be taken into account, not so much as rival claimants for the use of time, but as distractions precluding serious considerations of any issues but the most immediate and personal, and producing what Albert Schweitzer called "a mentality spiritually relaxed and incapable of self-collectedness". It was undoubtedly fostered in the present century by the triviality of the popular press. The distractions were conducive to 'apathy', a condition by no means restricted to the post-second-war era; apathy has a long history, compounded of many ingredients and conditioned by many factors, of which the inter-war thirst for distraction is both one cause and effect. And there were other important factors in the 'physical mobility' of the population from the 'thirties, through new housing schemes also on an unprecedented scale, through 'occupational mobility' in the late inter-war years, and even more so during and since the last war, all of which in association have produced a fluidity of population such as the country has never before experienced. The numbers of people of all ages whose break with a church followed a move of house, a move from district or town, must have been immense. It would follow logically that those denominations that traditionally held their members through local attachment, and local community pull, would suffer the greatest ravages—a fact that the non-Roman churches, and particularly the Church of England, have yet to appraise.

So a culture pattern emerged in the inter-war years that progressively excluded the habit of worship, even in social groups to whom the custom had been traditional. At the same time the long hard depression further defined and solidified the working class, with its traditional lack of adult participation in the churches. The passing of the aged explains the steep fall to a new low level before the last war. It may continue at that level for a long period—without an analysis of the numbers in the churches within different age groups, statistical forecast is not possible. But quite apart from the likely shape of the curve in the years ahead, any assessment dare not forget the social groups outside the churches, with their own long tradition of non-participation. What is not a matter of conjecture is that the church faces a missionary problem in the country as acute as anywhere in the world.

Chapter 6

THE MISSION OF THE CHURCH IN AN INDUSTRIAL SOCIETY

CONCLUSIONS

THE HISTORICAL SURVEY we have made of the relation of the Church at large to the industrial community of Sheffield, and the reactions and accommodations of each to the successive phases of the other, may make us question the dictum that history is a cordial for drooping spirits. Be that as it may, formidable facts are disclosed, standing proud and needing no highly selected array of evidence to substantiate them. They are the intractable facts of the modern missionary situation—rocks, obtruding from the past, upon which many mission ventures are wrecked, as surely as others look successful only by evading them.

It is important to stress this, since the mission initiatives of the Church at home are rarely based upon ascertainable historical and sociological data. The Church thinks and plans within the context of the Church instead of setting her mission and her obedience within the given context of society and the world at large. And her "zeal without knowledge" is responsible for grossly inadequate expressions of mission. It is important to face the inescapable facts, to understand the process of history that has brought us to the present situation, that we may be delivered from superficial analysis and equipped for more soundly based missionary advance. Dr. George Macleod tells a good story illustrating the point—of the attorney of Falkirk whose doorsteps were so worn that he feared accident to his clients and even litigation from them. Shrinking from the high cost of a new flight of steps, he hit upon the brilliant alternative of turning the old ones over—only to discover that his grandfather had the same idea! So often in our zeal we pursue as novelties and panaceas the ideas of our grandfathers, even if we adorn them with the paraphernalia of modern techniques, only to be less successful and without their justification and excuse. Missionary planning in the Church must measure up to the realities of the situation.

We select five main facts that emerge, which are summarized as follows, though it should be remembered that there are proper qualifications to be made from the detailed study:

1. *The historic estrangement of the working class*

From the eighteenth century, and progressively through the nineteenth, since emergence of the industrial towns, the working classes, the labouring poor, the artisan class, as a class and as adults, have been outside the churches. Everything had combined to keep them outside. From the earliest times that an industrialized proletariat came into being, there was inadequate space for them in the buildings from which they were also excluded. Poverty and wretchedness of material conditions as well as their own positive way of life bound them into a pattern of life that made them as foreigners in the midst of more stable townsmen, and rendered them content with their virtual exclusion, and apparently disinclined that it should be otherwise. There had always been the poor, but until the early part of the eighteenth century they were recognizably within and part of the community of township and hamlet, but with the rapid growth of population they became an undifferentiated group, lost to view except as a mass. This, coupled with the economic rise of a middle class that was increasingly religious in its habit, led to a social stratification in which religious and denominational lines ran parallel to the economic ones, so that the poor were excluded both socially and religiously; a fact that both hardened the separation of classes (even where the edges were blurred) and widened the gulf between the churches and the working classes.

In due course there came a positive social and political reorientation of the working class into a direction of its own, and in the twentieth century the crystallization of a strongly positive and solid working-class pattern of life without the practice of religion being part of it. It was simply not there to be inherited and embodied in the new culture pattern. Though less open to the direct impact of "nineteenth century ideas" than the intellectual levels of society, the same ideas were at work, though appropriated in a bowdlerized form, where they could

find congenial lodging in an instinctive attitude of mind conditioned to living for the immediate present, for practical affairs,
and for such pleasures as came their way. If the intellectuals
had discovered that the heavens were closed, the workmen
had never expected them to open. The material job of existing
precluded the luxury of 'religion', as of culture in general.

It is an academic but a pretty question to ask what might
have been the situation had the Liberal Party, with its strong
religious dynamic, become a 'Labour Party' vigorously pressing
the claims of labour, as it had once embodied the interests of
the new industrial middle classes. It is also interesting to consider what success a further Nonconformist secession at the
end of the nineteenth century might have had, if it had openly
espoused the political and social objectives of the working class.
The former, of course, was inconceivable, and the short-lived
Labour Churches suggest that by this time the disinclination
for anything that savoured of institutional religion was too
strong for the latter to have met with great success. But there
were men in the churches who saw the prophetic calling of the
Labour Movement, and many more within that Movement who
had been led there by their Christian passions. And some were
emphatic that the Labour Movement would continue to need
an ethical and religious dynamic, as there were others who saw
that, if the churches were truly to be incarnate in the society
to come, some positive relationship to that Movement was inevitable. For the Western World as a whole none expressed it
more clearly and brutally than the American Walter Rauschenbusch, famous and infamous as a father of the 'social gospel'.

... The Church has a tremendous stake in the social crisis. It may
try to maintain an attitude of neutrality, but neither side will permit
it. If it is quiescent, it thereby throws its influence on the side of
things as they are, and the class that aspires to a fitter place in the
organization of society will feel the great spiritual force of the
Church as a dead weight against it. . . . Protestantism throve with
the class that had espoused it. It lifted its class, and its class lifted
it. . . . If the present class struggle of the wage-workers is successful, and they become the dominant class of the future, any
religious ideas and institutions which they now embrace in the
heat of their struggle will rise to power with them, and any
institution on which they turn their back is likely to find itself
in the cold.[1]

[1] *Christianity and the Social Crisis*, W. Rauschenbusch, 1907.

This was not as opportunist as it sounds; Rauschenbusch insisted that the demands of God and of conscience were to be heard within the claims of the working classes of America and Europe, and none more than he had earned the right to speak. The future was not to work out as simply as he visualized, but he was right enough in foreseeing that vast working-class groups growing to political strength, and dominating the social scene, without an historic association with the Christian churches would find those churches in an acute predicament.

The extent of working-class estrangement is still insufficiently realized inside the churches, partly because the churches do not ask embarrassing sociological questions, and also perhaps because we have grown accustomed to the situation, to smaller numbers of all social groups, and can always produce a handful of artisan swallows to suggest that the summer is with us. It is to deny the hard facts of history; and a sociological comparison of the congregation with the parish, or the churches with the industrial area in which they are set, would show the critical nature of the situation. It would show the almost total exclusion of adult men such as miners, steelworkers, engineers, general factory workers, dockworkers, transport workers, and so on. Nor is there a sufficiently skilful and sympathetic understanding by the churches of the working-class pattern of life, in which faith has to be born and the Christian community to grow.

There are some who dismiss the drag of the past, maintaining that the culture pattern is still in process of change. That of course is true, and it is not contradictory to say that the pattern is both crystallized and still in process of change. Great changes have taken place since 1939; the 'palaeotechnic' age of industrialism is behind us and greater changes may lie ahead, and the 'biotechnic' phase, if Mumford's happy term may be appropriate to the next industrial era, may render all our normal class terms obsolete. But there is no contemporary evidence that where poverty and insecurity give way to decent standards of life the working classes assume a greater attachment to the practice of religion, and to the churches. No longer does religious habit denote an escape from the abyss. We should be ill-advised to think that there is any inevitable force at work that could retrieve the situation. In this brief summary are to be found the sociological roots of the most intractable problem facing the Church in this country. It can be denied only by those who see human society as millions of isolated atoms, uninfluenced by one another, uncoloured by their history, environment and experiences, and unmoved by the currents of history. Unfortunately it would seem that enthusiastic evangelists all too.often do regard society in precisely this way.

2. *The loss of the middle classes*

It is also clear that the losses from the churches in the past two generations are substantially from the middling classes of society—the industrial and professional middle classes, the inhabitants of suburbia, shopkeepers, black-coated workers, superior craftsmen, foremen and such-like. Losses from the working classes have also occurred, but relatively less, since fewer of this class, as adults, were within the churches. The religious faith of the middle classes had always been weaker than its impressive expression suggested. A faith that is so widely conformist, and in the best sense of the word conventional, and at the same time, whether evangelical or catholic, prone to narrowness and pietism, is ill-equipped to wrestle with a world so heavily secular as the twentieth century was to become. At best it could maintain itself only by isolation from the realities of the time—a possibility not open to the urban middle classes, who were notoriously activist. And in the ensuing dichotomy between religion and the world, the latter was bound to triumph.

Such religion, granted all its good points, was not the best to resist the acids of nineteenth-century ideas and the blows of the twentieth, and where it was liberal, humanist and conformist, it was even more open to erosion. The impact of scientific and secular ways of thought, a broadening view of the world and its complexity and a greater pre-occupation with affairs, coupled with an easy acceptance of more hedonist ways of life, all left their mark and led to a weakening of moral fibre, a loss of verve at the beginning of the present century. Conservatism and social convention could still hold them in the churches, but with weakened faith, quite unable to survive the shocks of modern war, social crises, and the material exactions and seductions of twentieth-century living. Once the social habit began to dissolve, a widespread dissolution took place, with the inevitable tendency of the new social habits to maintain themselves.

It will be claimed that at the present time there is evidence of a return to the churches by the middle classes. It is true, and replenished churches can turn it to creative purpose. Despite the losses, the middling groups are still more easily embraced by churches of all denominations than working-class groups. Every industrial city proves the point. The well-attended churches are generally in the pleasant, middle-class, suburban and dormitory areas—and there are many such churches; and the struggling, denuded churches, those in the old downtown and slum areas, the 'East-ends', and on the huge new housing estates where industrial workers live. But a wariness is becoming. The reasons for the renewed interest in religion may not be wholly unrelated to the sense of insecurity in the raw world in which we are living; a rawness that the middle classes sense more than others. The desire for social stability, sound authority, and even nostalgia for past tradition are not uncommon, and a return to Church and orthodoxy can go far to meet them.

For this very reason the return could be more powerful witness to uneasiness than to a recovery of a robust faith that was determined to penetrate the world of to-day and to-morrow and to grasp the nettles of its challenges. It is a hard word, but if religious faith could be the expression of an optimistic and ebullient rising class, it could also be the expression of one in bewilderment, and even retreat. This is not to decry the habit of church-going or to be cynical about the significant shift of the middle classes towards the churches. Far from it—all men are called into the Church of God, and only the most hairy and inhuman of prophets would insist on wholly conscious and unmixed motives. But it is to insist that sociological questions are legitimate even of the body of Christ, that full churches do not necessarily denote prophetic witness, that the Church must be exposed to the real world and not a refuge from it, and that the Word of God within the Church must be an incisive word for our time. Unless this is clear we shall have learned nothing from history; on a smaller scale we might even repeat the errors of the nineteenth-century Church all over again.

3. *The sociology of faith and unbelief*

This leads to a third striking feature to be seen in the sociological conditioning of both faith and unbelief, of both the habit of worship and its neglect. Nothing stands out more clearly than this, and it suggests that the Church should be willing to submit herself to radical sociological self-examination, and take the conclusions into account for her own self-understanding and in the planning of her mission. Such scrutiny is rare, and yet it is important for the Church's own health of soul, since it is extremely easy for the Church to assume in a complex society, and without conscious Pharisaism, that she is the body of those who have responded (which may be true), and that the others are the outsiders who have denied the Gospel (which very few in fact have done). Even less justified are those sectaries (and they exist even in 'great churches') who equate the sum of their members, or those responding to their evangelistic work, with the saved and the elect, and the others with the unsaved and the lost. To do this would be to assume a remarkable predilection on God's part for the middle classes, and a singular distaste for, let us say, industrial workers! This is not to impugn the fidelity of those who have responded to Christian faith in a milieu that is conducive to such response, nor to deny that faith is a gift of God. But neither must infidelity be hastily impugned where adverse conditioning is effective, and where invincible ignorance is a general consequence. We need a modern exposition of 'invincible ignorance' that takes into account the monolithic conditioning of entire social groups in modern society, and it is the more necessary in that frustrated sections of the Church are greatly tempted to draw the line more harshly between believers and unbelievers.

But it is not only the Church's own health of soul that requires a recognition of this conditioning; it is of crucial importance to the Church's mission. For if there are sociological and conditioning factors intimately related to the likelihood or otherwise of man's belief in the Gospel, if some environments make response more probable and others more improbable, then it follows as night follows day that the Church must be acutely concerned with those conditioning factors, from the point of view of her missionary task, if for none other. There is Biblical precedent! The children of Israel, we are told, cried unto God by reason of their bondage in Egypt, yet "they hearkened not to Moses for anguish of spirit and for cruel bondage". It is not melodramatic to say that generations of industrial town dwellers have also made that cry, and remained invincibly ignorant.

Much study and research is required on the effect of modern society upon the mind and spirits of men, and on the complex relation of different factors that produce what we have called the working-class culture pattern, which in its turn becomes so potent a conditioning factor. The Church has no systematic and positive means of bringing the influence of the Christian faith upon the major conditioning factors of modern life. Such a concern would take into account the economic organization of society, and the industrial institutions of society which underlie the modern culture pattern. And if men are 'made' by their environment in the widest sense, as they so manifestly are, the Church's mission is not exhausted by mere awareness, but demands a direct impact on those institutions and within the culture pattern. It is the concern with what may be called "principalities and powers"—all-pervasive and determining factors that can enslave men or liberate them, stunt them or increase their stature as men, and which can be demonic or angelic. The Church must be more concerned with "principalities and powers" if she would more faithfully save "flesh and blood". This is the hardest lesson for the Church to learn.

4. *The lack of prophecy*

The theological weakness of the nineteenth-century churches also stands out from the story, and this at least is not a matter of dispute. It is evidenced from the successive phases of liberal theology, critical theology and the neo-orthodoxy both Catholic and Protestant, all of which in their ways are critical reactions to earlier nineteenth-century views. Yet, in spite of the reactions, it is questionable whether the failures of the past have been sufficiently defined and corrected. Nor is it only a matter of rediscovering a high doctrine of the Church and a massive orthodoxy free from the narrowness of nineteenth-century pietism or the dangerous taints of liberal humanism. It is a question of discovering a theology profound enough to apprehend the given facts of the modern world, and a Word of God relevant to man's existence and experience in the twentieth century.

The two factors above all others that emerge in the nineteenth century and patently in the twentieth, as the structural formative elements of the modern era, are the two great revolutions: the scientific revolution and the social revolution. These are the two basic constituent factors of the present age, that underlie its most complex problems. They are also the two factors, in separation or conjunction, that underlie the missionary problem in the industrial parts of Europe, and are probably determinative of that problem from now on throughout the world. And they are precisely the two factors that most disturbed the nineteenth-century Church, and against which rearguard action was continuously fought. It cannot be confidently asserted that the contemporary Church has understood them either providentially or prophetically, or that the contemporary Christian has a positive attitude towards them. Until this is effected for ordinary Christians we may continue to speak of the theological destitution of the Church. Here surely is a task awaiting the attention of theologians who are themselves sensitive to the secular atmosphere of the age, to justify the ways of God to men in things that modern men, without scales on their eyes, know to be momentous. It is surprising how little of the richness and variety of modern theological writing bites on the modern world.

5. *Inadequate structure of the Church*

A further fact that emerges is the ill-devised shape of the Church for the missionary task in a highly industrialized and urbanized society, not only in its failure to bear on the major institutions of an industrialized society which we have already noted, but in its manifest incapacity to impinge on more than a tiny minority of the parish, in mammoth populations. Taking the structure of the Church of England as an example (and the shape of the Church in all denominations is now substantially the same), it is clear that the parish structure, the notion of the large church standing at the centre of the small community, presupposed a Christian conformist society. It had been an adequate structure over centuries, from Saxon and Norman days. It met the case of the Middle Ages. It is inherent in Hooker's concept of the relationship between Church and State, where the Church and the Commonwealth comprise one society fulfilling different functions. It was not required that the Church should be the 'Christian community' over against the non-Christian world; the secular community was itself the Christian community. All that was basically required was a structure of the Church that could provide facilities for 'public worship'. This, of course, is not to say that everyone was a serious and devout Christian, but it does define the structure of the Church in relation to a wholly conformist Christian community, in which any dissenter became a social outcast. Certainly up to 1680 every county in the country had convictions for non-attendance on the National Worship and for not Communicating,[1] and the theory was still implicit up to the reign of William and Mary, when the Act was passed exempting their Majesties' Protestant Subjects dissenting from the Church of England from penalties imposed by Elizabeth for non-attendance at common prayer.[2]

But even from the early eighteenth century the theory on which the conformist expectation had been based had ceased to meet the facts in the swelling industrial towns, and any legal requirements were hopelessly obsolete—not because of the growth of Dissent and religious toleration, but through the concentrations of amorphous populations and the ensuing breakdown of community, in which religious conformity ceased to have meaning. It took over 200 years for the Church to begin to learn that one of the consequences of this breakdown was that she had to become the "Christian community" within the wider secular world. The tardy erection of new churches by the Establishment and Dissenters was no adequate solution, as perspicacious observers saw at the time. And when they called for parish churches to every 400 houses, or for 'Mechanics' Churches' and 'Ragged Churches', as when in the late nineteenth century the Settlement Movement appeared, and as, indeed, when John Wesley had insisted that every member of the Society should be in a class of known membership—in all of these cries there was open or tacit admission that the structure inherited from the past was inadequate to the new problems.

The case, if not any particular remedy, is fully proved once the Church's concern with the entire population is conceded (as the Church of England certainly is bound to concede), and unless the Church of Christ is for all time to be identified with any particular historical expression of it—and that very largely in terms of masonry! We may note too that the National Church suffered and still suffers the greatest ravages, since the greatest

1 Select Committee on Church Rates, 1851 : Appendix 3.
2 *I William and Mary*, c. 18.

losses of potential members are always from the 'great church' of a nation. The Free Churches have never claimed to be the churches of other than their members and adherents, even though they have assumed characteristics of a 'great church', and the Roman Catholic Church has always been able to count on the obedience of a high percentage of her members, and care for them as a known and manageable constituency if scattered over a large area. That is to say, if there are structural defects in the Church militating against her proper mission in the highly urbanized and industrialized areas, the Church of England has paramount reason to be concerned about it.

*   *   *

In drawing out these conclusions from the historico-sociological examination of the relation of the Church to an industrialized and urbanized order of society, the area and dimension of the modern missionary task are laid bare. It is a formidable task indeed and there are no neat solutions to overcome it. Reformation is not simple. We must neither minimize the gravity of the problems nor become paralysed by their enormity. Rather we should ask if the same analysis dictates any conditions that must be met in the mission planning of the Church, whether any remedial insights and lines of advance are suggested that might promise to measure up to the profundity of the problem as history discloses it. And can those measures be defined in any detail, beyond fine phrases and clichés that the Church must be the Church, more missionary minded, and so on? It is submitted that there are some positive suggestions to be drawn that provide presuppositions for modern mission, and the elements of a missionary policy. They can be classified under three headings and the remainder of this chapter delineates them:

1. *Theological*

The historico-sociological analysis suggests a certain theological perspective. It requires that the dimension of our customary understanding of Christianity must be stretched to apprehend the totality of human life and history. This in turn demands a concept of the Church engaged in persistent, purposeful permeation of the world.

It suggests too the communicability of the meaning of Christianity in secular terms, demonstrating its bearing upon all human activity even to those who are insensitive to the religious dimensions.

2. *Industrial*

The Church needs a structure and machinery whereby a continuous impact is exerted within the typical institutions of an industrialized society.

3. *Parochial*

The Church in its local expression needs to devise a structure and machinery whereby the congregation is broken down into natural and indigenous groups that at the same time promote the pastoral care and training of the laity, and produce working groups for the spontaneous expansion of the Church within large amorphous populations.

I. THEOLOGICAL PERSPECTIVES

Patience and urgency

Many indeed are the religious and theological insights directly suggested by the history of the problem, or born of a theological appraisal of its depth. We need to be humbled and sobered before the complexity of the world that God allows to exist, and to approach our missionary task within it in fear and trembling, and great patience. That task promises to be with us for a very long time. The penetration and permeation of our modern technological civilization constitutes a task as immense as ever faced the Christian Church, if not greater. It is more complicated, unprecedented and vaster. It calls for a divine patience and a distance of perspective comparable to that of the Apostolic Age or the Dark Ages, and yet paradoxically for an impatience, a sense of urgency and persistence, in that time seems foreshortened and the powers of this present world more formidable. True, the Church at large is predisposed to be patient, notwithstanding the ephemeral character of much of her mission activity. But patience by itself could be delusory. It could denote an unwarrantable conservatism, a retrenchment, even a return to the catacombs to await a more faithful epoch that may never come. On the other hand it could spring from too facile a theory of Church and Society, as though, the dispersed Church being salt and yeast at work, little had to be done but to carry on, with a reform here and a mission there. As theory, it is of course impeccable that the laity dispersed into the life of the world means permeation, influence and effective Christian transformation. But we should be naïve indeed to think that it happens so simply and so automatically.

Again, patience could spring from escape into a dialectical theology that hears its "No" but not its "Yes". It is true enough that soberness and humility might well drive us to believe that the only significant factor in a problem of such magnitude would be a change in the world outlook itself, so transforming the human situation, men's hopes, assumptions and the very air they breathe, that the Gospel could once again be heard and understood. That is to say, using the Parable of the Sower, that we do not sow the seed; *our* sowing, however diligent the scattering, may be of dead seed, and perhaps the very ground itself precludes germination of even quite good seed, of all but the best seed, perhaps of every kind of seed. Perhaps for a lengthy time the ground must lie fallow, men be radically without religion, to be cleansed of inadequate religion, and spurious pseudo-religions be discovered for what they are. Certainly it is wholesome to bear in mind that there are given conditions that men cannot alter, that men may play their part consciously and unconsciously in shaping the present and the future, but that God's Providential Will is both inscrutable and sovereign. It is a sobering word of Karl Barth that though we may be called to be His witnesses, "God has not called us to be His lawyers, engineers, managers, statisticians, and administrative directors". Barth's "No" to shallow confidence and churchly activism is healthy and timely, as though Atlas-like we would bear not only the world, but God Himself upon our shoulders. And yet he allows a "Yes" to obedient work in the world, with a trustful and sincere "Lord have mercy upon us", in belief that God's word must be relevant to the practical affairs of men and nations.

Self-criticism

Social and historical analysis can be a therapeutic, enabling the Church to understand the conditioning process through which she herself has passed and the extent to which she has become sociologically imprisoned. The value of self-examination and precise self-knowledge should not be underestimated. How otherwise can the Church at large know that the great industrial populations have never been at home in our churches, or sympathetically diagnose the antipathy and indifference that now marks so large a part of the population, or rectify her own deficiencies that have contributed to that condition? Does not the history of the case define the most acute area of mission with a crystal transparency? How else, to take a classic example, could Independency understand that once it moved as a powerful current, colouring the historical process, providing a critique and dynamic in society, yet with less and less effect as new currents began to run, forcing Independency away from its formative role, until it was left a small refuge for individuals rooted in that tradition? This is no selection for odious comparison—it but illustrates the predicament of the Church at large from a classic example.

Understanding can lead on to penitence. There is enough truth in the Marxist criticism of religion, certainly of nineteenth-century religion—that it is ideological, and epiphenomenal to the material economic forces at work to call for radical self-examination, not merely to weep over the past, but in order to scrutinize the present. Of course the summary Marxist repudiation of religion can never pierce the heart of the Christian faith and the Christian Church, and indeed there is a proper sense in which religion should reflect the material life men live. But to the extent that whole social groups can be shown to be within or without the churches for reasons sociologically explicable, and to the extent that religion can become ideological, a radical self-criticism is demanded by the Protestant principle of the Bible itself. A knowledge of history is the beginning of such purgation.

Again, an awareness of the process can serve to clarify the nature of the Christian witness, and to correct pietistic and individualistic deformations of the Gospel all too common in the evangelistic project, and which tend to become stronger as the social influence of the church declines. Often the missionary task is envisaged as the landing of a fish out of the sea on to the saving rock of the Church, as though the Church had escaped the pollutions and the colorations of the historical process;

whereas the Church also is part of the world, called to be immersed in the deepest waters, and to disclose the common
predicament all are in. Too often the Gospel is preached wide
outside the context of man's life in this world, thrown to him
from outside like a lifebuoy (or even a brick) inscribed with a
soteriological text that is meaningless to the secular mind and
indifferent to the social context in which men are rooted. One
is reminded of P. T. Forsyth's unheeded word that too often
"the Cross has been treated as a mere life-saving apparatus for
personal escape". If belief and unbelief are sociologically
conditioned to the extent that we have seen, and if in the West
the unprivileged and disinherited have been the more estranged,
the gravest question-mark is placed over a preaching of the
Gospel summoning men to faith and personal holiness, that
omits the social context in which God is to be discovered and
obeyed, and in which men are to be served and redeemed.
Nothing obtrudes from the history of the problem more clearly
than this, and to ignore the lesson is to deform the Gospel. It
was precisely this that Forsyth had in mind when he insisted
that "we need a better Gospel far more than we need more
gospelling", and when Rauschenbusch spoke out that:

> . . . We are not disposed to accept the converted souls whom the
> individualistic evangelism supplies, without looking them over.
> Some who have been saved and perhaps reconsecrated a number
> of times are worth no more to the Kingdom of God than they
> were before. Some become worse through their revival experi
> ences, more self-righteous, more opinionated, more steeped in
> unrealities and stupid over against the most important things,
> more devoted to emotions and unresponsive to real duties. . . . It
> is time to overhaul our understanding of the kind of change we
> hope to produce by personal conversion. . . . The form which the
> process of redemption takes in a given personality will be deter
> mined by the historical and social spiritual environment of the
> individual. . . .[1]

To ignore this lesson is at best to restrict the Christian ministry
to 'sick souls'; at worst to lay the Church open to the most
elementary criticisms of Marxism.

The relation of the Church to the world

This in turn raises the question of the proper mode of

[1] *A Theology for the Social Gospel*, W. Rauschenbusch, 1918, p. 96.

relationship between the Church and the world, and this study assumes that in fact, willy-nilly, the Church is enmeshed in the life of the world. Enmeshed in the secular order she is, yet also signally uninfluential, largely through a widespread ignorance of the proper role of the Church in the world and the required relationship between them. There are at least three distinct modes of that relationship, and the Church is under debt to Dr. Paul Tillich for a useful terminology to describe them.

First there is the Church as a reflection of the secular, common society. At its highest, and to which history has provided some approximation, there is the magnifical if potentially questionable condition of 'theonomy', in which grace and nature co-inhere, and in which, to use Tillich's words, "the ultimate meaning of existence shines through all finite forms of thought and action, and the creations of culture are vessels of a spiritual content". It is a condition where the Church reflects the total life of the Christian community, of which she is the crown and glory, and the community without sense of restraint or dichotomy embodies in its life the insights and valuations of Christian faith. We may note in passing that the Church of England, in its structure and constitutional aspect, assumes such a condition as the ideal norm. But at the other extreme it can degenerate into a debased condition of mere conformity, either of nation or class, not free at least from partial criticism of being 'ideological superstructure'. It is what happens when the 'laws of God' cease to be reflected in the total culture, where the religious and the secular fall apart and cease to co-inhere, yet where religious conformity persists and the accepted constitutional relations between Church and society remain. Radical self-criticism within English bourgeois Protestantism would reveal debased characteristics illustrating this condition.

Secondly, there is the 'heteronomous' relationship, to use Tillich's term, where a 'theocratic' church, refusing any adaptation to society, is set within an 'autonomous' society which it regards as secular and foreign. In the modern industrial areas of Europe it is one of those characteristics that the massive Roman Catholic Church and the sectarian groups have in common, although it is maintained far less than the theory suggests, since their members cannot avoid the influence of the world in which they are compelled to live. But it is not confined to these groups. One of the temptations to any Church frustrated by a debased conformity or an intractable mission situation is that it should seek rigorous disengagement and purification by adopting measures consistent with the theocratic position. Were the Church of England to fall to such temptation, it would turn her into a diminutive episcopalian sect, however imposing a role she might continue to play on ceremonial occasions.

But there is a third mode of relationship, although Tillich gives us no term for it, which is appropriate to a 'great church' called, though in a period of recession, to make its witness in a secular society. According to Tillich this is the true role of the Christian Church. It is the situation where the Church is acutely conscious of belonging to the world, subject to the conditions of the world, yet a catalyst within the world which is its only sphere of obedience. It seeks neither to manipulate nor dominate the world, nor to escape from it, nor merely to reflect a voluntarist religious aspect of it, but to understand it, prophesy within it, interpret it, and stain it. This, of course, has been the role of the Church wherever the theonomous relationship has been approximated. It is also the role to be undertaken, in fear and trembling where society as a whole is not confessedly Christian, but where Christians are free men, men of their age, and members of an autonomous culture. Nor should it be regarded as a weaker role imposed on the Church by reason of adverse circumstances, but rather as a normative role, implicit at all times, but peculiarly relevant in a world grown for good or ill beyond the stage of pupilage and determined to be master of its own destiny. It defines the Church in its relation with the world neither as a monolithic rock unmoved by the currents of history, nor as an ark for the saved, nor as flotsam and jetsam floating on the surface, but as a deep current itself running in the seas. The imagery brings to mind Kierkegaard's definition of faith, not as fair-weather sailing in the ship, not as clinging to the rock, but as swimming in the deep with 70,000 fathoms below!

No doubt this is a concept that gains the assent of many intelligent Christians, suggesting as it does the role of the laity dispersed into the world, the secular obedience of a Christian man, the notion of the 'Christian Frontier', all of which are seminal ideas in the Protestant understanding of the relation of the Church to the world. Yet in fact these ideas are not widely actualized in the life of the Church. Where they are brought to

birth, the premature death rate is high, and the few that remain are exceptional prodigies.

The reasons are several—the catalytic action of the Church ✓
through a dispersed laity presupposes an understanding of the
secular implications of the Christian faith, and a clear understanding of the role of the Church in the world, that are both
comparatively rare. And the structure of the Church is inimical
to the required clarity of understanding—there is no organiza-
tional expression of the Church deployed into the secular
'frontier' positions; and the idea is completely secondary, if it
has place at all, to the nigh exclusive understanding of the
Church as "the visible congregation of faithful men, in which
the pure Word of God is preached, and the Sacraments be duly
administered"—a concept adequate enough in a conformist
society, but wholly inadequate in the missionary situation. Most
seriously, it is in part due to a deformed understanding of the
Christian faith; were it enough to understand the Church as an
earnest of the Kingdom, a city on a hill, a kind of receptacle to
hold the faithful, the existent structure would be adequate, so
long as the lines between the Church and the world could be
sharply drawn, and a strong heteronomous attitude engendered
in the minds of Christians.

We may note in passing that any such attempt would spell the
demise of orthodox Protestantism, which could never win a
race between heteronomous churches! But this restricted understanding of the Church as the assembled worshipping body,
reinforced as it is by the existing structure of the Church, is a
wholly inadequate understanding of the Church as part of the
Gospel. Either it leaves the world to its own devices, or it
assumes too easily that its salt and yeast are effectively at work
in the lumpen world. Whatever theory may say, it is fact that
the impact of the Church becomes minimized, her prophetic
role becomes almost extinct, while the world assigns the Church
to religious people and to occasional ceremonial use. In the
process, the *meaning* of both Church and Gospel are lost. To
ask for a structure of the Church that measures up to the true
role of the Church in the world is not to be perfectionist about the
Church, as though all God's people were apostles and prophets.
Far from it—the blind and the lame also live in Jerusalem, and
the sick, the broken and the weary should find in the Church
their most proper consolation and refuge. But this does not

negate the catalytic, prophetic role of the Church in the life of men and nations.

A secular understanding of the Gospel

This mode of relationship between the Church and the world is not dictated solely by missionary necessity, but by the very nature of the Gospel of which the Church is part. There is no space for a long exposition of the Biblical and theological sanctions for this, but a few points may not be amiss. We must be wary of imprisoning the meaning of the Gospel into a sentence—the perennial error of revivalists seeking a neat formula to win a simple "yes" from the convert. Nor is it enough, because the apostolic creed was a simple "Jesus is Lord", to tear that phrase out of the context of apostolic events and shear it from that understanding of reality of which the Work of Christ is both effective part and hall-mark. There is a sense in which the New Testament is an appendix to the 'Bible', a key to the travails of Israel and of the entire cosmos, and to tear out the appendix is to misunderstand it; the key, without the door before it, is robbed of meaning. That is to say that Christianity is not theosophy or the revelation of esoteric truth; Christianity is about the meaning of human life and history, of ordinary secular history which is the only kind there is, and if true, true for every man.

This is surely implicit when we assert that Christianity is an historical religion, which not only means that God has wrought mighty works in history, but also that all secular history permits a unique interpretation in relation to which those acts themselves have meaning. This is not to dispense with the concept of revelation; on the contrary it is to insist that among the various interpretations that men can put upon the meaning of life and upon the sequence of events that make up history, Christianity gives us a certain interpretation that is no less than the situation as God Himself sees it. The words "as God Himself sees it" look outrageous and blasphemous in print, but for Christians the Biblical perspective on history and man's nature and destiny is not less than this; for them it is the true interpretation, yet not accepted because it is Biblical, but because ultimately, when discovered through all those devious ways in which it is disclosed to us, it is found to be profoundly adequate, not just as it were to a religious instinct, but to our experience of life. If this is so, it follows that we should have a mode of communicating the meaning of Christianity regarding which, although men may reject it, they at least ought to understand what it is saying.

The major theme of that revelation and interpretation is that there is a potential in history that God wills to realize, and an end for which the whole creation groans and travails—a potential and end to which man is blind as he follows his natural bent and makes his own history, as indeed he does. Men make their history, and it is written in blood and sweat and tears, ever on the verge of greater possibilities of good and evil, of blessing and curse, as their powers of making history are enlarged. And though we may not trace His Hand, God too is at work in His creation, confronting men, calling them, inspiring them, and in ways we may not define—only leaving them men, with some remnants of His image and likeness. Nor is He without witness —in reason and wisdom, though it decays into rationalism and cleverness; in good law, though it rots into convention, tyranny and class rule; in man's heart and conscience, though it is corrupted by self-interest, rationalization, and the claims to infallibility and 'guidance'. And servants and prophets are sent, and even the Son, and more servants and prophets, some of whom know not that they are.

That potential and end of history is delineated and hinted in a variety of ways in the Bible. Some are wholly symbolical and eschatological as the new heaven and the new earth of the Book of Revelation; some in the imagery of nature like the eleventh chapter of Isaiah, and some prosaically, as though spears could be turned into pruning-hooks, uranium into industrial and domestic power, and every man sit in his own council house, under his own vine and figtree, and call every man his neighbour. It is hard to know whether we are speaking of earth or heaven—and indeed it is the same thing, as the one is subsumed into the other. But if the Christian faith is concerned with ends, it is not concerned with dreams. Men are making their history, and in every generation and epoch there are lesser ends, modest ends to be realized, by hard means, all of which are to be tested by the meaning of history and the greater purpose to which the creation travails. And here the qualities of the Kingdom are demanded, to do justly, to love mercy, to walk humbly, to realize good law, good political and economic organization, good relations, and a second mile to pull the law on to a higher level. And here is the arena of hard decisions where Utopian blueprints, moral absolutes, and 'religion' are singularly unhelpful and may even do damage. Here men have to decide and act, to govern and work, without infallibility, in given situations, balancing interests, rights and duties, and striving for relative justice. And it is easy enough to be crucified. So is history made by men, the present conditioned by the past, future possibilities determined by the present, and the action of God's grace and of His wrath working inexorably. For the sins of the fathers are visited on the children and we are destroyed by the hand of our own iniquities, as every Marxist knows—yet also His mercies endure for ever, and the whole revelation is testimony to His grace.

If we may set out the substance of the Biblical theme in this way much else is directly and transparently deduced that might otherwise at best be appended as useful theological insight. It is clear for example that the Church is subservient to the Kingdom, a primary theological truth that is imprisoned in the textbooks. It may impede our drawing lines and painting in black and white, yet on the other hand it enables us to recognize that there are those who are "not far from the Kingdom of God", an important discernment indeed in the Church's mission in the world. It demands that the Church be continuously under judgment, the lack of which has led her so astray in the crucial years in which the modern world was in making. It roots Christian obedience in the world, from which it so easily escapes into 'religion', and it demands that Christian men seek God's will for the world, with which the Christian faith is seen to be patently concerned. And the hard facts of a scientific and technological organization of society, and the welter of social revolution the world over, can be seen, not as awkward difficulties that we must somehow live with, but as the raw material of which our age has to be built, and through which the Living God confronts our century. These are not slight elements to be apprehended in the Christian faith.

And does this 'secular' interpretation dishonour the centrality of the Person of Christ? He is the Word made Flesh, the supreme sanction and fulfilment of the truth; He is God revealed in history in the only way that man could understand Him, in whom the Kingdom is supremely established, who wills to incorporate all men into Himself making them instruments of His Kingdom, who will subdue all things and subject them to the Father. What is that to say but that He saves the world? But it is a very shrunken world unless the full dimension of human life and history is included. And does this overlook the 'individual' to save some historical abstraction? But men are not isolated units; they are members one of another bound together in a bundle of life, common victims of evil for whom salvation must also be realized in common. And does it reduce to insignificance the personal will and the little realm in which men are free to act and work out their own salvation? But obedience to the Word ranges from the given cup of cold water to world economic integration, from the care of the family to the lying down together of the bear, lion and eagle, and from the concern for personal wholeness to those things that belong to the world's peace. And through the whole gamut Christ is served in His brethren, and the individual finds high meaning and history on his side in the little life so orientated. And does it seem to disparage the Church, the means of grace, worship and personal devotion? God forbid! The Church becomes the conscious instrument of the Kingdom, and the ordinances of grace take on new relevance as the dimensions of the Christian concern lift us from a narrow pre-occupation with one's own soul. Prayer is energized with work. The sense of sin is widened and deepened to include man's corporate guilt—with all the creative consequences that can follow. The Eucharist is illuminated in a score of ways.

Hooks and eyes

This 'secular' mode of stating the meaning of Christianity, demanding as it does a continuous scrutiny and critique of the history that man is making and of his self-making in the process, enables us to communicate the Gospel in terms that men may more easily grasp. 'Communication' we are told is to-day a major problem in the mission of the Church, which is but a succinct way of saying that the generations conditioned into new categories of thinking cannot understand the categories in which the Christian religion has traditionally been formulated, and that the Church is unsuccessful in expressing the meaning of Christianity either intellectually or existentially in the secular culture of the present. Certainly the human beings most typical of the modern era seem the least persuaded of its truth. It is as though the Church propounds her truth in three-dimensional terms in a world reduced to a two-dimensional experience of reality—they do not correspond and there is no *rapport*.

It is singularly useless and unjust to denigrate the unresponsive world for this incapacity to understand the Gospel. This is not to abrogate man's moral responsibility, nor to suggest that if men saw the truth they would follow it. But it is to say that religiously speaking, from the three-dimensional point of view, the offence is largely technical, and that if the human mind is in fact an idol factory, the production is carried on automatically and almost unconsciously. If the Church is the more blameworthy, it is through the neglect of her specific role to assist the world to understand itself and to see the things that belong to its health. It is the failure of prophecy and interpretation, understandable though it may be in the rapid evolution of a wholly new society. But it is not enough to diagnose; we have to declare truth in such a way that its relevance is conceded, if the Gospel is to be communicated. If our reasoning is correct, it follows that the two-dimensional, the secular interpretation is vitally important, dictated not only by missionary exigency but by theological and Biblical truth. The German theologian Dietrich Bonhoeffer raised this very question—how we do in fact communicate the meaning of Christianity in a world radically without religion, how we speak in secular terms of God, and how Christ can be Lord even of those without religion—audacious questions, but not too extravagant where the mission project goes beyond traditional revivalism and really engages the modern world.

This mode of understanding the Christian faith, wilfully related at all points to the secular order, forces us to engage the world, work and converse within it in ways that compel our faith into relevance. To use William Temple's metaphor, we have to find the 'eyes' and discover 'hooks' that fit them, demanding on our part both a sensitive and informed understanding of the real problems of our time and place, and also the bearing of Christianity upon the secular problem and the human predicament in terms of judgment, promise and practical implication. There are many instruments at our disposal if we can learn to use them theologically. Thus, as prolegomena, the very interpretation of the historical process through which the modern world has evolved can be therapeutic—for the world as well as the Church. Just as the mentally and spiritually sick can be helped by good psychological diagnosis and analysis, so men can be helped by an analysis of the cultural air they breathe and by the theological commentary upon it. This is no academic point. Nothing is more striking and terrifying than the extent to which intelligent men, with no particular ill-will, can be imprisoned by their inherited and unconscious axioms and prejudices, and the disclosure of facts and a Christian interpretation upon them can be part of the truth that makes them free. So also of man's impotence to apprehend the Gospel, an understanding of his tortuous pilgrimage by which he came into an arid two-dimensional view can help to make the vertical dimension more intelligible.

There are many illustrations that come to mind, in which the theological and secular can use the same language about the same concerns. We need to prise people's eyes open to see how community has collapsed in the urban society leaving man a stranger to his neighbour, a mass of faces in the High Street, and point the quality of natural community that the Church could once baptize, and the positive task of creating it in the new society. Certainly the creation of community and the Christian mission go hand in hand in our modern society—and not solely in the Christian concern for the community of the Body of Christ. All the fertile insights that Martin Buber has given us are beyond value in this context—that there is a "sacrament of dialogue" where "there are no gifted and ungifted, only those who give themselves and those who withhold themselves" —a theological insight profoundly relevant to the common events of every day for every man, so qualitatively different from mere social activity. Again, we need to expose how men on such a wide scale are seduced by distraction, activism, and the purely pleasurable, and show the high stakes in more purposeful living—an approach quite different from the Mrs. Grundy role of churches belabouring the wickedness of what men feel to be the most trivial misdemeanours. A Nonconformist conscience is still valuable enough, but it needs sorely to be brought up to date.

In no area of life is it more crucial for us to learn how to communicate Christian truth than in the field of politics and industry, so important from the point of view of this study, since it is in the broadly industrial context that the technological and social revolutions most clearly join hands, and where the promise of both must be realized or thwarted. Again, we may say that if the appropriate disciplines are mastered, there is a way of speaking theologically about the social problems of industry and of an industrialized society, just as there is a Biblical way of speaking of the social and political issues of our time. And in both cases the dialogue—for dialogue with the world now becomes possible—is about the world. There are no neat solutions or Christian blueprints, but there are social principles of the Bible, 'middle axioms', a moral and dynamic view of history, and an understanding of man's nature, which bear upon the problems. Nor is prophecy impossible, for prophecy is not crystal-gazing or clairvoyancy; prophecy is the reading of the present through a profound discernment of the past, and a realization of the possibilities, even the certainties that lie ahead, in the light of our handling of the present.

These are but a few brief illustrations of how the theological perspective can be expressed in secular terms, in a way that impinges on the secular affairs of men, and speaks into their precise situations. Clearly it implies the deep immersion of Christians in the affairs of the world. We must confess that we are poorly equipped to communicate the truth of Christianity to the age in which we live, either in words and ideas that awaken a response, or in a relevant spirituality of being and doing. Both are desperately important; the latter may prove the more converting power and we should not separate them, but the discovery of a relevant, existential pattern of Christian living is dependent upon the former, upon our capacity to interpret the Gospel in secular terms that men can understand. If there has been place for religion without secular relevance in the past, there is little hope for it in the future. Nor should we wish it to be otherwise.

*   *   *

II. INDUSTRIAL MISSION

While it is true that the deepest questions posed by the historical and sociological study of the mission problem in an industrialized society are theological, other questions, theological but also supremely practical and strategical, present themselves. How, for example, is the Church to bring effective influence upon the new society, with its new structures and typical institutions which, as we have seen, elude the existing structure of the Church? How is she to become informed on the nature of the missionary problem, and the social problems of an industrialized society? What is the bearing of the Christian insights on those problems of industry and society? What machinery of engagement needs to be devised by the Church? These are all practical questions, but at all points the theological must be related to the strategical, as closely as thought to action in any healthy organism. But there is a prior question even to these—does the Church in fact need new organs of thinking, a different perspective, and new machinery of engagement? Many would say "No", and with them we must argue the case.

The Church, as we have seen, has not been without prophets; nor has she lacked men who have seen that the social concern of the Church goes far beyond the narrow evangelistic outreach. The twentieth century is the age of conferences; in these at least the Church has not lagged, and not a few of them have been devoted to the social problems of an industrial society. There was the superb report of 1918 on Christianity and Industrial Problems which sprang from wartime thinking within the Church; it was not universally welcomed, but it was the first concerted attempt in modern times to scrutinize the industrial and economic order from the standpoint of the Christian conscience. Much dated, it still asks incisive questions of our society. Then came the series of ecumenical conferences, including study of the social order, that were directly or indirectly inspired by William Temple. There was Copec—the Conference on Christian Politics, Economics and Citizenship in 1924. There was the Conference on Church Community and State at Oxford in 1937, the economic section of which went to the heart of the inter-war problems. From the Second World War and since there have been the Malvern Conference that Temple chaired in 1940 for the Industrial Christian Fellowship, and the conferences of the World Council of Churches at Amsterdam and Evanston which sought to define the characteristics of a 'responsible society'. None of them provided detailed solutions or programmes, which was not the task of the 'Church' as such to produce even were she competent to do so, and which could have constituted an unwarrantable intrusion into the proper technical autonomy of the spheres of politics, economics and industry. But they provided clear criteria of moral judgment, suggested fruitful avenues of approach, and the later ones stressed the crucial role of the laity if the impact of the Christian faith was to be effective in the social and institutional life of the nation.

These conferences and their reports were but milestones on a road with many lesser signposts. And behind them was that golden if thin line of individuals in the nineteenth century who had sought to extend the rule of God to the material and social affairs of men. There were those who conceived the 'Christian Frontier' long before the term was coined, like Charles Gore, who before 1890 was insisting that "the moment has come for the Church, and particularly the Church of England, to put social morality and Christian living in the forefront of its effort. At present we are making too much of the development of the outward exhibition of worship. We trust too much to Church building and the organizing of plant. We try too much to get people to come to Church . . . it would be possible . . . to form small circles of representative men in each district, where special occupations prevail, to draw up a statement of what is wrong in current practice, and of the principles on which Christians ought to act". Significantly, his paper was published as a Fabian Essay.

It adds up to a remarkable tradition, much greater than any realize who look only at one denominational contribution. And yet, in terms of effective consequence, it adds up to . . . nothing! No, that is overstatement; individuals who took part in the thinking process behind and within these conferences were greatly influenced, including in their number many of the ablest laity in the contemporary Church, whose contribution in society is far greater than their number would suggest. But they comprise a handful. As far as the mind of the Church at large was concerned they had come to nought. It showed and still shows an alarming capacity of the Churches to produce ideas and ignore them, or to absorb them and smother them, though their monuments remain, periodically garnished to suggest a state of thinking and work that hardly exists. Yet the rank and file of the churches were teachable, capable of new attitudes of mind, where new ideas were persistently expounded and embodied in the life of the Church—as for example the remarkable growth of Anglo-Catholicism has shown. So it could have been with a theology of the Kingdom that emphasized the secular concern of the Gospel, the true role of the laity, the elements of a Christian social critique, and that encouraged, up and down the life of the nation, the appropriate machinery of thinking and involvement. It did not happen.

We need not look for sinister reasons, although such a departure from the customary understanding of 'religion' would no doubt have evoked opposition both within the Church and outside it. It was assumed rather, when a word had been said, a report published, an assembly at Lambeth or a conference concluded, that somehow work had been done, and that consequences would follow automatically. The most 'red-hot' subjects have been handled, whatever we may say of the conclusions reached—like the report of the committee on Socialism of the 1888 Lambeth Conference. But from all these reports, conferences and encyclicals there was hardly a ripple on the smooth surface of the churches and none on the world. A few eccentrics, some at high levels of the Church's life, might remain concerned, but the issues were wholly subsidiary to the main continuing pre-occupations of the Church with maintaining the organization of public worship, the circle of social activities around it, and such obvious ambulance work as was found on their doorstep. It is not necessary to question the intrinsic value of such a massive expression of the Christian Church throughout the land. But its sum total was a woefully inadequate expression in the face of a rudely autonomous society, new nation-wide institutions that were dominating the life of the nation, and social problems beyond the capacity of the most generous works of mercy. The Church was maintained, but impinged neither on the crucial issues nor the power points of the national life. Perhaps the imposing role of Church leaders at national and local level and the deference still accorded them in English life were conducive to the assumption that the Church still exercised a formative influence in society—and neither Church, State, nor the élite of society wished to expose so congenial an assumption.

A more basic reason was that the Church was simply not organized to engage the new society. Her structure served valuable and essential purposes, but not this one. For obvious reasons we take the Church of England as our example, which by its very constitution is called to be 'established' in the life of the nation. We have seen that her structure is inherited from ancient time, and ideally presupposes a conformist population, and even a 'theonomous' society. In pre-industrial England that structure was capable of bringing influence upon the entire community, including its power points whose place and influence fell within the parish, in the persons of landowners, masters, farmers, magistrates, and so on. And at the upper reaches of county and national life the Church had its own hierarchical structure that met the powers of the world. Social power was largely concentrated in distinct geographical localities, and the Church had a geographical structure and a hierarchy of *personae* largely coincident with the political and social hierarchy of the country. Indeed, from Crown to village community, the Church was herself an integral part of the single social structure of the nation. The fact that the intimacy of social and ecclesiastical power was so close, and that the patronage system was calculated to produce the most courteous and uncritical of churchmen, does not annul the *theoretical* adequacy of the Church to have engaged the total life of society in pre-industrial England. It is precisely this structure, come down to us almost without change, that has been left so woefully inadequate by industrialization, and the new social structure of the nation reared upon it.

This is not to condemn the existing structure for what it can do, but for what it cannot do. It can still express the Church in local visible congregations, and bring an influence upon personal and family life in the locality, but even here it is lamed unless it can devise new living means and permanent machinery of engagement with mammoth populations, for churches even filled to capacity with two or three hundred people can hardly satisfy a missionary church set in parishes of twenty thousand. It is even less equipped to bear upon the social and institutional life of the area and nation, which hold the personal and family life of the nation as prey. Here, wholly new structures of engagement must be devised if there is to be dialogue, influence and impact. Churches may continue to consume their own conference reports, individuals may continue to be heard on this matter or that if their reputations and pulpits are of sufficient interest to the Press, and others, thank God, will continue to be significant wherever they are in spite of the Church—but without planned machinery of engagement the impact will be exceptional, ephemeral, mere token.

Let us consider the structure of the Church and the shape of the mission project were continuous engagement with the institutions of industry to take place. Industry, of course, is not the only "principality and power" determining the life of the country, its health, or lack of social health, and the Church of the nation has a proper concern with them all. But industry is the most important and uniquely relevant to our study, creating as it does the economic basis of society, the shape of urban society, and being as it is, the fruit of the scientific revolution, and the matrix of the forces of social revolution. If Sheffield has provided us with an historical analysis of the Church's problem in an industrialized society, she can also provide some of the clues pointing to the way in which the Church can engage the basic industrial institutions. For Sheffield has been a crucible of modest though concentrated experiment in this field in recent years. Some of the conclusions can be formulated, and they too need to be argued.

(a) A supplementary non-parochial structure

A church whose structure is mapped out in a wholly territorial and geographical shape cannot impinge effectively on the functional structures and social projections of a highly industrialized urbanized society.[1] It is from now on a permanent characteristic of the new society that it cannot be exhausted in terms of local territorial community. It can be illustrated in many ways. One expression of it is to say that men live in one district, work in another and go elsewhere for their leisure pursuits and community of interest. Another aspect is to say that the industrial principalities, certainly the basic ones, colour the life of the city, throw up its typical social groups, and have a permanent life and community of their own. They make the town and determine its social structure, as steel has made Sheffield, and the pit makes the colliery towns, and the miles of light factory development make the 'Great West Road'. Not only men but towns too are fashioned in the image of their craft. A further important expression is

[1] See Appendix IV.

seen in the city-wide projections of modern institutions such as political parties, municipal authorities, industrial associations, trades unions, and a host of others, throwing their huge pyramids from a base of the entire city or area to points of decisive power that cannot be tied down into local territorial areas. And the basic industry of an area is the largest of all the projections, not only as a projection of power, but as a continuing association of thousands of men, in social groups and communities that in years of high population mobility can be more stable than the local community. In the pre-industrial village community, all the various expressions of community life were projected within the parish. That is no longer so, and with the change the social projections have taken on a power and significance quantitatively and qualitatively different from anything hitherto.

Thus individuals are now dependent on the whole economy as never before, and the role of industrial institutions of decisive importance for the entire nation, as well as the local area. It is for such reasons that we may rightly speak of them as "principalities and powers", manned by persons yet supra-personal, and in the most complex and subtle ways able to determine the lives of everybody, capable of providing the foundation of good social life and able to derange and dehumanize entire communities. Normally, except on the ceremonial occasions of a Mayor's Sunday or an Industrial Sunday, the Church takes no cognizance of these institutions, nor of men in their functional capacity within them. The Church assesses people as men, women or children, communicants, 'fringers' or outsiders, the hopeful or the hopeless—but not as industrialists, managers, city councillors, trades union officials, shop stewards, etc. And fair enough in one sense, for in the gathering of the Family of God to worship Him, and to receive His gifts, the Church is a primary meeting of human beings, without regard of function, rank, sex, power or intellect. But in terms of man's obedience to God in this world, in terms of the impact of the Church on society as a whole, in terms of the Kingdom of which the Church is instrumental, the secular role is of supreme importance.

Some special agency of the Church is required to be concerned with this expression of the Church's life and impact. The reasons are really quite clear. The local church must be pre-eminently concerned with the homes of the parish and the building up of the Christian congregation, a many-sided task that must take precedence in emphasis over the secular obedience of Christian men in the larger institutions of society. In heavily industrialized areas the proper sphere of that secular involvement will almost certainly fall outside the parish; the people one should work with will be scattered over a wide area, while the problems Christians have to grapple with are too specialized and technical to be dealt with in the parochial context. But even were it otherwise, it is in the very nature of the problem that the men who are most significant in the industrial field, whom the Church most needs to engage, are often precisely those who are furthest away from the churches and therefore simply not accessible to the influence of the parish church; though we should note in passing that they may be among the first to concede the relevance of the Christian insights where they are expounded in terms that bear upon their situations, and among the first to welcome the initiative of the Church, where she demonstrates a disinterested concern with society in its own right, and not merely as the pool in which converts may be fished.

In the light of these points, it is not unreasonable to conclude that effective and efficient engagements with the representative persons who man the great industries and industrial projections can only take place where there is a permanent specialized agency of the Church, of trained man-power, deployed to cover an entire industrial area, and able to create that web of personal relationships which is the very heart and foundation of any serious contribution that the Church might make. Of course this does not preclude the friendly contact of a local minister with the little factories, workshops and garages of his area, but it does apply to the large, basic industries and the area-wide projections that are thrown up in an industrialized society. It is important to stress that this specialized industrial agency of the Church must be continuing and permanent. Continuity in the local church is maintained through the historical continuity of the place of worship; not so in the engagement of institutions. Here, engagement is based on a web of relationships, and continuity can only be maintained by personal contact over a large area and within large institutions. The phrase 'Industrial Mission'—an obvious term—has been coined in Sheffield to designate this industrial agency of the Church: a structure supplementary to the parochial organization.

The difference between the two can be expressed, properly enough, in military symbols—for both are part of the Church Militant. Until the last war, forces on a battlefield were represented by oblong shapes representing battalion concentrations. In the last war, battles were represented by arrows and prongs, expressive of a more fluid, mobile war, in which points to be reached and engaged were more important than territory to be occupied. The metaphor illustrates the difference between the more static territorial concentration of the Church organized parochially, and the additional structure required if the formative influences of modern society are to be engaged. But we must not press every aspect of the metaphor! The forces to be engaged are not 'the enemy'. Nor could the oblongs ever be obsolete or even secondary, while human beings are creatures of time and space, living in homes, with a place in the Church of God from cradle to grave. But the more fluid, dynamic structure is equally necessary and it can be devil's work to set the one against the other, or to suggest that the one is not important because we have the other. The Industrial Mission supplementary structure is demanded by the new society.

(b) Day to day work of Industrial Mission

It has been proved that where such an agency is set up, representatives of the Church can come to know great numbers of men in industry who are never met through the normal work of the Church, and in a context quite other than the existing shape of the Church could ever meet them. Through discriminate visiting in industry, at offices and in their homes, the functional representatives of a great industry can become known—directors of companies, management, labour managers, educational and training officers, trades union officials, shop stewards, conveners of shop stewards' committees, works' councillors, city councillors, and so on. . . . Nor are they known solely in a 'functional' way, but as men with peculiar burdens and responsibilities, and as friends. And through these contacts, areas are opened to the work and influence of the Church that she would otherwise never penetrate.

Engagement can never be restricted to representative people in the industrial institutions, as though men were important only in their functional capacity, and to the extent that they occupy places of high responsibility. Even if some questionable organizations think in terms of influencing and working through 'key' people, the Church of God can never think in those terms. She acknowledges and respects proper authority, and recognizes the powerful role of influential leadership both for the service of society and of the Christian mission, but the Church must be concerned with all men. An industrial mission therefore is concerned with face-to-face relationships with everybody in industry. And in many cases it can happen. It is proved that, notwithstanding widespread criticisms of the churches, there is a remarkable reservoir of active goodwill, and countless opportunities for meeting men and for projects involving them, men who are among those furthest away from the life of the churches. It can happen where single-minded and long-term work has engendered mutual confidence, and a common understanding and language have removed suspicion, inhibition and a cautionary fear about 'religion'.

In the Don Valley it has proved possible over the years to engage and maintain continuous contact with the largest works in the heavy steel industry, to which full-time and trained ministers have been deployed after negotiation with managements, works' councils, and shop stewards' committees. As status and trust have grown over a long period, the work becomes easier to initiate, and more generally assumed as a perfectly natural thing for the Church to do, and as a natural part of industrial life.

It has been possible to visit men with regularity, as individuals, and as groups within departments of the works, in melting shops, mills, foundries, forges, machine shops and offices, and to become accepted by the working teams of men there. It is possible to talk with men during working periods where the processes allow, at lunch breaks and shift changes, and after working hours in informal groups, many of them specially convened for the purpose. These meetings, if such a euphemistic term should be used to describe them, are informal, 'matey', humorous and yet serious, and will deal with every conceivable issue. And out of such shop-floor contacts many other projects develop. Clearly the minister seeks to be unobtrusive and incidental; he wants few facilities other than the opportunity to fit into the informal pattern of the works, and to discover such opportunities as may present themselves for making contact. In fact they are many—many more than the formal pattern of works' life would often suggest, for industry has its own informal works' organization with its own community and means of communications. But the industrial mission respects the primary function of the works—to make steel! The importance of such contacts and meetings is not to be measured in terms of education, although they may constitute informal and unconscious adult education on a considerable scale; nor in terms of church-membership from a milieu where almost the entire population is unchurched; but in terms of genuine meeting and encounter through which the Church is engaged on a project which the bulk of men concede to be its most proper function— "coming among us", and "going into the highways and hedges". They have some good theology on their side. Reactions of men are countless of course; much indifference, indifference-plus, hardly any opposition, and the possibility of a positive group attitude to Christianity and the Christian viewpoint as it becomes raised in a public way. Through it all new laymen emerge in an intractable area of mission—there is more to be said on this at a later point.

In formal ways, though again in a most informal manner, a large contribution can be made in the field of education and training in industry, in which the steel industry is well to the fore in British industry. The staff of the Industrial Mission in Sheffield are asked by the companies to make regular contributions in the whole range of training, from induction courses and day continuation school for new boys, study groups for apprentices and junior operatives to foreman and manager training, both at company level, and at inter-works and national level through the training courses of the British Iron and Steel Federation. In all of these the minister will fit in with other lecturers and training personnel, but he will have his own angle. His role will be more critical and at the same time more integrative; he will have his own special presuppositions—the bearing of Christian faith and Christian axioms and values on personal and social life, and particularly on industry where human and social problems are posed in quite distinctive ways. Necessarily he will be more general in his scope, yet raise perhaps more searching questions about our practices. Not least he is there to listen, to answer if he can the multitude of questions that men want to ask of the minister when he is on their ground.

Part of the changing character of modern industry is the recognition that education and training, bound up with selection and deployment of men, is of the very lifeblood of industry, and the more far-sighted see that the scope of training goes well beyond the technological concern to include the human-social aspect of industry. It ties up with a new concept of industry—in some quarters—as a community of people engaged in a common project and service, and with a new concept inherent in the modern productive method: that it is the organization that produces rather than the worker, so that social skills and human attitudes and relationships are of great significance. Often it is seen from the point of view of industrial efficiency or social psychology, which are perfectly valid points of view within their own limits. But some go further and see that this raises social, political and philosophical issues, that in turn depend upon value-judgments, social objectives and the meaning of life and history, which are the very stuff of theology. Thus Mr. Graham Hutton, in his analysis of the post-war Anglo-American Productivity Reports, makes the point that productivity and efficiency must be the basis of any modern viable society, but are not ends in themselves. They can be the basis of the bad society as well as the Good Society, and our task is to ensure that they do assist in the achievement of "non-material ends, ethical, social and even spiritual ends".[1] Christianity is precisely concerned with such ends, and with a critique of means, as the end illuminates them.

Industry will not state the issue in this kind of way, naturally enough, but this is how the Church should see it, and it illustrates the significance of a Christian critique of modern society and the importance of machinery that impinges on the industrial scene; without the latter the former is sterile; where the engagement takes place Christianity can be shown to be relevant. It is of interest therefore that in the Sheffield–Rotherham–Stocksbridge area, almost all the large steel works regularly send men from all levels to residential training conferences that are wholly concerned with this theological aspect of the social and industrial problem. They are organized by the Industrial Mission, and are the only regular training projects that include both management and workpeople.

In many other ways there is face-to-face encounter with

[1] *We Too Can Prosper*, Graham Hutton, 1953.

men in the industry—in managers' groups, foremen's groups, professional associations, trades union branches, and through personal and pastoral work of every description. The programme of work built up by the missioners constitutes permanent engagement on a wide front with the basic industry of the area. It also represents the most concentrated visiting of men who are furthest away from the institutions of the churches. With appropriate deviation in method to meet the differences in industries, it suggests a structure that could be evolved and developed in every industrial area of the country. Its justification is written in the long history of the past, and in the progressive accomplishments where such a structure has been devised.

(c) Laymen, lay-training and lay-projects

There may be stalwart defenders of the lay initiative who will interject that, without any 'industrial mission', the Church is always present in industry in the persons of her laity dispersed into their secular callings, so that, at most, all we have to do is to provide suitable schemes of training them. Would that there were many more who held this view and accepted the challenge implied by it!

Unfortunately the admirable theory breaks down for many reasons. Thus because the churches do not embrace a proportionate number of all social groups, there are wide areas, particularly on the ground-floor of industrial life—but by no means confined to this area—where the number of practising Christian laymen available to the Church's training schemes is infinitesimal. Where there are such laymen, they rarely see that an impact might be made beyond personal example—though this of course must not be lightly esteemed; but they do not feel constrained to bear a particular burden and responsibility in terms of social or missionary action. They are rarely "men with a mission", unless they belong to a sectarian group or a highly self-conscious church group, in which case their witness tends to be morally narrow, and religiously either pietist or aggressive. Christians have little understanding of the nature of the secular obedience required, of the kind of critique they should adopt, or the kind of spirituality that might commend the faith they hold and demonstrate its relevance to the real affairs of men. Nor should they be blamed where the concept of the 'good churchman' has been defined so largely in terms of personal religion and loyalty to the Church. But nonetheless, the proper Christian impact goes by default. It simply is a fact that all too often the Christians are not to be found in those places where the issues are most vital, where decisions have to be taken, and where the hard wrestling takes place. And contrariwise, in precisely those places, the men best fitted to make the right kind of impact—who indeed may well be making it—are outside the churches and removed from their influence. It raises the question whether the most studied training of the laity can lead to significant impact in those places where it is most important. That rare beast, the layman, has certainly been discovered by the contemporary Church, but current theory about his whereabouts, his training and use needs realistic scrutiny.

In many of the most important cultural areas the laymen, the potential laymen, simply have to be *discovered*. It is an additional justification for a structure or shape of the Church that gears into industry. And indeed even were there large numbers of laymen from the crucial sections of industry inside the churches, it would still call for special machinery, trained personnel, and supra-parochial training schemes, for training is not exhausted in theological instruction. Its essence is the wrestling by men in the same secular situations with their own problems in the light of common basic insights deduced from their faith. There is a technical aspect to all 'frontier' thinking that calls for special agencies, were it to be developed on a wide scale. It could not happen without specialist agencies set up and deployed to foster it.

Training, whether of men within the Church or of men discovered in the situation by an industrial mission of the Church, is but the beginning, no more than the mere promise that significant laymen might be born. We can assume too much from the mere machinery of training.

Lay training has been developed by the Church to a considerable degree in the past five years, but if the mountain of stimulation is not to bring forth a mouse of consequential action, that training must be less casual and indiscriminate than it often is; it must have more cutting-edge and be tied in to actual work. And from the angle of the industrial world, it must be tied to a practical policy and a concept of the Church permanently at work through the attitudes, insights, decisions and pressures of men engaged in political work, in committees, in board rooms, unions and workshops. General statements on the secular witness of the laity always sound lame and inept, but the generality can cover an immense amount of influence, vision, leadership, boldness and restraint brought to bear by men who are immersed in secular activity, and continuously thinking about the problems of society in the light of their beliefs about man and the world. It is not to say that Christians have unique solutions, blueprints, or infallible 'guidance'. On many issues, indeed on most, the Christian will find men in agreement who would not profess to Christian faith, though his sanctions should be firmer, his questions more penetrating and his illusions fewer. He should have a perspective, a sensitivity, some conscious values and axioms in the light of which his questions are asked even if addressed only to himself, and his decisions made. That is to say, Christians should have pre-suppositions, and the policies, judgments and decisions they make should reflect them. Had there been through the years more disciplined, concentrated and expert thinking by Christians on many social issues, it is conceivable that a far greater unanimity upon many of them would have been the case.

The role of the laity in a missionary church set within an industrial society can go beyond this normative catalytic action. Not perhaps all, but many have a responsibility for expressing a structure of mission within their own orbits of influence, and this constitutes a further extension of a structure of the Church that impinges on the industrial scene. Thus in the steel industry the most advanced expression of the Industrial Mission is where a layman organizes others around him in an informal group. A senior manager may himself convene fellow-managers for a study of their common problems and interests. Not all will be in the churches, probably only a minority; but they share a common situation, have common problems and are colleagues, and in their discussions together the Christian perspective is seen. A younger manager may gather a dozen other young managers to his home periodically. Or twenty men spend their lunch-time together once a fortnight, gathered together and led by one of their number. A lad will organize a meeting for other apprentices, putting up their own speakers, and inviting people to meet them from other parts of the company. Or where regular meetings are impossible, in a melting shop or a rolling mill, a man, often the trade union representative himself, represents a certain point of view and a certain interest in the bearing of Christianity on industry, and is known as a man who has this concern.

These '*lay projects*' as they are called represent a stage in industrial mission where the layman carries a project entirely himself, his leadership accepted, and the missioner is only present when called to make some particular contribution in which he may be expert. These projects are the finest fruits of an industrial mission structure that gears into the industrial scene with unremitting persistence. They are young, and often frail, but where they exist they demonstrate the most genuine objective of industrial mission, in the discovery and stimulation of laymen who in turn can engage those nearest to them. The lay-projects are not 'cells' or underground movements, they are not meetings of 'militants', though within them must be some men of wise and sober militancy; and they are not meetings of committed Christians, whose visible assembly should surely be in the 'church' and not in the 'world'. They must be open to all in the department, the office, the workshop, the natural environment of the man who takes the initiative. Such projects suggest an immense range of possibilities, and the most tangible expression of the engagement of the Church and the world, not as an attempt to capture the world, but to engage it in a natural, infectious, and 'theonomous' manner. But they do not happen by accident, but as a consequence of continuous mission, in which the missioners can be likened to fuses laid to the barrels of gunpowder!

In all soberness it can be said that action of this kind could become a commonplace up and down the life of the nation, in industry, in other cultural areas, and—however we define it—within Caesar's household itself. If this concept is not entirely illusory, ten years of concentrated work based upon common policy could establish the Church in an industrial society in an entirely new way. So Industrial Mission seeks to become a laymen's movement, expressed in a cadre of laymen engaged in projects within their own areas of influence. It suggests the most proper and permanent mission of the Church in the world, of far greater significance for Britain than a 'priest-workman' movement or the ordination of laymen in their secular callings. It is unthinkable, even undesirable, that there should be ordained men enough to penetrate the natural communities of the secular world. But the multiplication of active laymen holds the promise of a 'theonomous' relationship of Church and society; it shows concern, but also respect for the proper autonomy of the secular, and guarantees a bulwark against an improper intrusion of the Church as an official body; a matter on which the Protestant churches should be as cautious as the secular institutions of society undoubtedly are.

(d) A national policy

We have seen that a project of the Church designed to engage the principalities and powers of modern industry, certainly those basic industries of the country that set the industrial tone of the nation's life, cannot be restricted to a parish or district. It must have freedom to range over the industrial field, and its area of operation should be dictated by the structure of industry, and not by the shape of ecclesiastical jurisdictions, whether of parish, diocese or even province. The churches have initiated industrial projects of various kinds in recent years, but each has been set within its own area of ecclesiastical administration, and set up by the will or permission of that authority. Inevitably, it is fair to say, the work has been piecemeal, uncoordinated, based on quite different presuppositions, and dependent for initiation on chance factors and personal decisions, as a result of which work has been weak, and easily terminated. Sometimes the lack of intensity or continuity and the absence of adequate theological and industrial insights have failed to give justification to the work; not infrequently the second five years were not done to reap the harvest of the first five, and the possibilities of the third five not even glimpsed. Always there have been inadequate resources of man-power and money. Let it be said emphatically that the Church is not likely to justify work in so huge and hard a field without a clear vision of what should be done, without a masterly efficiency, great persistence and considerable cost.

Efficient development of industrial work calls for concentrated, deepening and permanent work in each of the large industrial centres, with local status and local roots. But the local work should not be isolated from other pieces of work in the country. Efficient development also calls for a national co-ordination of work and the operation of an over-all national policy. It is required in the interests of common policy, common presuppositions, and common objectives. It is also required by the need to train ministers for industrial mission work, and to secure a planned deployment and continuity of staff—for at present there are few competent men available for this work, and they are easily drained away from their fields of operation by Church authorities who want to initiate industrial work without the cost of training men for a planned expansion of the work.

But, most important of all, a national structure and policy in the Church is dictated by the national structure of the basic industries themselves, which not only have their various local manifestations, but also area and national projections. Nor of course is this true only of the industries as such; the trades unions too have their local expressions, but also their district and national expressions. This industrial structure is still developing, the consequence of many technological and economic factors, company-grouping, rationalization and integration, nationalization and so on. It follows that basic British industry is more than the immense lay-out of factories, plants and mines up and down the country; it is also an integrated organic system, analogous to the arterial or nervous system of the human body, and the intelligent engagement of this integrated structure by an agency of the Church itself calls for a national structure with its own national projection, ensuring at one level continuous local work, capable at another of relating itself to the national projections of industry wherever they are, and able to develop work from one area of the country to another along the lines of *industrial* communications.

Thus if a large steel combine has plants in, say Sheffield, and its administrative centre in that city—with works also in other parts of the country, any negotiating of work at the centre should take all the plants into consideration, and contacts made through the Church's work in one area should lead to developments in plants in other parts of the country. This is to follow the lines of industrial communication. It is even clearer in such an industry as coal-mining—for coal seams are no respecters of ecclesiastical boundaries! A single administrative area of the National Coal Board may cover three or four dioceses, and clearly any discussions and negotiations with the industry or the trades union organization should take cognizance of the whole area. Many illustrations could be given. And London, of course, is as important in an over-all policy as Rome was to St. Paul, for many of the basic industries and largest companies of the country find their administrative centres there, as also the highest points of trades union administration. Not that the contacts could be fruitful in London without the local and area development taking place at the same time—otherwise one might be discussing work that was never initiated. Moreover it can be assumed that industrial powers, whether companies or unions—particularly unions—are not likely to be impressed unless what they deem to be significant work is already happening in their industries, unless spurs have already been won and men on the ground-floor of industry behind the work.

An efficient policy of the Church therefore would need to reflect this national and integrated structure of British industry, in the evolving of its own appropriate structure of engagement. The development of work in one place should play into another, and the negotiating of work in one place should take others into account. The experience and 'know-how' should be available for the whole field. It would require over-all co-ordination, an integrating point, and easy communication piece with piece. Such a scheme may seem extremely formal and over-organized —organized it needs to be, but formal, no! We have already made the point that industrial mission work is based on a web of personal relationships at all levels of industrial life; experience also shows that these personal contacts naturally lead on to others, along the many lines of industrial communication. It may look very complicated; in fact it is clear and simple, if the children of light would learn from the children of this world! It is the alternative, piecemeal, unco-ordinated and ephemeral work that is muddled and inefficient. It may sound an ambitious and audacious project. No doubt it is both. But it does not mean flamboyant demonstration, mass attack by the Church or 'aggressive evangelism'. Rather is it a task to be undertaken discreetly, advisedly and soberly, presupposing serious, long-term and permanent attempt on the part of the Church to engage the national life, aiming at a more positive and informed participation of the laity in what are already their proper fields of responsibility. The institutions of society should welcome that. It should not appear excessively ambitious to a Church of the nation.

Undoubtedly such a mission structure should be ecumenical in composition, though a basic theological unity would be necessary. The strong emphasis that the secular obedience of the Church dispersed into the world is a means and instrument of the Kingdom should reduce to a minimum those difficulties that wreck so much inter-denominational work, which is solely concerned with adding to the churches. Indeed, a widespread movement of laymen engaged together in the world might well put the ecumenical problem into an entirely new context.

(e) Organs of thinking

It is patently clear that a policy of engagement with the institution of industry will call not only for efficient mechanics of engagement but also for disciplined thinking within the Church upon the nature, problems, and potentialities of our new society—thinking of a high order. A Church away from the main stream of society's life can avoid this hard discipline, but not so a Church deliberately and deeply immersed by its own planned mission. If there is any truth in the claim that the Church should seek to express at least something of the conscience of the nation, and if there is any truth in the thesis that men are conditioned by the principalities and powers of this world, by social, political and economic systems and industrial institutions—if any of this is true, it lays upon the Church of this age an intellectual task before which that of any earlier age pales. We desperately need organs of good thinking, and God deliver us from a Church religiously determined to engage the world, without the intellectual capacity to speak intelligently to its real problems! Nor is this a matter of mere exhortation; it is a plea for the promotion of deliberately planned thinking as part of the Church's mission in an industrialized society.

This is not to say that the Church can come to infallible judgments. Indeed, a Protestant understanding of the Church precludes the notion that ecclesiastical authority can make judgments on matters requiring technical competence for an obedient laity to observe. But that is a wholly different thing from saying that the Church has no responsibility for seeking the most expert thinking and judgment on social matters, in the light of all that can be deduced from the Christian faith. In the last resort a man must be spiritually free to make his own decisions, but that does not absolve the Church from seeking a good judgment and a common mind in the Body of Christ. At least the right questions should be posed, and able thinking upon them be available in the Church. Nor does it follow that Christians will necessarily be in agreement with one another. There is a proper secular autonomy, and it is inherent in the Protestant understanding of the secular that Christianity does not provide exact social programmes, political, economic and industrial directives—it is for such reasons that Christians should be opposed to the formation of 'Christian' parties, or 'Christian' trades unions, which always create an ambiguous relationship of the Church to society, and actually foster the growth of the autonomous society.

But Christianity should provide a theological perspective, an understanding of the interests of the Kingdom, a knowledge of man's nature and destiny, basic values that should be reflected in men's social relationships, that add up, if not to a social philosophy, certainly to a social critique, in the light of which human society, social programmes, and economic and industrial organization can be scrutinized, attitudes adopted and decisions made. Christianity can provide a context within which the "ethics of the situation" become clearer. One of the most serious weaknesses and indictments of the contemporary Church is the lack of such a critique, and no amount of fidelity to the Church or even devotion to her Lord can make up for its absence.

There are clear reasons for its absence. Partly, the structure of the Church does not dictate its necessity, for the Church is organized for worship and not for mission and secular engagement. Even where material exists, it is foreign to what the Church expects as her proper intellectual food. And partly, there is no planned means of continuous thinking within the Church, either on the nature of the Christian critique itself, or on the contemporary issues upon which such a critique should bear. Hence the need for organs of thinking to serve the Church at large, and indeed areas far beyond it, and at the service of such machinery of engagement as should be devised. Without it, Christians cannot possibly make the contribution to the life of the world that they should; without it the thinking within the Church is not consciously and distinctively Christian at all, but chameleon-like, reflecting the instinctive views of the social group of which it is part. There can be no word of prophecy where there is no critique. Perhaps the Church cannot make prophets, but whether there is a dearth of prophets, or whether their judgments are heard throughout the land, or whether they prophesy outside the camp, the Church should be concerned to foster a prophetic school: organs of thinking on the problems of society at the very time that they are emerging.

To anyone of theological acumen, and in continuous contact with men in their industrial life, the issues on which good thinking is required stand patently clear. First of all, we need a modern exposition, well documented with contemporary illustrations, of the elements of the Christian critique itself. We need to grasp the idea of the 'middle axioms', to use William Temple's term, that there are axioms, assumptions, or principles to be deduced from the great Biblical doctrines, which are commendable to reason and an enlightened conscience, but which find their ultimate sanction in the declared nature of God and of His word for men. In the light of such axioms men can approach the empirical problem, in analysis, judgment and social purpose. Hence the term 'middle' axiom—between doctrine on the one hand, and the concrete situation in which men have to decide and act on the other. If there is a Christian perspective from which men may look at the totality of the secular world, as distinct from a purely religious outlook that bears on some part only of the personal moral life, it can only be created out of such assumptions and axioms, and it is tragic that in the modern world in which the ideological conflict is at its deepest, the Christian critique and perspective is so generally wanting. For lack of vision people perish, or pseudo-Christian ideologies like Moral Re-Armament or crude anti-Communist crusade are enabled to masquerade as prophetic Christian judgment. Even the very elect are seduced, and the truth is crucified.

This is no place to delineate the diverse elements that go to make up a Christian critique, nor the range of questions upon which they should bear in our modern society. It is precisely the task crying out to be done. Suffice it to say that those tremendous Biblical axioms—that God wills righteousness, justice and fair dealing among men, that His justice is slanted to the weaker, that the human race is one, that sin is lodged in man's own nature and the social entities of his making, that history is the scene of man's freedom and of God's wrath and grace, and that His mercy to men is extended in both Law and Gospel—these, and many more, provide a point of view wide and deep enough to apprehend the world of our time. It cannot be said too often that we are not given 'answers' and 'solutions' in the field of practicalities where limits of what is possible are set by many factors, where moral relativities are inevitable, where men have no infallibility, and where any plans have to be generally acceptable and worked by men. But the perspective permits a common language and a common frame of thought that set some limit to the reign of Babel that must otherwise obtain. To provide a perspective from which men look at their world has always been the proper role of effective religion; how much more so that of the Hebrew-Christian religion supremely concerned with a theonomous world, the obedience of men to God in their handling of it, and with the establishment of His Kingdom on earth.

The critique must bear on the range of economic and industrial problems with which we are beset, and which are posed in quite new ways in the post-war world. Men are still prone to make ephahs small and shekels great, but the consequences in an economy ever increasing in complexity and one so delicately poised can be ruinous. Has the Christian perspective any bearing on a situation where the life of the nation is held in the grip of economic factors which men feel to be beyond the influence of their own personal contribution, or beyond the area of their own personal responsibility? In the light of the Biblical axioms, and in the light of the facts of social history, what commentary should be made on the issues of wealth and its distribution, and on the burning question of wage and salary differentials and the complex but clearly recognizable problems stemming from them? What should be said of the trend to the more efficient, necessarily planned and streamlined society, based as it is on greater equality of opportunity than ever before obtained in our industrial society, and yet in danger of producing a functional class structure in the nation, with the threatened dangers of a 'managerial society', and its accompanying 'rabble hypothesis'? And at the level of industrial organization, what are the factors that can make for common purpose, interest and community, and how can they be strengthened? How can industrial relations be improved, and men at all levels give of their best without reliance on 'whip', 'carrot', or paternalist 'soft-soap'? What do justice, fair dealing, honesty, responsibility, care for others . . . demand of us in terms of industrial life? How can men discover a higher status in their work, pride in the group accomplishment, and what are the necessary satisfactions they should find in the project of industry?

And these in turn raise wider questions. What is the nature of the 'good society', its proper 'feel', its picture of social relationships and its common orientation, to which efficiency, planning, political programmes and social welfare are the means? Clearer understanding, more sensitive intuition, and stronger conviction at this point could do much to deliver contemporary politics from the doldrums of apathy and cynicism.

All of this is to insist that there is a huge intellectual task requiring the disciplined co-operation of the best minds of the Church and indeed of many who may be outside it; the co-operation of theologians who understand the secular problems, laymen with their appropriate expert and technical knowledge who live with the problems, 'lay-theologians', men of wisdom and good counsel who know the social temperature and have a finger on the social pulse. A Church seeking to help her own members, let alone a Church seeking engagement and dialogue with the world, would require more effective machinery for thinking, good minds corporately focused on the hardest issues of our time, some *planned* use of brains at the service of the Christian mission in the contemporary world. Tawney's devastating word that the Church has ceased to count because it has ceased to think is not without point. Its implications would be even more urgent if the Church were more closely geared into this problem-beset world.

*   *   *

III. THE MISSIONARY STRUCTURE OF THE LOCAL CHURCH IN AN INDUSTRIAL SOCIETY

Because a strong case can be made out for supplementary, extra-parochial machinery that bears upon the institutions or functional structures of an industrialized society, it does not follow that the present territorial, parochial shape of the Church is the perfect design for the discharge of its own proper local task in the highly urbanized society. The emergence of a new form of society has not only left the Church unrelated to typical and formative social projections; it has also shown the 'local church' to be inadequate as a missionary structure in its own territorial area, a fact that has contributed to the general estrangement of the populations in the industrial areas. We should not, of course, draw the conclusion that effective industrial mission could in any way obviate the need of effective local territorial churches—a point unnecessary to make but for stupid conclusions drawn in some quarters whenever an industrial mission case is argued. Indeed it is presumptuous even to compare an industrial mission structure, hardly existent as it is, necessary though it may be, with the massive parochial structure of the Church covering every square inch of the country. Each has a proper and different function in the total life of the great Church of the nation, and rather than engage in odious comparisons we should concede the argument for the one, and face the predicament of the other.

The predicament of the local church in the industrial town is not new—a fact that stands out from our study of Sheffield where the swamping of the Church by population increase can be traced to the early eighteenth century. From the time that extensive urbanization destroyed the small community character of the town there has been an ever-widening missionary problem, partially concealed though it may have been at some periods by crowded churches and chapels. To-day, but for very favourable areas, the nakedness is conspicuous in the desolation of many churches. For those with eyes to see, the problem was always there; the advance of time producing ever greater populations estranged for all the reasons we have examined, amorphous groups, without defined community shape, whatever smaller social groupings were enjoyed in the submerged classes. The fluidity of population in the present century has greatly increased the problem. The cost in membership to the Church of England and the 'reformed' churches in general through this process has been immense—the more so, in that traditionally they have held their members by community pull, by local attachments and personal 'belonging', factors all dependent on reasonable stability of population, rather than by strong doctrinal and ecclesiastical authority. In theory, no doubt, fidelity should be enough to hold Christians in the life of the Church wherever they may find themselves, and whatever social convention in their milieu might be; but men in general are weaker than this—they need dykes and supports, the external disciplines if they are Roman Catholics, and the personal attachments, the community pull, the feeling of belonging to the local church, if they are Protestants. And if this is so, in a society where community is weak, mobility of population high, and the bulk of the people estranged, the Protestant churches, the Church of England and the Free Churches will suffer the greatest losses, through erosion of their membership and the incapacity to embrace and hold potential members. It clearly happens.

It is tempting to think that if we had more clergy and ministers we could deal with the problem. Certainly the shortage of ministers in recent decades has aggravated it, and an increase in their numbers with the consequent probability of longer incumbencies would undoubtedly be good. Certainly, too, no missionary policy in the parishes would have any chance of success without a halt to the present rapid movement of clergy. But the history of the case does not allow us to think that this by itself could substantially change the situation. For even in the heyday of successful evangelicalism, when churches and chapels were full, entire social groups were outside, and the very size of congregations held together by strong social habit precluded effective mission without, minimized pastoral care within, and dwarfed the individual into insignificance. In neither case, of those outside or those inside, were pastoral care and the converting relationship very effective. It was implicitly or explicitly recognized by such men as Thomas Arnold and Horace Mann, and local Sheffield ministers like John Livesey and Samuel Earnshaw; it was precisely why they pleaded for many more smaller churches, and smaller gatherings of Christian people, and why the former two pointed to the Methodist organization as an example. And rightly so, for the organization of the Methodist Societies into classes of a dozen or so members undoubtedly provided the inner strength and cohesion of the Connexion, the strongest dyke in the most adverse days.

Hopes and fears

The contemporary Church is in fact much concerned with the shape and witness of the local church, and indeed her very pre-occupation with the parochial problem is liable to blind her to those broader relationships with society at large, with the nation as an entity, with social institutions such as industry, which we have maintained to be proper interests of the 'great church'. The signs of awakening at the grass roots of the Church's life are many indeed, to be seen in liturgical renewal and parish meetings as means of strengthening a common life and common mind in the Body of Christ, in parish visitations by the laity, ecumenical assemblies of local congregations, house-meetings, house-churches, and even 'para-churches' if so dangerous a word may be allowed. All these are incomparably healthier than the mass demonstrations of renowned evangelists that have featured in the post-war British religious scene, and which are so often associated with Biblical literalism, individ-ualist concepts of salvation, and a neglect of the social conscience.

But good though the signs are as experiments and evidence of the possibilities, in the face of the long-standing and chronic missionary situation as history discloses it, it must be questioned whether the new expressions of vitality are completely adequate. Often, as parish communion and parish meeting, they define the inner shape of the church, rather than an external shape impinging on the parish—they can even become "the thing to do", cutting away the 'fringers' without inducing new vitality in the faithful. Parish visitation by the laity is usually related to occasional missions, and the house-meetings and house-churches, more admired than reproduced, are dependent for their creation and persistence on the continued ministry of particularly gifted men. The promising engagements therefore are localized, spontaneous—even evanescent, as ministers come and go, lay people move, and the Church, Gamaliel-like at best, leaves them in splendid isolation.

This is not to disparage genuine signs of vitality—the very opposite—the real weakness is that they are neither the product of long-term mission policy on the part of ecclesiastical author-ity, nor built into the structure of the Church at large. The Church has no policy except that of maintenance; there is no attempt to work out the required shape of the local church if it is to be a missionary instrument, as distinct from a centre for public worship. And let us have no doubt that a missionary structure has to be planned and organized. There will always be outstanding men who can produce a missionary parish with the bricks to hand, even in the midst of ruin, but the Church cannot hope to man every parish with outstanding men. This surely is the point of a missionary policy, structure and organization, and a theological training of ministers to serve it—for ordinary mortals can operate a good system, but only extraordinary ones can work effectively in a bad one.

There will be those who despise all policy and planning and even claim the Holy Ghost for their support; there will be those who regard all attempts to produce a new shape of the church as new-fangled nonsense, resting content with maintaining the inherited plant of the Church, with providing the opportunities for public worship, not wanting to bother people who come. They may be able to do this in more favourable districts but not in the industrial areas, the huge new estates and the downtown wastes. In these intractable areas a missionary church is bound to exert pressure, put out feelers, engage the life of the parish, plough up the ground and sow. Moreover a missionary structure must ensure all this in a *permanent* way. Some of the finest contemporary expressions of mission have been done before on a large scale, and yet have fallen away into desuetude. Thus Sheffield had over a thousand 'district visitors' up to the 'twenties, and, as we have already seen, a vigorous parish like St. Mary's, Bramall Lane, had fifty lay workers visiting in the parish, cottage-meetings, and regular visiting of the small local works, at the end of the last century. And yet it all fell away. True, many factors, as we have seen, were responsible; but nonetheless it shows that the missionary character of the local church was a matter of chance, no part of official policy, not built into the very structure of the Church.

Whatever the inside shape of the church—and here there is bound to be diversity of opinion reflecting differences of theology and church order—the case for an outward shape designed for missionary engagement is unanswerable. But it must be based upon over-all persistent policy, largely sustained by the laity and not subject to interruption and new beginning on different lines every three or seven years as ministers come and go. One of the hardest lessons to be learned is that continuity of public worship in a parish and even of pastoral care is quite a different thing from continuity of *mission*—a lesson that the Church of England has more cause to learn than any other communion.

Methodist precedent

Historically the most creative and tested external shape of the Christian community, related to the greatest expansion in "modern Church history", was that devised by John Wesley, and maintained as a basic structural element in all the successive waves of Methodist revival for over 150 years. It is a long way back in search of precedent, to be sure, but in our enthusiasm for evangelistic techniques that are themselves 'throwbacks' to the nineteenth century we should be singularly biased to ignore the mission of a slightly earlier period that reduces any subsequent revival to insignificance. True, different winds blow to-day; the mood within the churches and in the estranged masses outside is wholly unlike that of the eighteenth and early nineteenth centuries. That is to say, the sociology of the situation is quite different to-day—and the mood and sensibilities of an age are of crucial importance in determining the content, shape and probable expectation of the Christian mission. And it is unlikely that a "Wesley redivivus" could awaken the people in the same way to-day. But there are some features in the present situation akin to those of earlier days, in the large concentrations of people alienated from the Church, indifferent and antipathetic, and feeling it is "not for us". It is not inconceivable that the structure he devised in the course of the greatest missionary expansion of English history has something to teach us to-day in spite of the immeasurable changes in intellectual outlook and social conditions that have taken place.

Certainly there are conditions and needs to be fulfilled by the modern missionary project that were met in a quite remarkable way through the early Methodist organization—notably in the 'class-meetings'. Thus there is the need for smaller, warmer, more community-minded expressions of the Christian community than attendance at public worship alone can provide; and in a secular society the image of the Gospel and of the Church is grievously distorted both to those within and to those without, when the Body of Christ is reduced, seemingly, to "going to church". This is now in fact widely realized in the

Church, and much has been done to make the assembling of the Church, whether for worship or for deliberation, a real community of people, sharing a rich common life; though it is often secured only because the smallness of numbers permits it, and, as we have already noted, the community created all too often defines the inner life of the church rather than the shape of a missionary instrument bearing on the parish. There is no certain evidence that the class-meetings as such were very spear-head and cutting-edge in the Methodist expansion, but undoubtedly the 'militants' were made there and the new members were held within them. Certainly too they provided a structure through which a close pastoral care was exercised even where the ministry was remote and itinerant—a structure moreover that could be manned by ordinary intelligent laymen.

It seems therefore that the early Methodist precedent met some conditions that must still be met in a missionary planning of the Church. And most important, where there is psychological and sociological resistance to church attendance, the case for the "para-church", the "church outside the church", the "church without walls", which is more easily met and existentially experienced, is strong indeed, as some of the most audacious and creative mission experiments in recent years have shown. And where this can happen a rallying-point is squarely set within the estranged culture-pattern itself, capable of bearing upon it, engaging it, staining it—which does not happen or happens in quite inadequate ways where isolated individuals contract out of that pattern at specified times on Sundays to worship in the local church, and whose impact within the culture-pattern must be weakened by being individualized and representative of an institution itself outside the pattern.

The case for the small, local, indigenous expressions of the Christian community, defining the external shape of the church impinging on the parish, can be argued on theological, missionary and pastoral grounds, the last by no means the least important when the weaker brethren drop out of sight so easily under the exactions of modern living, and when the population by its very size is beyond the care of the most diligent and stable ministry. Though in such a different world, many needs analogous to our own were met in Methodism by the subdivision of the larger Society into the classes—manageable groups of definite known membership, for whom a 'leader' was responsible, and with whom the little flock was bound to meet as a normative expression of their life of corporate faithfulness. It was not an alternative to worship in the larger chapel—nor merely supplementary; it was an integral structural part of the Methodist Society, and its inner strength. It is clear that the purpose they could serve was not realized from the beginning, even if the structure was ever subjected to a scientific examination! Indeed, originally the method had been adopted in Bristol in 1742 as an efficient means of collecting money to defray the debt on the first chapel built in that city. Very soon afterwards, however, it was adopted in London for pastoral reasons, as Wesley himself writes:

> . . . I appointed several earnest and sensible men to meet me, to whom I showed the great difficulty I had long found of knowing the people who desired to be under my care. After much discourse, they all agreed, there could be no better way to come to a sure, thorough knowledge of each person, than to divide them into classes, like those at Bristol, under the inspection of those in whom I could most confide. This was the origin of our classes in London, for which I can never sufficiently praise God; the unspeakable usefulness of the institution having ever since been more and more manifest.[1]

The importance Wesley put upon effective organization cannot be over-emphasized; we have already seen his criticism of revival preaching in Sheffield that awakened the people and left them to fall asleep again. At Norwich he discounted the members who failed to meet in class—"they hang on but a single thread".[2] And the Church of England he described as "a rope of sand", surely because of the casual relation of so many of its conformist members. It would indeed be interesting to know the extent to which purely sociological perceptions led him to this view. In fact the class-meetings became the strong ground-floor structure of the Methodist societies, accomplishing ends that were never envisaged—not only religious and pastoral but also creating vital centres of responsible community life often set in the midst of misery and debauchery. They produced an active and articulate laity—at least great numbers of them—such as no other denomination has produced, not only within the Connexion but in secular society, as the leadership

---

[1] *Journals*, Apr. 25, 1742.   [2] *Journals*, Sept. 3, 1759.

given by great numbers of Methodists in the early Friendly Societies, Trades Unions and Co-operative Societies shows.

The extent of this lay initiative was in marked distinction to other denominations, and associated with an itinerant ministry it made Methodism, at base, a lay-movement, even in the Wesleyan Connexion, the autocratic character of its Conference notwithstanding. No wonder that Horace Mann in his comments on the 1851 Religious Census recommended the "plan fforded by the Methodist community, in which some ten or fifteen thousand laymen are employed not merely in the work of visitation, but also in that of preaching. . . . Nothing probably has more contributed than this to their success amongst the working population". Of class leaders at this time there were probably not less than 25,000, apart from all those other lay offices that Methodism provided.[1] It is interesting indeed to note that to-day the best thinking in the churches and in the ecumenical movement is stressing the urgency of an active laity, not only as theological propriety but in the interests of mission and of secular obedience in the world.

So many of the requirements of modern mission call for smaller purposeful organizations of Christians that this early Methodist structure deserves minute examination. If the mission of the Church is to go ahead in a serious, business-like, persistent way, whether in the territorial parish field or in the wider field of social structures of our modern society, some kind of working subdivision of the larger Christian community, both of the congregation and in vocational groups, seems imperative. Not of course that we could transpose the old class-meetings into the present, just as they were. They were *closed* groups, full membership requiring a term of probation; to-day the lay missionary project must be *open* and inviting to others in its milieu as part of its very justification, although the basic membership, the committed core carrying the project must be known and completely reliable. 'Sheep-stealing' should still be forbidden as in the early days, both in the interest of efficient organization and to ensure the maintenance of the various outposts—the gregarious habits of Christians need to be watched.

The pietism of the early classes would be quite inappropriate to-day in a missionary structure; Christian disciplines are no

---

1 *Methodism and the Working Class Movements of England, 1800–1850*, R. F. Wearmouth, 1937: p. 11.

less important, but pre-occupation with the narrowly religious is ruled out for all the reasons we have already considered. Nothing human can be alien to them—in relation to which they constitute centres of infection, affection and disaffection! Undoubtedly they were too inquisitorial! A Church under judgment is essential, and at present we have no effective means for securing it, but "full inquiry into the behaviour of every person" with appropriate reproof and advice from the leader would hardly serve in present days—any more than some of the quaint old rules prohibiting "the putting on of gold or costly apparel", the wearing of "needless ornaments, such as rings, ear-rings, necklaces, lace and ruffles", "the taking of snuff or tobacco, unless prescribed by a physician", or even the "evil speaking of magistrates or of ministers"! But others are still sound enough—"To be at a word at buying and selling", "to pawn nothing, no not to save life", to avoid "softness and needless self-indulgence", to feed the hungry, clothe the naked, and visit those who are sick and in prison; not to speak of the practicalities that ensured the pastoral care—the weekly meeting, the weekly contribution, the mark on the class-paper —D if the member is distant from home, S if sick, B if prevented from attendance by business, N if neglectful, a P if present, and an A if the reason for absence is not known, all to receive the appropriate follow-up.

The Rules for the Society that John and Charles Wesley promulgated in 1743 make fascinating reading, and demonstrate their conviction that serious Christianity cannot be produced in a casual, conformist way, but only by discipline, good organization and purposeful witness. That is why this brief excursion into early Methodism is no antiquarian pursuit. Wesley was right; the casual, conformist adherence to the Church, every man left to care for himself, is a rope of sand in a missionary situation, the grains scattered by any wind, capable neither of giving inner cohesion to the members nor of tying in those without. He forged a chain of steel, flexible yet each link with its own strength, and the "glorious failure" of Methodism may not be entirely unrelated to the gradual neglect of his premises in the palmy years of great congregations.

A missionary structure based on the deployment of lay forces for meeting, witness, and catalytic action within their own indigenous areas, whether geographical or cultural, presupposes elements of strength within the Church, and it can begin where the Church is strong and courageous. It depends upon the quality of the Church, or quality within the Church, rather than on quantity. Yet on the other hand it does not 'unchurch' the weaker brethren where it does not succeed in fortifying them. While at the core and base of a missionary structure must be committal and planned deployment, it does not follow that the Church shrinks to a fellowship of 'saints'—which is no picture of the Catholic Church. The very fact that the sub-divisions of the total structure must be open and infectious and secular in their concern is recognition that a missionary structure must merge the stronger with the weaker, the Church with the world, which is the very essence of its purpose. It is designed for radical engagement, not radical disengagement. And early Methodism, that in some ways seems sect-minded, was in fact saved from the sect-mentality, becoming a missionary movement, a 'great church' with adherents who numbered twice and thrice the number of those who were actually members of Societies—and how many who came to the chapels in more casual ways must have become members in course of time, strengthening the core and becoming active in all those ways for which there was provision. An early defence of Methodism that some were wholly 'Methodist' while others still went to the Church for baptism, the Sacrament, and for burial maintains that "the Methodists believe, that they were not raised up to do good to any one denomination of people only, but to rush through every open door, to spread scriptural holiness over the land, and in some measure over the world; till names, and sects, and parties fall, and all Christians be one fold under one shepherd".[1] This is no sectarian view.

Wesley did not seek to form a new denomination: he sought a method and machinery whereby awakened Christians could be nurtured and held together in a new order of serious-minded laymen, the ultimate object of which was missionary engagement with the world. However unhappy some of the consequences of his magnificent work, that is precisely what we need to-day. It is of the very nature of our situation (as of his) that there should be a 'great church', open to society, baptizing, marrying and burying all who come—and yet because of the desperate weakness of a Church no more than this and in a

[1] *Portraiture of Methodism*, J. Crowther, 1815.

far more intractable missionary situation, that there should also be planned machinery for engagement within the very fabric of our secular society. There is a tension here that must be held at all costs, since the triumph of one over the other would be ruinous, but it is part of that proper tension between the Church and the world which in the 'great' Catholic Church must be held within the Church as well as outside it. In fact it is implicitly accepted in any concept of lay-training, but lay-training is but the beginning and could itself be casual; it must pass on to permanent planned lay-projects that engage the secular world. It would seem that degrees of fidelity, strength and militancy must exist in a Church that is at once a 'great church' and yet set within an acute missionary situation; and if this is so, there should be planned machinery to ensure the polarity.

The strongest case can be argued from the historico-sociological evidence we have cited, that the subdivided structure is required not only for missionary engagement within mammoth estranged populations, but as a permanent structural element in a 'great church' set in the highly-populated society. It is required as a balance to the expression of the Church in large congregations, without which a mass conformity is the best that could be expected: an expression of the Church that is bound to lack some of the most crucial marks of the New Testament. The tragedy of the break between the Church of England and Methodism is not only that the forces of Christianity were split across the nation during the most formative period of modern history; it has also precluded the use of the Methodist structure—whatever deviations might have been required in it—by the National Church. Were each to give of its best to a united Church of England, a renewed modernized missionary structure—for the old one has fallen into disuse—would be the richest contribution from the Methodist tradition.

Reformation

It is fair to say that since the decay of religious conformity set in, and in the working-class areas since their very beginnings, the Church at large, planted out over the nation, has failed to devise a missionary structure; and to that extent she is a survival from the past. Humanly speaking it is not conceivable that the situation can be retrieved by a laissez-faire policy of leaving the inherited plant of the Church as it is, with a few reforms and a little streamlining dictated by a weaker position in the national life. This is in fact no policy at all. Retrenchment, a *reculer pour mieux sauter*, is a temptation, but it is unrealistic in the national situation. Periodic spurts of so-called 'aggressive evangelism' are subject to a score of criticisms and are hopelessly enervating. And reliance on a few chance if laudable experiments, whether in the parish or in the field of industrial mission, that are mere token unless embodied in national policy, is like taking drugs. What is required is no less than over-all reform. But reform is native to the Christian Church, and the test of reform will be the capacity of the Church to engage the life of the nation, from its great "principalities and powers" to its base in the common life of the people, in planned, persistent, sensitive and relevant mission. It will call for courageous leadership, and for that Biblical, existential understanding of faith as courage, that grows with committal and work, even where it fails. We should not delay the hard national planning of it.

Appendix I

RELIGIOUS CENSUS FIGURES. SHEFFIELD, 1881

Church of England

	Sittings	Morn.	Even.	Total
ST. MARY'S	2,000	416	548	964
ST. PHILIP'S	2,000	410	1,251	1,661
ST. GEORGE'S	1,800	1,047	1,408	2,455
PARISH CHURCH	1,200	956	1,234	2,190
			[842 afternoon	
ST. PAUL'S	1,200	420	528	948
—— MISSION	100		171	171
CHRIST CHURCH, ATTERCLIFFE	1,135	303	479	782
ALL SAINTS	1,000	525	667	1,192
ST. MICHAEL'S	1,000	319	440	759
HOLY TRINITY, WICKER	1,000	331	472	803
			[324 afternoon	
ST. MARK'S	900	630	620	1,250
ST. JOHN'S, RANMOOR	559	267	245	512
ST. ANDREW'S, SHARROW	800	605	497	1,102
ECCLESALL CHURCH	750	298	290	588
ST. SILAS'	800	439	515	954
—— MISSION	120		52	52
ST. THOMAS', CROOKES	600	348	274	622
CHRIST CHURCH, PITSMOOR	842	741	802	1,543
—— MISSION	200		139	139
ST. STEPHEN'S	636	333	430	763
ST. MARY'S, WALKLEY	650	274	338	612
ST. JAMES'	750	350	502	852
			[250 afternoon	
ST. BARNABAS	680	337	424	761
FULWOOD CHURCH	368	181	166	347
ST. SIMON'S	850	132	228	360
ST. MATTHEW'S	540	152	239	391
ST. JOHN'S, OWLERTON	560	510	357	867
—— MISSION	100		62	62
ST. JUDE'S, ELDON STREET	600	276	452	728
ST. JOHN'S, PARK	750	387	316	703
SALE MEMORIAL CHURCH, ST. LUKE	778	166	283	449
SHREWSBURY HOSPITAL	200	33	32	65
ST. MATTHIAS	761	401	562	963
DARNALL CHURCH	500	184	215	399
CARBROOK CHURCH	700	200	471	671
			[227 mission services	
CHRIST CHURCH, HEELEY	360	87	97	184

275

Church of England—cont.

	Sittings	Morn.	Even.	Total
ST. LUKE'S, HOLLIS CROFT . .	500	147	197	344
ST. THOMAS', BRIGHTSIDE . . .	500	118	157	275
ST. BARTHOLOMEW'S . . .	200	83	200	283
ST. PETER'S IRON CHURCH, HEELEY .	600	521	661	1,182
ST. JUDE'S, MOORFIELDS . . .	600	127	201	328
EMMANUEL	250	149	220	369
THE INFIRMARY	112	47	45	92
	30,551	13,250	17,487	32,380

Wesleyan Methodist

BRUNSWICK	1,350	625	556	1,181
—— MISSION	75		89	89
EBENEZER	1,090	262	364	626
—— MISSION	100		120	120
BURNGREAVE	1,040	380	435	815
—— MISSION	100		63	63
ELLESMERE ROAD . . .	1,040	231	395	626
NORFOLK STREET . . .	1,006	340	366	706
—— MISSION	120		79	79
FULWOOD	700	236	206	442
CARVER STREET . . .	950	535	669	1,204
—— MISSION	150		120	120
PARK	800	289	319	608
WESLEY COLLEGE . . .	450	308	175	483
MONTGOMERY	400	139	139	278
HEELEY	611	202	181	383
HILSBROUGH	525	206	232	438
RANMOOR	260	74	97	171
CROOKES	250	72	150	222
FULTON ROAD . . .	180	95	98	193
CARBROOK	250	40	130	170
ATTERCLIFFE . . .	450	241	236	477
DARNALL	350	44	80	124
MANOR	130	26	85	111
TRINITY, HIGHFIELD . .	960	385	560	945
ST. JOHN'S, CROOKES . .	350	153	297	450
DON ROAD	700	80	250	330
MILLHOUSES	80	32	30	62
PRINCESS STREET . . .	400	70	262	332
	14,867	5,065	6,783	11,848

Independents

NETHER CHAPEL	1,050	323	357	680
—— MISSION	90		68	68
GARDEN STREET	1,020	108	336	444

Independents—cont.

				Sittings	Morn.	Even.	Total
QUEEN STREET	.	.	.	770	331	347	678
—— MISSION .	.	.	.	100		54	54
MOUNT ZION	.	.	.	700	263	315	578
BROOMPARK .	.	.	.	438	153	99	252
—— MISSION .	.	.	.	300		165	165
CEMETERY ROAD	.	.	.	600	405	380	785
ZION, ATTERCLIFFE	.	.	.	850	380	504	884
—— MISSION .	.	.	.	100		74	74
TABERNACLE	.	.	.	800	190	284	474
BURNGREAVE.	.	.	.	650	132	214	346
WICKER	.	.	.	950	206	303	509
—— MISSION .	.	.	.	140		149	149
HOWARD STREET	.	.	.	650	136	220	356
LANGSETT ROAD	.	.	.	350	81	192	273
DARNALL	.	.	.	210	83	161	244
TAPTON HILL.	.	.	.	200	41	82	123
RINGINGLOWE	.	.	.	60		35	35
BRIGHTSIDE .	.	.	.	600	70	160	230
				10,628	2,902	4,499	7,401

United Methodist Free Churches

HANOVER	.	.	.	1,350	524	681	1,205
PYEBANK	.	.	.	850	466	564	1,030
—— MISSION .	.	.	.	50		19	19
OXFORD STREET	.	.	.	750	136	313	449
SHREWSBURY ROAD	.	.	.	750	138	217	355
SURREY STREET	.	.	.	500	141	155	296
CHERRYTREE	.	.	.	450	128	121	249
MOUNT TABOR	.	.	.	923	321	709	1,030
CUNDY STREET, WALKLEY	.	.	330	81	245	326	
OAK STREET, HEELEY	.	.	.	620	231	291	522
GRIMESTHORPE, HUNSLEY STREET	.	355	195	214	409		
DARNALL	.	.	.	250	43	97	140
CARBROOK	.	.	.	100	26	60	86
LOPHAM STREET	.	.	.	400	250	360	610
EBENEZER	.	.	.	500	170	250	420
				8,178	2,850	4,296	7,146

Primitive Methodist

PETRE STREET	.	.	.	1,250	174	450	624
BETHEL	.	.	.	900	100	219	319
STANLEY STREET	.	.	.	900	250	500	750
JOHN STREET	.	.	.	625	141	270	411
HOYLE STREET	.	.	.	700	80	251	331
—— MISSION .	.	.	.	60		13	13
MEADOWHALL	.	.	.	300	55	95	150

18

Primitive Methodist—cont.

	Sittings	Morn.	Even.	Total
BRIGHTSIDE, JENKIN ROAD . .	78	36	38	74
WOODLAND VIEW	100	29	50	79
HODGSON STREET	300	26	74	100
HEELEY	260	87	250	337
LANGSETT ROAD	600	177	248	425
ATTERCLIFFE	350	133	217	350
CORBY STREET	100	14	60	74
NEWHALL	570	80	150	230
—— MISSION . . .	50		29	29
CARLISLE STREET	200	36	80	116
BIRCH ROAD	80	25	80	105
DARNALL	200	21	76	97
GRIMESTHORPE	300	33	46	79
FIR VIEW, WALKLEY . . .	250	107	111	218
CROSS TURNER STREET . . .	90		44	44
UPPER HEELEY	140		83	83
WEIGH LANE	150		80	80
CRABTREE	150		70	70
	8,703	1,604	3,584	5,188

Methodist New Connexion

SOUTH STREET, MOOR . . .	900	250	301	551
BROOMHILL	800	121	184	305
TALBOT STREET	650	106	226	332
ANDOVER STREET	600	151	255	406
SCOTLAND STREET	700	112	169	281
ATTERCLIFFE	450	88	208	296
WALKLEY	250	32	58	90
FIRTH'S ALMSHOUSES . . .	100	72		72
PARKWOOD SPRINGS . . .	300	27	67	94
FRANKLIN STREET	150	15	24	39
OWLERTON	300	34	120	154
MALIN BRIDGE	142	26	80	106
	5,342	1,034	1,692	2,726

Wesleyan Reform

OWLERTON	500	50	126	176
WATERY STREET	450	80	133	213
WESTON STREET	300	109	201	310
PHILADELPHIA	250	83	148	231
ATTERCLIFFE	300	114	176	290
EBENEZER, BRAMALL LANE . .	250	62	145	207
GOWER STREET	274	104	240	344
GRIMESTHORPE . . .	384	53	102	155
MOUNT GERIZIM	200	26	66	92
EBENEZER, CARBROOK . . .	200	56	104	160
SHARROW VALE	180	24	46	70

Wesleyan Reform—cont.

	Sittings	Morn.	Even.	Total
HAMPDEN VIEW	60		40	40
MOUNT OLIVET	72	24	21	45
MAYFIELD PREACHING ROOM . .	100		49	49
DARNALL	200		52	52
	3,720	785	1,649	2,434

Salvation Army

	Sittings	Morn.	Even.	Total
4 BUILDINGS	2,800	579	2,155	4,054
			1,320 afternoon	

Unitarian

	Sittings	Morn.	Even.	Total
UPPER CHAPEL	700	301	556	857
UPPERTHORPE	400	120	211	331
	1,100	421	767	1,188

Society of Friends

	Sittings	Morn.	Even.	Total
MEETING HOUSE	680	172	191	363

Presbyterian

	Sittings	Morn.	Even.	Total
ST. ANDREW'S	470	230	193	423
—— MISSION	70		60	60
	540	230	253	483

Roman Catholic

	Sittings	Morn.	Even.	Total
6 CHURCHES	2,965	3,602	1,871	5,473

Catholic Apostolic

	Sittings	Morn.	Even.	Total
1 CHURCH	200	65	118	183

Plymouth Brethren

	Sittings	Morn.	Even.	Total
2 CHURCHES	300	187	188	375

Workhouses

	Sittings	Morn.	Even.	Total
SHEFFIELD		84	356	440
ECCLESALL		134	80	214

Workmen's Christian Temperance

	Sittings.	Morn.	Even.	Total.
1 BUILDING	300	110	257	367

Barracks' Church

	Sittings.	Morn.	Even.	Total.
1 CHURCH	250	80		80

NOTE.—There is a slight discrepancy between this abstract, published November 24, 1881 in the *Sheffield Independent*, and the summary published November 26 (see page 148), the latter including various emendations.

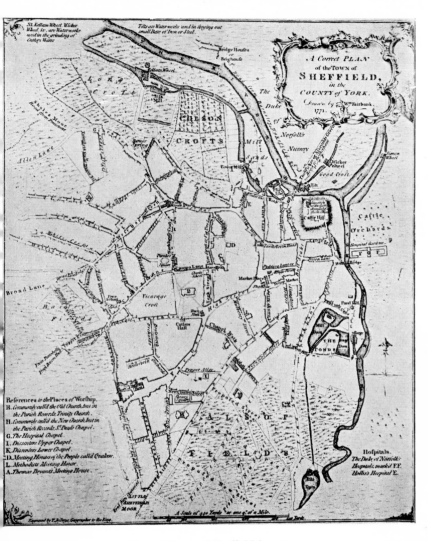

Plan of Town of Sheffield in 1771

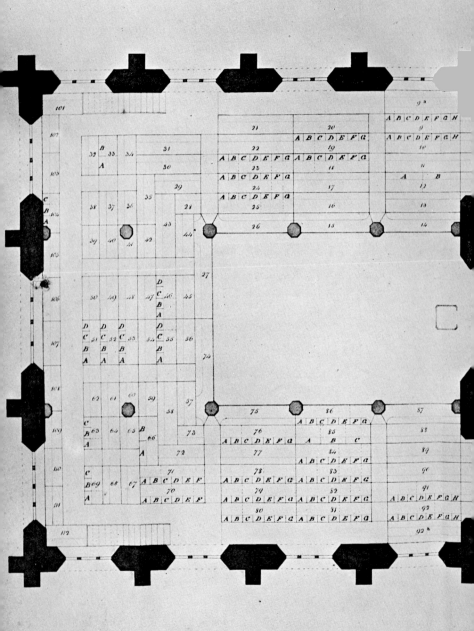

The Gallery Plan

Pew Plans of the Parish Ch
Ordered to be free pews in 1807:
Gallery Floor: KLM in No. 8, M in No. 93, No. 109. No. 10
(The stoves t
(Minute Book of the Church Burgesses, July 2, 1807. See n

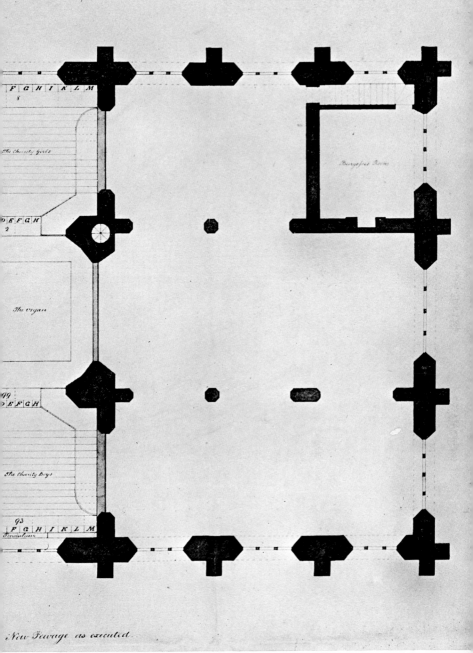

New Savage as executed

eld as executed in 1806.

r : Nos. 13, 14, 15, 16, 17, 18, 21, 60, 61, 102, 103, 104, 105.
 and 105.)

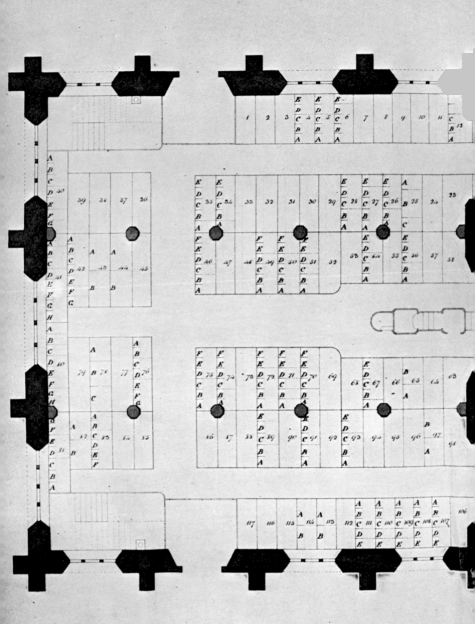

The Ground Plan

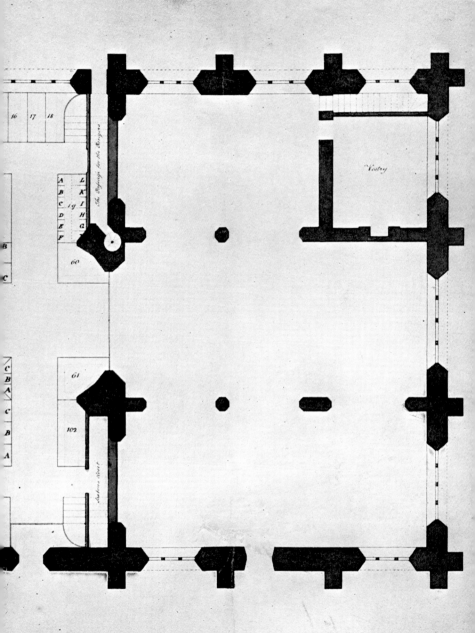

New Pewage as executed.

HISTORICAL CHART SHOWING COMPLETE PROVISION OF PLACES OF WORSHIP BY ALL DENOMINATIONS FROM 1841 TO THE PRESENT

NOTE.—The mark ⊗ signifies original date of the place of worship although it may have been enlarged, rebuilt, or even reduced in size, but on the same site as the original erection.
The mark √ denotes that the building is still in use.
The mark † beside numerals indicates the number of buildings brought into the City through boundary extensions in the years 1900, 1912, 1921, and 1933.
The disparity between the numbers of Church of England buildings in the 1851 and 1881 Census figures, and the chart is due to Census figures including some mission churches which appear on the chart at their later dates of consecration.

Year	Pop.		Church of England	Independent	Unitarian	Quaker	Baptist	Wesleyan	Meth. New Connexion	Primitive Methodist	United Methodist Free Church	Wesley Reform	Presby.	Salvation Army	Rom. C.
1841	112,492	Number of Buildings in use in 1841:	13(10√)	9(4√)	1(2√)	1√	2	15(2√)	6(2√)	1	2(1√)				1
1851	135,310	Accommodation	19,562	4,486	900	800	2,220	10,479	1,952	1,000	670				950
1861	185,172														

Year	Pop.	Accommodation	Church of England	Independent	Unitarian	Quaker	Baptist	Wesleyan	Meth. New Connexion	Primitive Methodist	United Methodist Free Church	Wesley Reform	Presby.	Salvation Army	Rom. C.
			32,731	10,900	1,100	680	3,200	14,917	5,342	8,904	8,178	3,720	340	2,800	2,715
1866															
1867															
1867															
1868	239,946														
1868															
1869															
1869															
1870															
1870															
1871															
1871															
1872															
1873															
1874															
1874															
1875															
1875															
1876															
1877															
1878															
1878															
1879															
1879															
1880															
1881	284,408	Accommodation													
1881															
1882															
1882															
1883															
1883															
1884															
1885															
1886															
1887															
1888															
1889															
1890															
1891	324,291														
1892															

6 other
barracks,
exact
dates not
known

1907: United
Methodist Ch.
formed by
M.N.C., U.M.F.C.

4,610

6,120

18,600

12,300

28,100

5,200

14,050

40,800

Accommodation

409,070

454,632

482,798

1893
1894
1895
1896
1897
1898
1898
1899
1899
1900
1900
1901
1901
1902
1902
1903
1904
1905
1905
1906
1907
1908
1909
1910
1911
1912
1913
1914
1915
1916
1917
1918
1919
1920
1921
1925
1924
1925

Year	Pop.		Church of England	Independent	Unitarian	Quaker	Baptist	Wesleyan	Meth. New Connexion	Primitive Methodist	United Methodist Free Church	Wesley Reform	Presby.	Salvation Army	Rom. C.
1926			⊗	...	...	⊗√	...	⊗√	...	...	...	...	...	...	...
1927			...	...	...	...	...	...	...	...	...	...	...	⊗√	...
1928			...	...	...	...	...	⊗√	...	...	⊗√	...	...	...	...
1929			⊗√	...	...	...	⊗√	1932: Methodist	...	...	...	...	...	...	...
1929			⊗√	...	...	...	...	Church formed	...	⊗√	...	...	...	⊗√	⊗√
1930			⊗√	...	...	...	...	by Wesleyans,	...	...	...	...	...	...	⊗√
1931	511,757		⊗√	...	...	...	...	U.M.C. & P.M.	...	...	...	⊗√	...	...	...
1932			...	...	...	...	...	⊗√ ←				...	...	...	...
1933			⊗√	⊗√	...	...	...	...	...	...	...	...	...	...	...
1933			†5√	†1√	...	...	...	†3(2√)	...	†1√	...	...	...	...	...
1934			⊗√	...	...	...	...	...	...	...	...	...	...	...	...
1934			⊗√	...	...	...	⊗√	...	...	...	...	...	...	...	...
1935			⊗√	...	...	...	...	...	...	...	...	...	...	...	...
1935			⊗√	...	...	...	...	⊗√	...	...	...	...	...	...	⊗√
1936			⊗√	...	...	...	...	⊗√	...	...	...	...	...	...	...
1936			⊗√	...	...	...	...	⊗√	...	...	...	...	...	...	...
1937			⊗√	...	...	...	...	...	...	...	...	...	...	...	...
1937			⊗√	...	...	...	...	...	...	...	...	...	...	...	...
1938			⊗√	...	...	...	...	...	...	...	...	...	...	...	⊗√
1939			⊗√	...	...	...	...	⊗√	...	...	...	...	...	...	...
1939			⊗√	...	...	...	...	⊗√	...	...	...	...	...	...	...
1939			...	...	...	...	...	⊗√	...	...	...	...	...	...	...
1940			⊗√	...	...	...	...	...	...	...	...	...	...	...	...
1940			⊗√	...	...	...	...	...	...	...	...	...	...	...	...
1941			...	...	...	...	...	...	...	...	...	...	...	...	⊗√
1942			...	...	...	...	...	...	...	...	...	...	...	...	...
1943			...	...	...	...	...	...	...	...	...	...	...	...	...
1944			...	...	...	...	...	...	...	...	...	...	...	...	⊗√
1945			...	...	...	...	...	...	...	...	...	...	...	...	⊗√
1946			...	...	...	...	...	...	...	...	...	...	...	...	...
1947			...	...	...	...	...	...	...	...	...	...	...	...	...
1948			...	...	...	...	...	...	...	...	...	...	...	...	...
1949			...	...	...	...	...	...	...	...	...	...	...	...	...
1950			⊗√	...	...	...	...	...	...	...	...	...	...	...	...
1951	512,834		...	...	...	...	...	...	...	...	...	...	...	...	...
1952			⊗√	...	...	...	...	...	...	...	...	...	...	...	⊗√
1953			...	...	...	...	⊗√	...	...	...	...	...	...	...	...
1954			...	...	...	...	...	...	...	...	...	...	...	...	...
1955			...	...	...	...	...	...	...	...	...	...	...	...	...
1956			...	...	...	...	...	...	...	...	...	...	...	...	...
1957			⊗√	...	...	...	...	...	...	...	...	...	...	...	...
		Number of Buildings in 1957 (√)	71	23	4	4	12	88	...	...	...	16	2	7	18

INDEX